Elizabeth Barrett Browning

Elizabeth Barrett Browning

A Psychological Portrait

Peter Dally

MACMILLAN
LONDON

First published 1989 by
MACMILLAN LONDON LIMITED
4 Little Essex Street London WC2R 3LF
and Basingstoke

Associated companies in Auckland, Delhi, Dublin, Gaborone, Hamburg, Harare, Hong Kong, Johannesburg, Kuala Lumpur, Lagos, Manzini, Melbourne, Mexico City, Nairobi, New York, Singapore and Tokyo

A CIP catalogue record for this book is available from the British Library

ISBN 0-333-48197-6

Typeset by Wyvern Typesetting Ltd, Bristol

Printed and bound in Great Britain by
WBC Ltd, Bristol & Maesteg

Life, struck sharp on death,
   Makes awful lightning. His last word was, 'Love –
Love, my child, love, love!' (then he had done with grief)
'Love, my child.' Ere I answered he was gone,
And none was left to love in all the world.

Aurora Leigh
Book 1 lines 210–14

To Anne, with love

Acknowledgements

I am more than grateful to the Browning Society, from whose members I have learnt so much, and to Elizabeth Barrett Browning's great-grandnephew, Edward Moulton-Barrett, in particular, a source of knowledge and kindness.

The book would never have been completed without the patience and good humour of my secretary, Anne Lingham.

Contents

Edward Moulton Barrett,
1785–1828

Elizabeth's father was born in Jamaica on 28 May 1785.

Barretts had lived on the island since the English had ousted the Spaniards in the seventeenth century, but not until the eighteenth century did they prosper and grow to become one of the wealthiest families. As commerce between the West Indies and Europe expanded, so the Barretts seized opportunities and increased their lands and riches. Edward Barrett, Edward Moulton Barrett's grandfather and head of the family, was successful; he owned large estates and tracts of land and hundreds of slaves. Sugar and rum were much in demand and highly profitable, and the plantation slaves were worked to the bone to maintain supplies.

Edward Barrett's great-granddaughter Elizabeth regretted that the Barretts' fortunes, on which she lived so well, were derived from such a source. From an early age she questioned the morality of benefiting from the toil and suffering of slaves, the concepts first picked up from her father's talk or from one of the radical authors in her father's library, and woven into the elaborate system of guilt and penance which so often grips the thoughts of a sensitive, anxious child. She came to believe that the family was cursed by 'the blood of the slave', and she more than any other Barrett; in consequence those she loved were at risk.

In fact, among the West Indian planters the Barretts had a reputation for treating their slaves better than most. But this was relative, and until slavery was abolished in 1833, recalcitrant and runaway slaves were put in stocks with iron collars fastened to their necks and flogged, even to death.

The beauty and fertility of the island were offset by sickness and high mortality from endemic diseases like malaria and yellow fever, spread by the mosquitoes which bred in the stagnant pools and swarmed cloudlike everywhere; the terrifying hurricanes which swept in from the Atlantic and

Caribbean, destroying ships and installations and laying waste the canefields; and the erratic droughts which caused the sugar cane to wither and the cattle and sheep to die – until the more enlightened planters, Edward Barrett among them, began to construct aqueducts, build tanks and tap the plentiful supplies of water which lay below the surface. Over and above these natural hazards were raids by bands of escaped slaves, invasion from the sea during wars, and the slave rebellions which broke out intermittently, when planters and their families were murdered and their homes burnt, and which were suppressed with barbaric ferocity.

There was increasing restlessness among the plantation slaves towards the end of the eighteenth century. Missionaries had started to arrive and their influence on black unrest was sometimes considerable. Many of the planters forbade them to visit their slaves and strongly resisted the promulgation of Christian ideals. Meanwhile in England public opinion was building up against slavery. It was useless for the plantation owners to argue that their slaves were better off in Jamaica than in the primitive lands of Africa where their chances of becoming food for cannibals were high. Change was on the way and in 1807 the slave trade was abolished.

Edward Moulton Barrett's mother, Elizabeth, was the third of Edward and Judith Barrett's five children, and very much the darling of her parents. Her two older brothers left for school in England when she was seven or eight and her third brother followed them within a few years. Her sister Sarah was twelve years younger, too young to intrude upon Elizabeth's pampered life at home. She became an attractive if spoilt young woman and, in all likelihood, headstrong and obstinate.

There could have been no shortage of suitors, given her looks and wealth, but when she was eighteen she chose to marry an outsider whose family were newcomers to Jamaica and comparatively unknown. Legend has it that Charles Moulton's father had been captain of one of the local inshore frigates, and on retirement had remained in Jamaica. He came originally from Norfolk, where his family were said to have estates and be entitled to a coat of arms – which was the only aspect of his father that Edward Moulton Barrett coveted and troubled himself to obtain after his father's death.

Charles Moulton was older than his wife. Prior to the marriage on 28 August 1781 he had been living on the island of Madeira, and earning his living as a merchant. He seems, in fact, to have been an entrepreneur, dealing in anything that came his way, from slaves to wine. He was invariably short of money, and it may have been his pressing debts that later led to his leaving Jamaica and moving to New York and to England for a time. That he was attractive to women is suggested by his having at least four separate families and a number of mistresses.

The Barrett family's reactions to Elizabeth's decision to marry such a man are unrecorded, but cannot have been altogether favourable. Elizabeth was not to be persuaded to change her mind and so, hoping for the best, her parents gave their consent. The wedding took place amid scenes of devastation, for the third hurricane in eighteen months had swept across the island four weeks earlier – a fitting augury to what lay ahead.

The marriage never seemed to settle down, although the couple continued to live together intermittently as man and wife for almost eight years. Theirs was probably one of those love–hate relationships that are so hard to break. Each expected too much of the other and was unable to compromise. An entrepreneur like Charles Moulton was usually being pressed for money, and it is easy to imagine that he quickly used up his wife's dowry to pay off debts and gamble in some fresh commodity. Their sex life was, one imagines, satisfactory, and one reason for the marriage continuing for so long; Elizabeth was pregnant four times in eight years. It is not known how long Charles Moulton remained faithful, given his powers of attraction and the widespread West Indian practice of having at least one mistress in addition to a wife.

Elizabeth's sheltered and privileged upbringing had not fitted her for being married to a philandering adventurer who was unable to provide for wife and children, and expected support from his in-laws. Bewildered by what she discovered she left her husband and ran back to her parents. She was already pregnant, and her first child, Sarah, was born, like all her children, at Cinnamon Hill. Her husband was solicitous, the disagreements were sorted out, and Elizabeth went back to him, only to leave when she became pregnant again. Back and forth she went between Charles and her parents until, after the birth and early death of their fourth child, the seesawing finally came to a halt.

The Barrett family united to condemn Charles Moulton, and persuaded Elizabeth to make a clean break from him. After eight years it must have become plain that the leopard would not change his spots and she would never be happy. Yet the prospect of living out her life in her parents' home as a separated woman was a gloomy one and continually kept alive the hope that a rapprochement might still be possible. She was unsettled, restless and unhappy. To her father it was manifest that the only way to ensure that Charles and his daughter did not continue their destructive relationship was for Elizabeth to leave Jamaica. The two boys were destined soon to go to England for their schooling. Their sister must accompany them and their mother follow as soon as possible. It is not known if Charles raised any objections. He may have been out of the country in 1793 when this plan was conceived – he was certainly in New York in 1798 – or, more likely, he was bribed to acquiesce. He displayed no strong paternal feelings for his children; his main interest was financial.

Edward Moulton Barrett was born and lived his first eight years at his grandfather's house. He saw little of his father, and his filial feelings must have been influenced by his mother's reactions, and what he overheard among the Barrett family and domestic black gossip. At no time in his life did he have anything good to say of his father, and his later experiences of Charles Moulton's double-dealings only confirmed his low opinion.

Edward was a quiet, withdrawn child who kept his feelings hidden. Yet he was prone to outbursts of temper when frustrated, especially against his mother who spoiled and over-protected him which was understandable, given her unhappiness and the uncertainty of her future. She enjoyed the presence of all her children. Her daughter was a delight and Sam was charming and outgoing. But it was to Edward, her elder boy, that she gave her deepest love, the affection that an unhappy mother so often feels for one particular child. He grew up to idealise and adore his mother, and she bore the brunt of an explosive temper and his general dissatisfaction with the world and himself – a characteristic he never lost with those he loved.

Edward Barrett senior was astute, hardworking and, unlike many of his contemporaries, a God-fearing man. While other planters 'ate like cormorants and drank like porpoises', to quote a female observer, and amused themselves with the Creole women, he led a sober, ordered life, was devoted to his wife and children, attended chapel regularly and held daily prayers at home. He was liked and respected by his fellow whites, who sought his advice and were amused that so wealthy a man insisted on 'looking after the pennies' and visiting his plantations and sugar works dressed in patched clothes. All his family loved him and none more than his elder grandson, who idealised him.

In 1791 he was absent from Jamaica, visiting his sister in London and discussing business and pleasure with his old friend John Graham-Clarke in Newcastle. He left his eldest son George Goodin Barrett in charge of the estates and to care for his sister and her children. That George took a lively interest in the children is suggested by his will, in which he left large legacies to Edward and Sam, provided they altered their surnames to Barrett. As his father was, so George Goodin must have been seen by the young Edward – six at the time – as a surrogate father, much admired and to be emulated in later life. George Goodin, still in his early thirties, was already influential and powerful; a member of the Jamaican Assembly, an Assistant Judge of the Supreme Court and Controller of Public Accounts, and a Captain of the Trelawney Militia. He appeared a giant of heroic qualities to his small nephew.

Edward's life was enlivened in the spring of 1792 by the arrival of a tutor, Francis Murphy, whom Edward Barrett had chosen in London. He tutored all three children and got on well with them and with the adults of Cinnamon Hill. His influence on the formation of Edward's character and opinions is not known, but it is just possible that, like Edward's tutor Thomas Jones[1] at Cambridge ten years on, he was opposed to slavery, or at least the harshness of the system, and made no bones about his sentiments.

In 1794 the children and their tutor sailed for London, followed later by their mother. They stayed at first with their great-aunt, Edward Barrett's favourite sister. She took Sarah and Sam to her heart, but considered Edward to be a sullen, unattractive boy, only redeemed by the fondness shown to him by his brother and sister. It was hardly to be wondered at. To have been uprooted and separated from everyone he loved, including his mother, and deposited in a strange land among relatives known only through hearsay was deeply upsetting. While Sam and Sarah, with their more outgoing natures, could hide their depression beneath a screen of jollity and noise, Edward sank into morose melancholy which persisted until his mother's arrival.

Edward was sent to Harrow School when he was twelve, none too happy at the prospect and no doubt protesting volubly to his mother. He did not remain there long, certainly for less than a year.

Some 300 boys attended Harrow School at that time, under the brutal chaotic conditions that characterised public schools before the mellowing influence of Thomas Arnold. The fagging system required junior boys to serve their seniors, who were monitors or in the sixth form, clean shoes, prepare breakfast, cook snacks and prepare hot drinks, and generally be at the fagmaster's beck and call.

Edward could never have fitted easily into the rôle of fag. He was not accustomed to subservience, and the indignity of being treated like one of his grandfather's slaves incensed him. One day he burnt the toast and was cursed and shouted at roundly. Furious, he refused to make more. His fagmaster lost his temper and beat him savagely. Edward complained to his mother who came post-haste to the school and removed him at once. She also had the fagmaster expelled, no mean feat at that time, and an indication of her forceful personality. Thereafter he and Sam were tutored at home until, at sixteen, he went up to Trinity College, Cambridge.

A series of tragedies struck the Barrett family in London and Jamaica in the mid 1790s. At the end of 1794 two of Elizabeth's brothers died, probably of yellow fever,[2] followed a year later by the remaining one, George Goodin. The deaths devastated their father, who never fully recovered, and spent the next two years putting his estates and will in order in preparation for his own death in 1798. In the midst of all this, Edward's sister Sarah died suddenly at school in Greenwich. Why she was away at school is uncertain, but it may have been that her mother had gone to Jamaica at around that time to support her parents in their loss.

The effect of these four deaths on Edward must have been enormous. Until the death of George Goodin, the uncle he so much admired, he had probably seen himself returning to Jamaica and entering into the life of the island. Afterwards he must have had doubts, and these crystallised into certainty when his grandfather died. The tension and sense of insecurity which had developed when he left Jamaica, and only gradually lessened, were reactivated by these family losses. The lesson he learnt was that the family alone was capable of giving him safety and comfort, and it was important that the family itself should keep together; separation was hazardous. Forever after, Edward's peace of mind required that his family should never be far distant, a characteristic acquired early in her life by his eldest daughter. Especially after his wife died, the absence of even one member for long was liable to raise his anxiety.

At thirteen Edward had lost both the men he idealised. His mother was unnerved and, one can imagine, did not recover quickly from the grief of losing her daughter, her father and her brothers. Edward and Sam were closely united, but he needed a wider circle, another family. One was in fact already made.

The Graham-Clarkes were family friends and business partners of the Barretts. It was to their home, Fenham Hall in Newcastle-upon-Tyne, that the Moulton Barretts had gone after their arrival in London. Edward and Sam stayed there in the holidays and when their mother was away from home.

John Graham-Clarke was almost the same age as Edward Barrett, wealthy, powerful, and held in high respect. He was an aloof man, always impeccably dressed in contrast to Edward's grandfather, but like him a stickler for observing Christian practices and social conventions. Edward looked up to him, and saw him as the natural replacement for his Barrett father figures. He felt safe under his protective wing.

The Graham-Clarke family contained seven children, five of them girls, and Edward, during his mid teens, fell in love with the eldest, Mary, and married her when he was nineteen. She was five years older than he, an attractive, lively, capable young woman. He felt at ease with her. She liked him and responded to his needs. At times she mothered him as she did her younger siblings. In Edward's mind she came gradually to supplant his mother and he transferred to her his childlike dependence and need for security. She became his ideal, the wife he adored – and whom he criticised bitterly when she failed to reach his expectations, as had happened with his mother.

Edward's mother liked her – although Mary, after marriage, never found her an easy companion – and Sam doted on her. Mary and her parents had no hesitations over accepting Edward. He was, after all, a good-looking young man, wealthy, and seemingly reliable and amusing on his good days. Only Edward's guardian, James Scarlett, later Lord Abinger – appointed by his grandfather when Edward came to England – had reservations at first, but he soon changed his mind after meeting her; 'I hold out no longer,' he cried, 'she is far too good for him.' They married on 14 May 1805 and moved into Coxhoe Hall, a mere fifteen miles from the Graham-Clarkes.

Edward inherited property and slaves, and a large amount of money, from his grandfather and uncle. Early on he began to concern himself with his business affairs, under the guidance of his guardian and the latter's lawyer brother in Jamaica; the two

7

were responsible for Edward's and Sam's properties while they were minors.

At the time of Edward's marriage the plantations were in disarray. James Scarlett summed up the situation succinctly: '. . . financially you are in a scrape,' he pronounced. This was in no small measure due to the underhand dealings of Edward's uncle, Robert Moulton, aided and abetted by Edward's father who was embezzling large sums of the money which should have gone to his son. Robert was the younger of the two Moulton brothers, and had been appointed to manage part or all of the estates by Edward Barrett, perhaps at the time of Charles Moulton's marriage to Elizabeth, before distrust had sprung up between Charles and the Barretts. Both brothers were intelligent, capable men, possessed of considerable charm, and while Edward Barrett and his sons were in overall charge and checked on what happened, there were no complaints or suspicions of any misdemeanour. After their deaths Robert Moulton had sole charge of the estates for several years, for Edward, unsuspecting, had sent him a power of attorney.

By 1805 it was all too apparent that the Moulton brothers could not be trusted and were attempting to transfer goods and property that were Edward's into their own hands. Money from the sales of sugar and rum went to them instead of to Edward's account, and every effort by Edward and his advisers to obtain an explanation was countered by prevarication. It was not easy, when travel between Jamaica and England took almost two months, to keep control of such a situation, and although Philip Scarlett was on hand in Jamaica he had no direct power to intervene. Edward tried to withdraw the power of attorney from his uncle, with the intention of making it over to the lawyer, but Robert Moulton immediately claimed that he had the legal right through his brother, who was Edward's father and guardian, to hold on to the estates.

As his minority neared its end he had at last to resort to law to compel Robert Moulton to give up his hold on the estates. But as James Scarlett remarked at the time, the law is slow, 'whereas force and fraud are prompt and choose their own time'. It seems strange that Edward waited so long before enlisting the law on his side, when his losses were so apparent. Perhaps the difficulties of taking effective legal action at long distance made his guardian advise caution. Even more curious is why Edward himself did not go out to Jamaica and attempt to settle matters by direct confrontation with his uncle and father. He did, in fact, suggest the possibility towards the end of 1806, but his guardian's response then was lukewarm, and his wife, who had just begun her second pregnancy, predictably objected strongly.

However, legal action eventually brought success and by his twenty-first birthday he had obtained full possession of his property. For several years afterwards he continued to receive demands for money from his uncle, who claimed he was owed large sums, all of which Edward ignored. He also received a number of requests from his father to settle debts! He had great satisfaction in sending £50 in response to one pleading letter for a large loan, with the comment, 'More I could not [give] for I had it not.' He was furious with the Moultons and ashamed to be related to them, as he told Philip Scarlett. When his father died in 1819 he showed no regret, and declined to be an executor or have anything to do with his affairs. 'You can guess the reasons,' he wrote cryptically to the solicitors.

Edward's income was considerably reduced, and not simply from the Moulton brothers' dishonesty. The price of sugar had dropped catastrophically in Europe and the economy of the West Indies was very depressed. There were constant troubles and disputes with the slaves and insurrections flared or threatened, with the result that the overseers and managers were jumpy and work suffered. The slave trade had been abolished in 1807 – emancipation of the slaves did not come until 1833 – which by rights should have increased the value of a slave, but such was the state of the economy that many planters were bankrupt or had to sell up and the price of a slave actually fell at this time.

Still, Edward was hardly povertystricken. His annual income in 1807 was in the region of £4000, which was a large sum in those days, and that was after deducting the annuity of £1000 he paid to his mother (contrast the £300 a year earned by Robert Browning's father).

Mary was happy living at Coxhoe Hall near her parents, but it was rented accommodation and Edward was determined to possess his own estate. He searched for a home of which he could be proud, big enough to hold his growing family, and sufficiently grand for him to entertain the highest in the land. At the back of his mind, perhaps, was the memory of Cinnamon Hill Mansion House, although the Graham-Clarkes' home Fenham Hall was much larger and more distinguished.

In 1809 he found Hope End in Herefordshire, placed in a valley among the Malvern Hills, a few miles from Ledbury, and central to what his mother's Creole companion Treppy called, 'Many gay places – Bath, Gloucester, Worcester, Cheltenham.' Mary told her mother that Edward was thrilled by the discovery, and she was equally delighted; it was 'surrounded with fine hills covered with wood . . . deer in the park . . . a stream running through it, forming a cascade . . . nothing in short ever was so picturesque and beautiful'. There were 475 acres, including woodland, and the asking price was £27,000. An agreement was struck and, before the end of 1809, the family moved there.

Then began six years of discomfort. Edward decided to turn the original mansion into stables and build an entirely new house in front of it. It was constructed in the 'Turkish' style which was then fashionable, and Edward probably had in mind the Pavilion, then being built at Brighton by the Prince Regent, as he discussed the design. Slowly an Arabian Nights' palace rose in the verdant Malvern valley, with minarets rising in the corners and the roof crowned with metal spires and crests. A massive glass dome gave light to the central staircase and ensured that the large hall was a chilly place in winter. The circular-ended drawing room was decorated in the Italian style by workmen specially brought over from Italy. The mahogany doors were inlaid with mother-of-pearl. The dining room was ablaze with crimson flock wallpaper.

Around the house Edward laid out gardens and parkland, planted thousands of trees, dug streams and constructed a lake, and enlarged the cascade which became renowned for its splendour. No expense was spared. Only the best would do. By February of 1815 most of the work on the house was completed, and a grand dinner party was given to which the local gentry were invited. It was, according to Mary, a success and the guests were full of acclaim and wonder at the house and its contents, which were 'very unique and striking'.

Edward was as dependent on his wife as he had been on his mother, and treated her to the same extravagant outbursts of affection and ill temper. In the beginning she coped with his moodiness, but the strain took its toll and in the end she was wearied and depressed by him. The move away from her parents had upset her and the inconveniences endured between 1810 and 1815 and the continual noise and dirt and dust of the workmen, almost overwhelmed her at times. There was only one room in which to sit and to dine, she complained to her mother in a letter composed while waiting for her husband to return from London; she expected him home 'any day', but confessed that she had a friend staying with her and she was apprehensive of Edward's reactions to her presence; he was capable of objecting and throwing a scene.

Even when she was depressed Mary loved Edward unreservedly. He was lucky to have a wife who came near to being the ideal 'mother' to him, always forgiving and understanding, despite the hurt she so often suffered. He could be thoroughly odious on occasions, but his warmth and the wholehearted delight with which he involved himself in family life inspired her love. His eldest daughter worshipped him, and much of her early poetry and her plays were written to attract his attention. Despite everything that happened later, Elizabeth Barrett Browning's devotion to, and dependence on her father never wavered. Nor did any of her brothers and sisters ever turn away from him, despite his treatment of the three who married.

Edward had many good qualities. He was hardworking, highminded and cultivated and, within his family, he had that great joie de vivre which made him such a delightful companion. His Achilles' heel was his fear of failure. In his mind he had to be the perfect husband and father, faithful, reliable, successful, financially secure and morally respectable, the very opposite of his father. With increasing age these qualities took on a life of their own, and anyone who opposed his views or offended him was guilty of a heinous offence not readily forgiven.

At Hope End he enjoyed and worked at all the responsibilities and diversions of a grand and respected country landowner. Twice he was appointed Sheriff of the County, and he took his duties so seriously that he sometimes wore himself out. 'Poor Papa!' his daughter wrote. 'He attends just to those pecuniary interests which no one cares for, with a scrupulous attention.' He was held in high repute on all sides and was made a Freeman of Gloucester and Hereford. He was prominent in politics, 'a most determined Whig', passionate about the Reform Bill which was passed in 1832, and was at one time asked to stand for Parliament by the Hereford Whigs. His brother Sam had been a member of parliament for the Borough of Richmond since 1820, and there is little doubt that Edward would have been successful had he accepted. Perhaps his refusal on the grounds that it would take up too much of his time was a valid one, or perhaps he feared the expense involved, but a more likely explanation lay in his dread of failure, that he might not be elected and that his worst fears would be realised.

By nature devout, he had been brought up Nonconformist,

and when the Moulton Barrett family were numbered among Herefordshire's wealthy landed gentry, they participated regularly in the surrounding Church of England services. Discerning churchgoers often went from one to the other, regardless of whether the ritual was high or low, in order to hear the best preachers in the neighbourhood. Edward also followed the practice of his grandfather and father-in-law, which was common in most large establishments of that time, of daily prayers at home. From the time of his wife's death in 1828, God and religion became increasingly important, and it was remarkable how often God's will coincided with Edward's needs. But in those heady youthful days, before tragedy struck, Edward kept God in proportion.

Over the question of slavery the liberal Christian in Edward conflicted with the slave owner. He approved of the abolition of the slave trade in 1807, and went along with the changes that followed in the thinking of Jamaican planters; marriage should be encouraged so that new slaves from within would take the place of those who should have come from Africa; punishment to be less harsh, and living conditions improved. Edward recommended to his own manager that flogging be replaced by solitary confinement, but otherwise his ideas were hardly original. When slavery was abolished altogether in 1833 his first reaction was that the West Indies' economy was finished – Jamaica might as well be sunk – but eventually he accepted that it was a good move. His liberalism was, one suspects, more cerebral and pragmatic than based on genuine feeling. In later life the Moulton Barrett children came to believe that their father looked on them as slaves, he being the slave owner who knew what was best for them.

By 1824 Edward's income was considerably less than his needs. The expenses of running Hope End were huge, and included the interest on the £10,000 mortgage taken out when he purchased the property. But Edward was not a man to worry about such trifles until they blew up in his face. Suddenly they did so.

When Edward's grandfather died in 1798 his will was found to contain one ambiguous clause over who was to possess ninety-two slaves and fifty steer, worth in all about £11,000. A dispute over it broke out between the Moulton Barretts and their cousins the Goodin Barretts which ended in their taking their differences to the Jamaican courts in 1801. The litigation dragged on for years, but in 1824 judgment was finally given against the

Moulton Barretts. It was an unexpected financial bombshell. Edward was faced with a huge debt, for he had to pay interest on the £11,000, going back more than twenty years, plus the money he would have paid had he hired the slaves and cattle. He and Sam appealed, but the prospect for success was not good.

It was clearly essential to increase his income from Jamaica. In 1826 Edward probably,[3] and Sam certainly, went to Jamaica to see for themselves the problems there and how the properties might be run more efficiently. It became obvious that one of the brothers must reside in Jamaica and assume personal responsibility for the day-to-day running of the estates if they were to become profitable, and the choice fell unhesitatingly on Sam. Sam had travelled to Jamaica several times in the past, and had even met his father there, and possessed none of the inhibitions that kept Edward off the island; although married, Sam had no children and his wife was not averse to improving the material and spiritual states of the slaves. It is very unlikely that Mary would have agreed to go. Not only was she burdened by eleven children, whose ages ranged from twenty-one to three, but she was depressed and already showing early signs of rheumatoid arthritis. Reluctantly Sam resigned his parliamentary seat and sailed for Jamaica in 1827.

Edward now struggled to save Hope End, and raised a further mortgage on the property. But even at this late stage he failed to make significant economies and live within his means. He could not bring himself to tell Mary about the state of their finances. He had never confided in her. To have disclosed his plight and the threat hanging over Hope End would have shown him up as a failure, much as his father had been. It would have been a mortal blow to his self-esteem. Yet the likelihood was that Mary guessed that trouble was brewing, and thereby had one extra burden to carry. Whether she ever shared her worries with her eldest daughter is guesswork; but Elizabeth did seem to be aware of the impending disaster before the news broke in 1830.

2

Elizabeth,
1806–1821

Elizabeth was born on 8 March 1806 at Coxhoe Hall in Durham. She developed into an attractive child, taking after the Barretts in looks; long black hair, her father's dark complexion, grey eyes, heavy wide mouth and slightly receding chin. Her teeth were very white and regular. She had a large, broad forehead which in later years she chose to hide behind her dangling curls. In addition to looks she inherited her father's spectacular displays of temper and sulkiness when thwarted in her aims. She would on occasions 'upset all the chairs and tables and throw the books about the room in a fury'. She was renowned among the servants for 'self love and excessive passion'. But she was to learn in time that it was not always to her advantage to behave in such ways. She controlled her temper, although she would admit that she was 'still as proud, or wilful, as impatient of control, as impetuous . . . [but] Thanks be to God it is restrained', she added piously in her diary.

Elizabeth's passions reached their height in the nursery. There was to be 'no upstart' to dispute her authority, and she established her hegemony from the beginning over her brother Edward (Bro), who was born in June 1807, and over Henrietta, a year younger still. She organised their mutual games, sent them here, there and everywhere, and generally controlled their waking lives. Bro tried ineffectually to assert himself, but was only able to do so physically. Elizabeth was by far the smallest of her family – she was only about five foot one when fully grown – yet she continued to hold her own in combat with Bro until she was eight or nine. In time she was certain to be overcome, but tussling among children is not simply a matter of establishing dominance; along with it goes an intensely pleasurable sensuality, which feeds into imagination and fantasy, colours later sexuality, and enhances emotional bonds. A brother and sister near in age are often very close to one another, and so it was with Elizabeth and Bro. Perhaps it was this more than any risk of injury that alarmed their Barrett grandmother and made her warn the ten-year-old Elizabeth that she was 'too big to be fighting with Bro . . . I have seen him very rude and boisterous to you'.

Elizabeth loved Bro deeply. As children they were insepar-able. They made each other laugh, had their own private jokes and knew one another's foibles. Bro accepted her domination and she in turn protected him whenever possible from their father's criticisms. She trusted him completely and never ques-tioned his loyalty to her. He was '. . . my constant companion and a beloved participator in all my pleasures, and never allowed the rage for power to injure the endearing sweetness of his temper'.

The same could not be said for Elizabeth. The rage for power was present in her from the earliest years, as soon as she was conscious of the needs of others, and the necessity to assert herself constantly in order to gain her rights. She soon became aware that women did not have the same rights as men, and in many respects were second-class citizens, expected to be sub-missive, or even subservient to men.

She was the first born of the family, yet it was Bro's birth, not hers, which had been publicly celebrated by her father, with a day's holiday for his slaves on the Jamaican plantations. It was for Bro's sake that a tutor had been engaged, to prepare him for Charterhouse School when he was thirteen. It was all most unfair. 'A steady indignation against Nature who made me a woman' took root and grew, and she resolved that once she 'was free of the nursery' she would dress up in men's clothes and go into the world to seek her fortune.

Meanwhile she determined to maintain equality with Bro, and to prove to her parents, and especially her father, that she was not only as good as her brother, but even better. At moments, one suspects, she felt considerable jealousy towards Bro and resentment over the unfair advantages he had. How could she not, given the nature of their relationship? She knew she was more able than Bro and she set out to demonstrate it, and put herself in the limelight.

She attracted her parents' admiration from the moment she could read and write – as she said, she began writing poetry with her bread and milk. She wrote a poem on Virtue when six, to which her father responded by awarding her ten shillings and the title of poet laureate of Hope End, an heroic poem at the age of nine, and verse plays and tragedies in French and English which were performed in the nursery. At twelve she composed *The Battle of Marathon*, an epic in four books, dedicated 'to him to whom "I owe the most", and whose admonitions have guided my youthful muse . . . to the Father whose never failing kindness, whose unwearied affection I can never repay'. Her dedication to her father, written as she was about to enter puberty, summed up her ambitions and hopes. Her father held the key to her life. He alone had the power to let her follow her inclinations. She had therefore to ensure that his kindness and affection *never* failed.

Her father was sufficiently moved to have fifty copies of the poem printed privately. (Only one poem, 'The Sorrows of the Muses', written when she was eleven, did she dedicate to her mother.) Rarely did her father fail to respond to his daughter. He was delighted with each fresh achievement, like a child with a new toy. But it was no game to Elizabeth. Acclaim from her father was vital for her peace of mind.

She read voraciously, progressing from fairy tales to novels and philosophy and literature in general. Her father encouraged her by opening up his quite extensive library to her, and allowing her to read any book she wished, 'except those on the right and Gibbons' "Decline and Fall" and "Tom Jones" '; he thought they might corrupt her! Before her first illness at fifteen, she had devoured Tom Paine, Mary Wollstonecraft and Voltaire and a host of radical writers. Pope's translation of the *Iliad* precipitated her into the classical world where Greek gods and heroes became intensely real to her. She set up shrines in selected sacred places in the garden and sacrificed to Minerva, her favourite deity, without in any way disturbing her Christian habits. But all this fantasy play faded into insignificance with the arrival of Bro's tutor, Mr McSweeney, when Elizabeth was eleven or twelve. The tutoring was intended solely for Bro but Elizabeth badgered her father, wept, pleaded and demanded to be allowed to join the lessons so vigorously and continuously that all resistance – one suspects it was largely token – vanished. (The scene, and outcome, were remarkably similar to the one Elizabeth had had with her mother a few years earlier when her parents set out for a holiday abroad in Paris, at the end of the Napoleonic wars. A tearful Elizabeth had then clutched so despairingly, yet firmly, at her mother's coat as she was about to leave, so aghast at being left behind, that her mother had taken pity and allowed her to join them on the trip.)

It is not unusual for parents unwittingly to compete for a child's affections and loyalties, particularly when strong undercurrents of tension exist in the family. In the early nineteenth century, most wives accepted without much questioning that their rôle was secondary to their husband's. Edward Moulton Barrett adored his wife – she was his ideal – and gave fully of his affection, but he expected perfection and when anything went wrong, and especially if his comfort suffered, he exploded and behaved as though she were one of his Jamaican slaves. Throughout her marriage his wife was liable to be taken to task, loudly reprimanded and left humiliated and exhausted. Never mind that her husband had forgotten the incident almost as soon as it was over, his wife could not dismiss it so readily from her mind, and it became ever harder as the years passed. Elizabeth could hardly fail to observe what went on between her parents, for her father was never a man to respect the feelings of others or disguise his own from his children. Her mother, she told Robert, was 'very tender . . . and of a nature harrowed up into some furrows by the pressure of circumstances . . . a sweet gentle nature, which the thunder a little turned from its sweetness'.[1]

Mary was devoted to her children, and was very much the linchpin of the large family. Inevitably she turned to them for comfort and affection, and especially to her eldest daughter.

Although no better educated than any well-brought-up Georgian girl from a wealthy background, she was intelligent and tried to keep pace with her daughter's expanding interests. She was the driving force in her elder children's early education, and undertook most of the nursery teaching herself. It was from her, in all probability, that Elizabeth learnt to read and write and to become so much at home with poetry. Her mother spoke French fluently – her father understood barely a word – and enjoyed French literature, and it was from this source that Elizabeth's later absorbing interest in French novels arose. Altogether she was a potent force in Elizabeth's childhood and in practical terms did far more than her husband to form and spur on Elizabeth's ambitions. She made fair copies of Elizabeth's poetry and verse plays, discussed ideas sympathetically with her, was optimistic about her writing and proud of her achievements. But, unlike her husband, she had her feet planted firmly on the ground and she would not have encouraged Elizabeth to regard herself as a genius, as her husband was

Elizabeth Barrett Browning

inclined to do, or give her the notion that she might bypass feminine domestic virtues.

Elizabeth loved her parents equally, she would have maintained, but she also thought of them as unequal. How could she not, given her ambitious personality? She saw her father succeeding in the outside world, the possessor of huge estates in Jamaica, High Sheriff of Herefordshire, greatly respected on all sides, the wielder of power, the beloved head of the family, while her mother busied herself with the dull routine of family and domestic chores, and executed her husband's wishes.

Elizabeth was approaching puberty and confused. She looked down on her mother's 'feminine softness', important as she saw it to be in the home, and equated it with lack of strength, the inability to hold her husband's respect; why did she provoke him into scenes? She was led to criticise her mother, mostly in indirect ways, finding fault with marriage as an institution and with domestic lives. Her mother was often amused, but her patience must have been sorely strained when she was low in spirits. Elizabeth reserved her admiration, which lasted all her life, for 'heroes', outstanding men and women in literature, politics, war, who achieved fame; and in this pantheon she included her father. He and they could do no lasting wrong in her eyes.

A conflict of loyalties existed in Elizabeth over her mother and father. She could not condone her father's outbursts, and she was invariably upset by witnessing or hearing their rows. Yet her father could not be expected to be patient with domestic mishaps, despite his love for his wife. She identified with each parent and as a result felt resentment and guilt when they quarrelled, as though, in some irrational manner, she was responsible for their behaviour. This was to contribute to her illness at fifteen.

Her father's permission for her to study Greek and Latin with Bro under Mr McSweeney provided a temporary respite to these difficulties. Her attention came to centre almost entirely on her work and before long she could think of little else.

I felt the most ardent desire to understand the learned languages. To comprehend even the Greek alphabet was delight inexpressible. Under the tuition of Mr McSweeney I attained that which I so fervently desired. For months during the year I never remembered having diverted my attention to any object than the ambition of gaining fame.

18

The scenario was predictable. She and Bro worked together, and he was outclassed. She was so superior to him in quickness of learning and comprehension that it must have been hard for the tutor to remember his primary objective, to ensure that Bro gained entry to Charterhouse.

Bro had charm and intelligence, but none of his sister's ambitious power. Twelve years of domination by Elizabeth, of always playing second fiddle to her, had effectively ensured that he lacked drive and persistence, and avoided hard work. His father looked on him as unreliable and was increasingly disappointed in him. Elizabeth summarised his character with tenderness and precision: 'He had high talents – only not distinguished among men because the heart was too tender for energy.' For her, he remained the ideal companion. She could speak her mind, show her feelings, or ask him, 'Is this which I have written good?' and always 'be sure of a just answer'. He was never a rival. He provided his sister with ideas and comments on her work, but he did not try to emulate her or even co-operate over a verse or drama.

Elizabeth did not intend Bro to fail his entry exam. In the world's eyes, and above all in her father's, he must be seen to pass with flying colours. He was in a sense her alter ego and his success or failure was also hers. She encouraged him to learn his verbs, made him parse his sentences, bullied and bribed and cajoled him until he was word perfect in his Homer and Horace, and made sure that he passed into Charterhouse.

Elizabeth's energy during these childhood years was boundless. She studied and wrote and played with intensity and absorption. She ranged through the garden and parkland and explored the woods, chased with Bro, dared him to climb trees and in turn accepted his challenges to leap the stream and risk getting wet. She romped with Havannah, her dog, and galloped across the fields on her black pony Moses, imagining herself to be one of Byron's travelling companions.

Yet gregarious as she was within the family, she needed time to herself, quietness and solitude, not simply to read and write, for she seemed always to have had the ability to do so in the midst of din and disturbance by detaching herself from her surroundings, but to recharge her mental batteries. Her expanding imagination, aided by literature, needed to be balanced by action. She loved nature (one of her criticisms of Jane Austen's characters was that they are 'all unconscious of the sunshine and trees and running water – to say nothing of the God of nature and providence'). She had secret hideouts in the woods and thickets, and there were leafy caverns, safe and magical and awesome like the one she described in 'The Magic Bower', which she stumbled upon and could never rediscover despite long searchings. And there were very old gnarled trees with twisted arms, or jagged trunks blasted by lightning and thunderstorms. She knew the strange beings who dwelt in their depths, like the monstrous toad in the hollow of the root of a thorn who 'wore a jewel in his head' and had to be avoided, but possessed magical powers which pulled her towards his haunt, as someone with vertigo is pulled towards the edge of a high cliff. He was, perhaps, really a frog prince, waiting to be rescued by a good maiden, but that was not a rôle that appealed to her. She would rather slay a dragon.

It was most peaceful in the garden of white, scented roses, which was a favourite place of her mother's, and she often walked and sat there. As she developed she became increasingly at war with herself and disturbed by inner turmoil. At times she experienced intense anxiety, as though her mind was about to fly apart. Generalised anxiety is too painful to bear for long, and the nervous system has ways and means of protecting itself; phobic anxieties and obsessions form and the anxiety becomes displaced on to seemingly harmless objects or situations. The phobic object is terrifying and has to be avoided at all cost, but away from it there is calm.

Elizabeth had numerous phobias. She was frightened of the dark and would not go to sleep without a lighted lamp in the room, and until late in childhood a nursemaid had to sit with her until she fell asleep. Paradoxically she later came to dislike bright light and was notorious for sitting in semi-darkness with the curtains drawn, reading by lamplight during the day, and receiving visitors in the gloom. This eccentricity increased with the years, particularly when she began to be conscious of losing her youthful good looks. Bats terrified her as they emerged at dusk and fluttered around her attic bedroom window. All her life she was appalled at the thought of a bat entering her room.

Agoraphobia, though, was her most crippling fear, and was present on and off all her life, making itself felt increasingly after her first illness. This is a condition, particularly common today among women, characterised by a fear of open spaces, meeting people, and in extreme instances, of leaving home. The sufferer is liable to panic if she encounters people, even acquaintances and friends, and immediately tries to avoid them. Many agoraphobics are housebound and unable to leave their homes, or are only able to do so under the protective umbrella of night, or when accompanied by a trusted companion.

Such an insecure person invariably has a close relative or friend on whom she depends and around whom she organises her life. She cannot move from her house, even her room, in the absence of her 'protector'. She is ruthlessly demanding of him or her, and expects her own needs to come first; she almost always dominates the relationship with her companion.

The condition can have a crippling effect on the sufferer's life but there are usually advantages to be derived from it, although these may seem to be far outweighed by the disadvantages. For Elizabeth there were several advantages. Firstly it established her central position in the family, and the 'special relationship' with her father. Secondly it gave her the time and energy to devote to her writing and reading which she might otherwise have expended on social intercourse. A third advantage, after the marriage, was that the agoraphobia ensured that Robert Browning was never far from her side; in the early years he was the ideal agoraphobic's partner.

Another lifelong terror was of thunderstorms. Around Hope End great storms were frequent and Elizabeth quaked in her chair or, as a small girl, pulled the bedclothes over her head. One might imagine the house, with its metal spires and crescents, to be a natural target for thunderbolts. Sometimes, as is often the way when people are terrified, she was drawn to watch the flashes of lightning. Once, looking from the window, she saw lightning strike a large tree some 200 yards away, the bark rent from top to bottom as though by 'dreadful fiery hands' and the trunk left bare and peeled. Some time later she heard that two young women in the neighbourhood had been struck and killed during that storm.

From childhood Elizabeth linked her father with thunder and the awful power of the thunderstorms. In a letter to Robert Browning she told him that 'only one person holds the thunder', and at the prospect of this being turned against her (she was talking of the possibility of her father learning of her engagement) she quailed; 'I shall be thundered at; I shall not be reasoned with . . . '. In the usual course of events her father never thundered at her. He had no cause to do so. He saw her as the 'purest' of all his children, who gave him no trouble. He often thundered at the others, and no one more so than her spirited, coquettish sister Henrietta. Elizabeth could no more tolerate her father's thunder than the real thing; 'I would rather be kicked with a foot . . . than thundered at,' she confessed. She described to Robert the 'dreadful scenes' between her father and Henrietta when her sister's 'knees were made to ring upon the floor' and she was carried out of the room 'in strong hysteria', and Elizabeth in turn, although she suffered 'only by sympathy, fell flat down upon my face in a fainting fit'.

Elizabeth had early on observed that her mother was as likely to be the target for her father's thunder as his children. 'Her sweet gentle nature' was, like the milk, turned sour by the thunderstorm although not ripped bare like the tree trunk. Her father was a terrifying Jovian figure, 'king and father', whom she loved and worshipped and dared not upset. Any rebellion against him that stirred within her had to be quietened at once, for fear that the thunder might be turned against her.

At the age of ten she perceived her father and God in much the same light, and she developed an obsessional way of thinking. 'One day,' she wrote in her diary,

> I omitted a prayer wholly through forgetfulness, but having afterwards remembered the neglect, I was so impressed with the idea of having offended the god of my salvation that I hardly hoped for pardon. My whole mind was tortured and my prayers that it bespoke the anguish of my heart. It was not the humility of a sinner suing for pardon at the throne of mercy, but the violent entreaties extorted by despair from my heart. The next morning I renewed with tenfold ardour my agonising prayers. My god, my god, why has thou forsaken me I repeated in a tone of anguish.

In her early twenties Elizabeth wrote an extraordinarily moving poem, 'The Tempest', the setting of which is a violent storm which 'came in power' and tore down the woods. The narrator welcomes the storm and rushes to meet 'the riding Tempest'. In the midst of the destruction, in the dark, she stumbles over a body on the ground. As she crouches over it there is a flash of lightning which illuminates the dead man's face.

> I knew that face –
> His, who did hate me – his whom I did hate!

The reader is momentarily stunned by the shock of the statement, and the naked intensity of feeling. The poem continues:

> Albeit such darkness brooded all around,
> I had dread knowledge that the open eyes

Of that dead man were glaring up to mine,
With their unwinking, unexpressive stare;
And mine I could not shut nor turn away.
The man was my familiar. I had borne
Those eyes to scowl on me their living hate,
Better than I could bear their deadliness:
I had endured the curses of those lips
Far better than their silence.

The narrator buried the body beneath a 'mighty tree' which had
been 'blasted, peeled' of bark by lightning, and then she 'turned
and wept'.

Much of the poem strikes an autobiographical note, but
whose is the dead body, the narrator's familiar? It has been
argued that it is the ambitious 'masculine' part of Elizabeth
herself, her animus, that is killed by the thunderstorm (her
father) and which she buries. She is then ready to follow docilely
in her mother's footsteps. This seems an unlikely explanation.
Most critics see the body as representing either her father or
brother. In fact it makes psychological sense only if it is Bro. The
all-powerful father slays his rival son and ensures possession of
his daughter; the classic Freudian theme.

In the poem the 'I' joins with the storm and is not only fearless
but exults in the storm and urges the elements to ever greater
power and destruction. There is a strong sexual colouring to the
poem. The storm is described in vivid orgasmal phrases: 'As
brazen chariots rushing from the war, / as passioned waters
gushing from the rock, / as thousands crashed woods, the
thunder cried . . . '. The narrator touches the man's body and
finds it 'chill and soft', lifts his head on to her knee, and is
stroking his brow when the lightning flash reveals the features
of his face. She falls back horrified. She is revealed in a taboo act.

Father and brother are closely intertwined in Elizabeth's
psyche. In the poem, if father does indeed represent the storm,
he becomes the god who is irresistible and whose power is
terrible. Bro is slain by him, but what was Bro doing in the wood
at all? Was there a love tryst? Was Bro waiting there for the
narrator, or enticed there by her? Was this why he was slain?
The reader can choose. What matters is that the poem allows a
glimpse inside the youthful Elizabeth's mind, at the strength
and complexity of the ties between herself and her father and
Bro, and at her gathering if still diffuse sexuality.

Bro was now thirteen and about to leave for school. Elizabeth was distressed. It meant an end to Mr McSweeney's tutoring and structured learning, the loss of her dearest companion, and a hopeless future. For fourteen years she had pursued knowledge and acquired a reputation as a child prodigy. She possessed 'an extraordinary genius' the painter William Artaud, then at Hope End painting a composition of four of the Barrett children, remarked: 'She has a command of language and ideas that is quite marvellous', and her brother, 'though by no means deficient has no chance in competition with her'.

Her parents 'idolised her', yet they had no thoughts for her life ahead, other than following the conventional path of a well-brought-up young lady. Shortly after Bro departed for Charterhouse, her father decided that his three daughters needed a governess, and a Mrs Orme descended on them. Elizabeth felt isolated and abandoned by her father, and gained no comfort from her mother. She was angry with them both and miserable. She was developing from a child to a woman, but she abhorred the idea of learning to become one, of preparing herself for marriage and domesticity. All she wanted was to continue to absorb literature and the classics, and to compose poetry.

Mrs Orme seems to have been extremely accommodating and allowed Elizabeth to pursue her own interests, perhaps at her mother's suggestion. But no solution suggested itself to Elizabeth and the crisis within her continued to grow.

3

The First Illness,
1821–1823

Hope End, without the companionship of Bro, no longer held its old delights for Elizabeth. She thought of him, but although he often wrote, she was slow to reply. She imagined him to be happily occupied by the opportunities and activities of Charter-house – although he was probably as homesick and miserable at first as his father had been at Harrow – while she sat aimlessly at home. She felt that she had nothing to say. Mr McSweeney had departed at the end of the summer of 1820 and she was left to her own devices, pushing herself to continue her classical studies alone. There was no one to take Bro's place. None of the neighbourhood girls of her age interested her and in any case, given her bluestocking reputation, they may have been as hesitant to visit her as she was reluctant to see them. Henrietta was three years younger, a lively girl and very different in temperament from Elizabeth; she was sociable and outgoing, her mind already turning to young men and marriage and domestic pleasures, none of which interested Elizabeth. She kept to herself, angry, unhappy and sulky.

She attempted to approach her mother but met with no success. Her mother could not have failed to notice the change in Elizabeth, from an enthusiastic, confident girl, active and busy with family affairs and her own ideas, ready at any time to discuss a philosophical or political question, to a miserable, pale child, unsure of herself, bad-tempered and often rude, liable to burst into tears and then plead for forgiveness. But Mary Moulton Barrett was herself near the end of her tether and had little energy to spare for her daughter. Her tenth child, Alfred, had been born the year before but, more important, her own mother, Mrs Graham-Clarke, was depressed and needed her help. This was a complete reversal of normal procedure. Mary had never wholly lost her dependence on her mother and still relied on her for emotional support at difficult times. It had been to her mother that she had confided how fractious Edward could be and his unreasonable outbursts of temper. Her father had been senile for some years, and an increasing burden on his wife. He had died in the summer of 1818, but instead of his death giving his wife relief, she had lapsed into prolonged and deepening grief.

At this critical period in Elizabeth's life, therefore, her mother's emotional and physical energies were fully stretched, and she had nothing to spare for her daughter. Her father was incapable of helping her, and even had he asked what was wrong, she would have been hard put to give him a comprehensible answer. Her Barrett grandmother, whom she loved, or Treppy, her old nurse, would have told her to pull herself together and stop being silly. There was no one to whom she could turn. She was trapped.

In the spring of 1821 all three Moulton Barrett sisters became ill at the same time, with symptoms of headache, vague aches and pains and spasmodic jerks of the muscles. It was conjectured that they had eaten 'something deleterious', but it is just as likely that they had a minor infection. Whatever the cause Henrietta and Arabel recovered completely within a few weeks of being dosed with an innocuous medicine and encouraged to take exercise in the open air. Elizabeth, on the other hand, became increasingly ill, and her parents were so concerned for her that 'during the two years, [they] scarcely ever left me to go anywhere, not even to dine in the neighbourhood'; an exaggeration no doubt, but certainly a reflection of their anxiety. Their third daughter, and fourth child, Mary, had died seven years before,[1] and the possibility of losing Elizabeth, 'that prodigy in intellectual powers and acquirements', must have set alarm bells ringing.

Her body was at first racked with pain, but this gradually shifted until it came to centre around the right side of her abdomen. From this point, in the words of Dr Coker, one of the many doctors consulted,

. . . the pain spreads to the back, up the side to the point of the right shoulder and down the arm. The suffering is agony – and the paroxysms continue for a quarter of an hour to an hour and upwards – accompanied by convulsive twitches of the muscles, in which the diaphragm is particularly concerned. The attack seems gradually to approach its acme, and then suddenly ceases . . . there are generally three attacks in the day and during the night.

This description has all the characteristics of acute anxiety, punctuated by attacks of panic, during which the heart beats rapidly and violently, and the chest is tight and constricted; the sufferer gasps violently for breath and overbreathes or hyperventilates. Hyperventilation has the effect of depleting the blood of carbon dioxide, which in turn makes the blood less acid and this causes muscles to twitch and go into painful spasms. Understandably the victim becomes ever more panicky and a vicious circle of symptoms ensues until he or she becomes too exhausted to continue, and collapses or faints.

Anxiety states are particularly likely to occur in young adults and adolescents who have sensitive and highly strung natures, and are faced with seemingly intractable difficulties, as Elizabeth was. Throughout her adult life she would be prone to such bouts of anxiety and overbreathing.

Extreme anxiety is painful and terrifying, and when it is prolonged, protective mental mechanisms tend to come into play and the anxiety symptoms are replaced by other psychological conditions. In Elizabeth's case, this was anorexia nervosa.

The self-imposed emaciation in which anorexia results has a number of effects, both on body and mind. The production of many hormones is reduced, especially those concerned with sexual function; menstruation stops and libido diminishes or disappears. Circulation of the blood and thermostatic control of body temperature are upset and the anorexic complains bitterly of the cold. Sleep is shallow and broken. Available energy is reduced and the individual tires easily and is reluctant to exert herself physically. She becomes fearful of her peers and isolates herself, terrified of what others think of her.

The anorexic manifests two very different sides of herself. On the one hand she behaves as a small frightened child, clinging to her parents (or husband), asking to be cared for and protected. She has no will of her own and cannot make the simplest decision for herself. She is terrified of being left alone and pleads for her parents to stay continually near her. For a time this was very much the way Elizabeth behaved; the formerly competent, almost cocky, teenage girl, was changed into a wailing infant.

But starvation is a mighty weapon, and nowhere is this more apparent than in anorexia nervosa. Alongside the helpless child is a ruthless despot who comes to rule the household. Appeals fail, she ignores delicacies, threats are ineffectual, nothing can make the girl eat. She is all-powerful. She controls her world by the play of her appetite; to eat is a gesture of love, to abstain is a sign of anger and displeasure. And as she loses weight concern mounts, until parents are ready to concede anything within reason, if only she will eat.

What did she want? Elizabeth was both begging and demanding. She wanted the freedom to choose her future, and she wanted to continue to be the favourite child of her parents, especially her father. She knew a girl in the neighbourhood of Hope End with anorexia nervosa, one Harriet Cocks, 'wearing away like a snow wreath and becoming at last unable to take food, except . . . turtle broth and grapes . . . ' . Elizabeth had no intention of remaining in such a helpless position. But for the moment it was advantageous to her.

She lost weight steadily until she was so thin that her family feared for her life. At one time the only nourishment she would agree to take was highly seasoned food. She became constipated, understandably, from the absence of food and needed aperients, but in other respects her doctors could find nothing wrong with her stomach and bowels – although one eminent practitioner was convinced that the trouble was due to her 'bowels [becoming] loaded with vitiated matter'. When she woke in the mornings she complained of a tight sensation 'as though a cord was tied around the stomach', which later 'seems to break'.

She was unable to sit unaided or without being propped up by pillows because her back was weak and painful, and the smallest exertion exacerbated her discomfort. She made no attempt to read or write, and lay in bed listlessly, detached from those around her. Her family fussed over her, but Elizabeth seemed quite unconcerned by events, a feature remarked upon by more than one doctor.

Her medical advisers were mystified and unable to agree on what was wrong. Psychological causes were well recognised by doctors in 1822 but, given the state of medical knowledge at that time, it would have been a brash doctor who ventured to suggest this diagnosis to Edward Moulton Barrett. Tuberculosis was rife in the nineteenth century, and an emaciated girl who encountered the bacillus would stand little chance of resisting the disease. But there is nothing in the various accounts of Elizabeth's first serious illness to suggest this complication.

It was Dr Coker who raised the possibility of a diseased spine, not that he found any signs of such, on the grounds that he had once treated 'a lady in Hampshire' for the same kind of spasms as Elizabeth had, which resulted from an affliction of the spine. 'I should recommend . . . the treating Miss Barrett's case as for diseased spine,' he accordingly advised. It was this curious piece of logic which eventually created the myth that Elizabeth had injured herself while saddling her pony; a piece of non-sense, as she told Robert Browning.

She was given 'a variety of powerful medicines', along the lines advised by a contemporary medical pundit: 'Make up a mixture. Put into it a little opium, a little arsenic, a little prussic acid, a little strychnine and a little quinine. These I call my great guns, and it will be hard indeed if they all misfire.' But misfire they did in the case of Elizabeth. Even opium, which at first relieved the spasms, quickly ceased to be of help.

Elizabeth confessed to Robert Browning that she was seriously ill for a few months only, which may have meant that she soon began to eat more and stabilise her weight or, more likely, that the panic attacks and spasms diminished. But she continued to complain of discomfort and weakness and be a faddy eater, and her father, perhaps under pressure from his wife – who was again pregnant and probably at her wits' end trying to cope with all the responsibilities – decided to act on the advice of the physician first called in to see Elizabeth: 'An entire change of air would be desirable, and the choice of place, if dry, would be less material than the change itself.' Advice of that nature suggested that Dr Carden had recognised the mental nature of the problem, even if too tactful to say so. He was anticipating the wisdom of Dr William Gull, who coined the term anorexia nervosa and first described the condition in 1868. Gull wrote, 'that mental states may destroy appetites is notorious, and it will be admitted that young women at the ages named are specially obnoxious to mental perversity . . . the patients should be fed at regular intervals, and surrounded by persons who would have moral control over them – relations and friends being generally the worst attendants . . . '.

Elizabeth was moved to the Spa Hotel at Gloucester, near the spa itself, although she never used its facilities so far as is known. There she stayed for almost a year. At first she was treated actively, with cold showers, cupping* and, even if not

---

*A hot cup or glass was placed on the body which, as it cooled, drew up the flesh into a lump through which, it was held, the body rid itself of excess humours.

put into practice, threats of blistering and leeches. But it soon became apparent that drastic measures were not efficacious and she was treated conservatively with rest and quiet.

It seems likely that her doctors by now suspected the psychiatric nature of the condition; at least that Elizabeth's mental state had become the predominant feature. How much her father was prepared to acknowledge this is unknown, although in years to come he indubitably believed that she exaggerated her symptoms, and that her eating habits were responsible for her thin, frail condition. One suspects that her mother took a more robust line and, impatient with what she saw, told Elizabeth to pull herself together and return to real life.

There is always an element of malingering in neurotic and psychosomatic disorders, but to accuse the person of this is often unproductive. Elizabeth was probably upset and angered by such hints, and those feelings in turn were likely to have added to the anxiety and insecurity that were at the core of the problem.

It takes time for psychosomatic states like anorexia nervosa to resolve themselves. The patient has to develop sufficient self-confidence and assurance before she can securely resume her life. Elizabeth had the best of conditions for recovery. She was away from home, yet she had a steady stream of relatives staying at the Spa Hotel with her – her parents, Henrietta and Bro, her grandmother, Uncle Sam, and so on – people she needed to know loved her. And she had tolerant medical care.

A year is, by modern standards, a reasonably short time in which to recover from anorexia nervosa. Her mother had her eleventh child, Septimus, in the New Year, and in May Elizabeth returned to Hope End. She was still very unsure of herself, and she needed to play the invalid to ensure that she was not regarded as a normal young woman. She did not stir from her room for nine months. But she progressed, even though by inches, and on 21 February 1823, she walked unaided for the first time into her mother's room. A week later, shortly before her eighteenth birthday, her father allowed her to walk downstairs.

The crisis was past. She was free to pursue her literary ambitions. She began work on a serious poem, *An Essay on Mind*, as well as composing shorter poems and odes. Domesticity was of no concern or interest to her. She was, according to her brothers and sisters, 'the most useless person in the house'.

She felt deeply loved, the favourite child, and she determined to please her parents through her writing. She basked in her father's praises. She recalled with satisfaction and pleasure the dream that had recurred during her illness:

I used to start out of fragments of dreams, broken from all parts of the Universe, with the cry from my own lips, 'Oh, Papa, Papa!' I could not trace it back to the dream behind, yet there it always was very curiously, and touchingly too, to my own heart, seemingly scarcely of me, though it came from me, at once waking me, and welcoming me . . .

She would always see herself as her father's beloved child, even when he came to reject her. For the moment she had no need to play the helpless invalid, although she never allowed herself to look healthy for long. She maintained an ethereal appearance through limiting the amount she ate.

Now she was happy, with almost no restrictions on what she did. Admittedly she led a very limited life, seeing almost no one outside the family circle, but this was largely because she deliberately avoided neighbours. She could not be at ease with men or women of her own age; she had no common interest with them, and their conversation for the most part bored her. Except on literary topics, or in later years spiritualism and politics, it was never easy to talk to Elizabeth. She had what amounted to a social phobia. She was not relaxed, and was unable to let her thoughts flow readily and amusingly as in her letters. The fear of making a fool of herself was always a hindrance in ordinary social life, a drawback she never fully overcame. She was also prone to become anxious over leaving home, or separating from her parents, even for a few hours; at times this feeling was so strong as to prevent her going out and she would invent some disability: a cold, tiredness, a headache, as a suitable excuse. Only in conversation with older people, especially on the classics, could Elizabeth relax and enjoy intercourse, but even then she preferred to correspond by letter, and whenever possible she would have the visitor call on her rather than visit them.

The one good friend she had was the eighty-year-old Sir Uvedale Price, a landscape gardener and Greek scholar, who lived some twenty miles away, with whom she had a lively and, for her, valuable exchange of views. Sir Uvedale criticised her

'*Essay on Mind*' and she in turn commented on his *Essay on the Modern Pronunciation of Greek and Latin*. It was a loss when he died in 1828, but already her friendship with Hugh Boyd had begun.

4

Hope End,
1824–1832

In 1826 Elizabeth's poem *Essay on Mind* was published. It was a long, clever poem, displaying encyclopaedic learning. It attracted the attention of a blind scholar living in the neighbourhood, Hugh Boyd. His interest was further aroused by what he heard from neighbours, and he wrote inviting her to visit him, enclosing his comments on the *Essay* and some of his own publications. He was an eccentric character, aged forty-six at this time, living with his wife and only daughter at Ruby Cottage, outside Malvern Wells, a few miles from Hope End. His family came from Northern Ireland, and his income from the family estate. He had a prodigious verbal memory, and from his youth retained vast quantities of Greek verse, effortlessly reproducible at will. This was to prove invaluable when he developed ophthalmia in 1811 at the age of thirty and eventually became blind. His academic interest centred around the Early Christian Fathers and Greek Christian poets, whom he translated and wrote about. He also fancied himself as a poet and playwright – with little justification.

Boyd was a restless man, constantly moving his home in response to changing interests and inclinations. He was tetchy, dogmatic and readily offended, and prone to react with childlike impetuosity to any offence, real or imagined. Elizabeth was both flattered and delighted to be approached by him and at once began to correspond. For a year they exchanged letters, with Boyd becoming increasingly querulous when Elizabeth did not take up his reiterated invitation to visit him. She invariably had one excuse after another, usually that no transport or driver was available, or that the weather was too unsettled to risk the journey. The real reason for her procrastination was her social phobia or fear of meeting strangers. When Boyd at length threatened to take offence she put the blame on to her father; he considered, she said, a visit from a 'young female' to be 'overstepping the established observance of society'. Edward

Moulton Barrett may have been serious when he said this or, more likely, was attempting to protect her, as he had done since her illness. Even her father must have found it difficult to see a visit to a blind middle-aged scholar, living with his wife and daughter, as improper. Elizabeth, one suspects, could readily have persuaded him to change his mind at any time for Mr Barrett only became the rigid and unreasonable autocrat after the death of his wife.

The meeting which eventually took place on 17 March 1828 had all the qualities of *opéra bouffe*. Elizabeth and her two sisters set out to visit their cousin whose home was close to Ruby Cottage. On the way they passed Boyd and his wife walking on the road. Henrietta, who knew him by sight, told Elizabeth, who was thrown into such a turmoil that she made no attempt to stop the trap and rode past to her cousin's home. There, learning that a neighbour, Lady Knowles, was about to visit her mother, Elizabeth went to warn her that she was unwell and to suggest postponing the visit. Boyd heard that Elizabeth had gone to the Knowles's house and, in high dudgeon, immediately sent her a long letter expressing indignation that she had not only passed him without stopping but had gone on to visit Sir Charles Knowles – when her excuse for not calling on *him* was that her father had forbidden her to visit any man outside the family. The letter made her 'feel uncomfortable' enough to break through her social inhibitions. She apologised and explained what had happened with more directness than she had previously shown: 'If you knew how strong an impulse almost made me stop the carriage, when I heard of you being so near – and how my courage failed at the idea of introducing myself *there*, you would not blame my inclinations.' She added placatingly, 'I hope to be at Ruby Cottage almost as soon as this note.'

She set out to call there a few days later with her sisters, driven by Bro. As they descended a steep hill Bro lost control of the pony, and Elizabeth, panicking, grabbed the reins whereupon the trap overturned on the bank. Henrietta was badly bruised but Elizabeth, apart from shock, was unscathed. The trap was righted and Bro manfully put himself between the shafts and began to pull his sisters towards their cousin's house. On cue, the Boyds met them on the road at this point, Elizabeth and Boyd shook hands and they walked together to her cousin's house. The ice was broken.

On returning home her father was both relieved and amused, and accused Elizabeth of 'having contrived the whole upset for the sake of the dramatic effect, and of taking care to fall lightly myself'. But he offered no objection to her seeing Boyd again. 'Depend on my coming as soon as possible,' she wrote to him. 'I hope that we may have a great deal of personal intercourse this summer. . . .' And she ended with a final apology for her behaviour. 'You had a *right* to expect from me something better, than my *passing you* might seem to imply! But you have found *now* that my intentions and feelings towards you were *not* in fault, however appearance might belie them.' On 16 April she paid her first visit to Ruby Cottage.

She liked Boyd from the start. He was 'a rather young-looking man . . . moderately tall, and slightly formed . . . his face very pale with an expression of placidity and mildness'. His voice was 'harmonious and gentle and low – and seems to have naturally a melancholy cadence and tone – which is affecting when you look at his quenched and deadened eyes – totally and hopelessly blind. I did not see him smile once!'

The first visit went well, so well indeed that Boyd was kept from his dinner reciting passages from the Early Christian Fathers to an appreciative Elizabeth. Another visit was arranged and soon she was calling weekly, and reading aloud selected Greek passages.

Boyd's lease on Ruby Cottage expired at about this time and he moved to Woodland Lodge, on the far side of Great Malvern, some seven miles from Hope End. Elizabeth visited him there, and she was even allowed to drive herself singlehanded in the pony trap. She had not only overcome her agoraphobia but convinced her father that she no longer had to be wrapped in cotton wool. 'I need not take either of my sisters with me . . . ' she wrote to Boyd. 'I may assure you that "leaving home" will not appear in the least tremendous when I am going to see *you*.'

She was impatient to see her new teacher more often, and was excited whenever it looked to be possible. Her mother was ill that year and in consequence her father planned to move the family to Malvern for the summer, to spend it at the higher altitude then thought to be healthier. Her beloved Moulton grandmother was set to join them there,[1] and Elizabeth's joy was the greater because the chosen accommodation was almost within walking distance of Woodland Lodge. But at the last moment the move was postponed, and then cancelled by her father because of 'the continued uncertainty and tediousness of [his] business'. 'You may imagine how provoked I was,' she told Boyd at the beginning of June. Meanwhile, she added, it was

35

impossible for her to visit him for the moment because of her mother's illness. Vexatious as it was, she felt her duty was to remain with her. Had not her mother stayed by her side when she was so ill? But she did not regard her mother as seriously ill – nor did anyone else – and as soon as she appeared improved Elizabeth arranged a further visit, and for Boyd's daughter Annie (about the same age as Elizabeth) to return with her to Hope End and spend the night there.

Elizabeth set out to make friends of Annie and Mrs Boyd – although later on relationships became strained, and even frankly hostile. Both mother and daughter were bored with their lives at Woodland Lodge, and were delighted to acquire a new acquaintance – especially one from the landed gentry. Soon they were being invited to Hope End, 'to dine with us at half past three' and drink tea at six. They must have met Mrs Barrett there, but there is no mention of their encountering Elizabeth's father. At this period he was spending much time in London, trying to stave off financial threats, and may well have been absent from home.

Her mother's health was still causing worry and Elizabeth was 'harassed and restless, on her account'. A plan for her to go to London was dropped and replaced by a 'little excursion to Cheltenham', to Elizabeth's considerable relief, 'as the separation from her will not be a very long one . . . '. Mary Moulton Barrett, together with Henrietta, left for Cheltenham at the end of September 1828, waving goodbye to a tearful Elizabeth, and seemingly in good heart. On 7 October she died.

Elizabeth was mentally shattered by 'the deepest affliction of my life'. 'The affliction was unforeseen and unexpected by me,' she told Boyd. And in truth she had regarded her mother's ill health as less 'tedious' than her own illness had been, perhaps no more than an extension of the increasing depression which had affected her over the last few years. For a while she was numbed, hardly able to think or feel. She did not cry; she rarely could when deeply upset. 'I tell you, hopeless grief is passionless,' she wrote after the death of her brother Bro. Her immediate reaction was to withdraw into herself, preoccupied by memories of her mother. She could not be bothered to read the many letters of condolence. Her mother was buried at Ledbury in the vault where Mary lay, but whether Elizabeth cried on the day of the funeral, or even went to the service, is unrecorded. She shut herself up at home and read the Bible.

For Elizabeth mourning was always prolonged and difficult.

Her feelings for those she loved were complex and often ambivalent. She had loved and despised parts of her mother, and after her death one can imagine the guilt and anxiety that surged up. Perhaps she was also indignant with her mother for dying, for she complained that she was still only a young girl at the time. In fact she was twenty-two years old.

She took refuge from her feelings in religion. Unlike those mourners who curse God for taking away the loved one, she thanked Him.

Are we not of the earth earthy – and must we not cling with the strong clinging of natural affection to that which is of earth, – to that which is resolvable to earth? Perhaps I have done it too much, and too long – and God has reproved me, by cutting asunder one of the dearest and tenderest and holiest ties that can bind finite beings to finite beings. God's will be done; His will, not our will – is just and merciful and to be fulfilled.

Now I can . . . understand all the mercy involved in it by Him . . . I can understand that by this dispensation, He has intended blessing both unto *her* who has departed, and unto us who remain. It is good for *us* to be afflicted – and *she* is happier than we could be if she were restored to us. . . . we are no longer *too happy*.

Too much happiness was both dangerous and wrong, Elizabeth now realised, for it was certain to be succeeded by grief. It was sinful to become too dependent on any other person, for that dependency was God's right and should be reserved for Him. This was to be her fallback for the rest of her life, and would be stated and restated whenever she was bereaved anew. It was completely at variance with her natural inclination. It was second nature to her to depend on one or two people; her dependency on Bro, her father, Boyd, and later Robert Browning, was extreme in every case.

Elizabeth closeted herself at Hope End and refused to see anyone other than her family for eight months. That her grief was not more prolonged was largely due to Boyd's skilful handling of her. He wrote regularly, assured her that she continued to have his highest regard, sent her Greek texts to study and analyse, and lent her part of his valuable library. This did her more good than any words of comfort could have done. She began to push back the past and look again to a literary future. She started to enjoy her homework and earning Boyd's praises. Her letters to him became more tranquil and lighter in tone. She laughed at his account of a bellringing disaster that had occurred at Malvern, and told him that while 'Grey's idea of paradise was "to lie upon a sofa and read eternal new romances by Crebillon", yours would probably be – "to sit in the belfrey during an eternal succession of New Year's Days" '.

Naturally Elizabeth looked to see her father's reactions. He is, 'thank God, well and composed. . . . My father's fortitude has assisted mine,' she told Boyd. 'After all, *his* is the great affliction – and *he* has taught me to use exertion – and God has enabled me to do so successfully.'

Edward Moulton Barrett had been in London, struggling not only with his financial problems but attending also to his mother's ill health, when he received news of his wife's death. He set off for Cheltenham at once and arrived there on 9 October. Resting at an inn before summoning the strength to see his wife's corpse, he wrote a brief note to his brother-in-law James which expressed his feelings more directly than usual for him:

> I cannot tell you what I have felt, to be deprived of one associated with everything that was in the way of a desirous life, and enjoyment for so many years is bad enough to bear, but to lose the wife of your bosom, the mother of your children, when yet I had a right to calculate upon many remaining years for us is very grievous but let me not repine, God has seen fit to remove her from the tenement which her soul inhabited into the dwelling of his Son. Her lot, I am assured, is a gracious one. . . . I write in haste with a headache.

He arranged for Mary to be buried in Ledbury Church, beside the child the couple had lost fifteen years earlier. He inserted a terse notice in the *Hereford Journal*: 'On Tuesday, the 7th inst. died Mary, the wife of E.M. Barrett, Esq. of Hope End in this county.' At home he was 'strong in the consolation which is of God . . . and well and composed', and he comforted his children. He did not weep, nor did he ever speak again of his dead wife. He ordered a period of mourning, and shut up and preserved his wife's room for eternity – a not unusual attempt to halt time and make believe that the deceased is still alive. Apart from a maid entering the room for dusting, no one was permitted there. We are not told whether he visited the room. The likelihood is that he communed there, perhaps kneeling beside the bed and praying, as he was later to do with his daughter in her bedroom.

He had always been a religious man, attending church, both Anglican and Dissenting, regularly, and he held daily prayers at home. The grandfather he so revered had been a devout believer, and Edward Moulton Barrett had carefully copied him in this respect. But until his wife died his religious convictions were no stronger than those of many of his contemporaries. Now, he increasingly sought solace in God, through belief and unquestioning acceptance. 'God . . . in His dealings with his people brings them down in order to exact, to take away in order to give more abundantly. . . . A curse is but a blessing in disguise or rather a blessing follows hard upon it.' One can see clearly the origin of Elizabeth's sentiments.

In the four years that passed between his wife's death and the sale of Hope End, Edward Moulton Barrett was too heavily engaged in trying to save his financial position to give God and his family too much of his thoughts. But once he was more securely established, God's will came to feature prominently in his thoughts, and it was striking how often his and God's will coincided; it became apparent particularly to his family.

In June 1829 Elizabeth resumed her visits to Woodland Lodge. Her father was agreeable, and all three Boyds welcomed the visits. Almost every letter from Elizabeth contained messages of love to Mrs Boyd and Annie. Her father sent Boyd presents of game, no doubt at Elizabeth's behest, and he responded with a bottle of fine brandy and requests for advice on a legal matter. Annie Boyd and her mother again called at Hope End, and Annie came for a protracted stay; she had to sleep with Henrietta – sharing a bed was not an unusual practice then – who resented her presence, but this did not trouble Elizabeth or cause her to suggest Annie might sleep with her.

The following eighteen months, to the end of 1830, was a happy time for Elizabeth. She regularly visited Boyd, and her reading and understanding of Greek authors progressed steadily under his supervision. Her father, when she saw him, seemed relaxed and content, and although he spent much time in London he was affable and easy when at home, playing with his sons and conversing with Elizabeth on the Reform Bill and the abolition of slavery. She was both surprised and delighted when he expressed a wish to visit Boyd with her. 'Upon hearing this, I believe I looked nearly *half* as much pleased as I felt,' she reported to Boyd. She was desperately anxious that her father should like her friend. 'His feelings of esteem and obligation with respect to you are stormy,' she told him several times, but she added, 'You will like the character of his mind and conversation.' In truth, it is probable that her father was too worried by his business problems at this stage to concern himself overmuch with Elizabeth's friend, particularly as Elizabeth seemed so well and active; she probably put forward the suggestion herself at a good moment and her father accepted it. The meeting never occurred. When he was at home he threw himself into work on the farm, often not returning for the evening meal until after dusk. The recognition that he had no choice but to sell Hope End was beginning to crystallise in his mind, but he hid his sadness beneath a flurry of activity and merriment.

Boyd had long been pressing Elizabeth to stay at Woodland Lodge, but such an event was so momentous that she needed time to summon up enough courage to go. When she was at last ready, her father agreed to the idea, and on 20 September Elizabeth went there. She spent two and a half weeks with the Boyds and during this time she read more than 2200 lines of Greek. But for Elizabeth the visit was infinitely more than that. It was a unique experience. She had voluntarily left home and her father for the first time, and spent nearly three weeks of great happiness with her friend.

Did I not once tell you of the old charge against me, about my never *enjoying the present moment* – and must I not say that *you* have taught me that the present moment *may* be enjoyed. . . . Thank you for this lesson in philosophy tho' it has soon ceased to be practised – for now that the teacher is at a distance, now that the pleasure of being with you, like the pain of going away, is over – I find myself enjoying the past and dreaming of the future, in my own usual style. You will guess (will you not?) *how* I am enjoying the past – and *how* I am dreaming of the future. . . .

Her thank-you letter (and remember that all letters to Boyd had to be read aloud to him by his wife or daughter, or helper) certainly suggests that her feelings for Boyd were, to say the least, warm. The beloved teacher was no longer simply looked up to and admired, he was also 'the dearest and most valued friend I have in the world'.

Boyd himself returned her feelings and their meetings became immensely important to him. He relaxed his usual formal stance and told Elizabeth that having her to stay in the house was like living in clover – asphodel, she fondly corrected him – and before she left he urged her to repeat the visit. But she was uneasy at the idea of taking up Boyd's suggestion for a second visit, so soon after the first, and was afraid her father would be upset at her wanting to desert him again. 'It would not be politic and advisable to apply to Papa again as soon as your kindness proposed,' she told Boyd firmly, although at heart she longed to be with him.

She was apprehensive when she returned home. She had, after all, placed Boyd in front of her father in her mind and thereby been disloyal to him. She had worshipped other gods. But when she arrived back her father greeted her 'with a good humoured smile' and joked, 'So you have *condescended* to come back at last.' And when she told him how happy she had been, the reply was, 'I do not doubt *that*. I am only afraid that you will find it impossible to tolerate us, after Mr Boyd.' Mr Barrett's jealousy was minimal at this stage but could still be glimpsed. A few weeks later, at breakfast, he surprised her with, 'Are you going to Malvern today, Ba?' 'No,' said Elizabeth. 'No! What! Not going to Malvern. I thought you always went there every fine day. You ought to go by rights.' She reported the exchange to Boyd, not quite sure how to interpret it.

She anticipated visiting Boyd with as much excitement as before, and her pleasure in reading Gregory and translating *Prometheus* and receiving Boyd's commendation was as great. Yet there was now a nagging sense of unease and dissatisfaction which disturbed her. She sometimes questioned whether Boyd *really* liked her and enjoyed her letters. He never seemed to reciprocate the warmth she felt for him: 'I am not of a cold nature, and cannot bear to be treated coldly,' she wrote in her diary. She was aggrieved at not receiving an undictated letter from him; blind he was, but there was nothing to stop him scrawling a more intimate message in pencil to her, unread by anyone else. And why did he never allow her to take him for a walk? His excuse was that he was too untidy to be seen with her, but this did not ring true; other young women accompanied him.

The truth was that she wanted Boyd increasingly for herself, and was jealous of his seeing other females; none more than Miss Henrietta Muchet, who read Greek well and sometimes helped Boyd with translations. She was enraged when Annie suggested that Miss Muchet knew more Greek than she. At times she wondered if Boyd liked her company only because she knew the classics so well; he might have no regard for her as a person. Her thoughts circled endlessly in this style, upsetting her tranquillity and making her moody and anxious. If not in love, she was certainly infatuated with Boyd.

She felt guilty that so much of her thinking should be taken up with Boyd. She was neglecting her father. She worried about him. He was now spending long stretches in London. Already there were rumours circulating among the servants that he had suffered disastrous financial losses in Jamaica and that he was in great trouble.

Elizabeth was growing thin and nervous, and at the end of the year developed 'a hacking cough', bouts of breathlessness, and had to stay in her room for two months. Her torments over Boyd and the strain of coping with her feelings had weakened her physical resistance and heightened her natural anxiety. The event that finally felled her was the death of her grandmother on 29 December 1830. Elizabeth Moulton had been ailing for some time, but no one had suspected there was any immediate danger. She had had several 'attacks' over the past two years, probably related to a diseased heart, which had confined her to bed. On this occasion her symptoms were so slight that her son learnt of them only after she was dead.

Elizabeth was deeply shocked, for she had adored her grandmother, and had been the favourite grandchild. She had been to Elizabeth a second mother, in whom she could confide at difficult times. Elizabeth learnt of the death from her father, who had hurried to Hope End in order to be the first to tell his children. He was only able to stay one night, because of business pressures, but his distress was obvious to Elizabeth. He had been caught off his guard by the unexpectedness of his mother's death, and the barriers he had erected against the pain of his wife's death momentarily gave way; 'My wounds have been again opened at this lamentable event,' he confessed to his brother. Elizabeth responded to his grief and uncharacteristically burst into tears, weeping more for her father than for the loss of her grandmother, one suspects, and in the process relieving herself of her guilt towards him. Her father was alarmed by such an unexpected exhibition, especially as the other children received the news with comparative stoicism. Back in London, he demanded daily accounts of Elizabeth's progress.

The tears of 'natural grief' helped to calm Elizabeth and by mid January she had regained her composure. Henrietta, who was in charge of the sickroom, was able to reassure their father that the worst was over. But he was as much worried by her spiritual state as her physical condition and asked Mr Curzon, the Barretts' minister, to talk to her. Since they discussed Boyd, among other matters, and the minister expressed a wish to know him, it may well have been that her father was beginning to see Boyd as a danger to his daughter's health and peace of mind.

For seven years Edward Moulton Barrett had been striving to remain solvent without altering his style of life. In 1824 the long-drawn-out litigation in the Jamaican courts with another branch of the family over a clause in his grandfather's will finally went against him and his brother, resulting in massive losses. Other lawsuits followed. His plantations, until his brother went there in 1828, had been poorly managed, and the production of good sugar and rum had seriously declined. In any case the sugar market in Europe had collapsed and the price of sugar was at an all-time low. Hurricanes had been exceptionally frequent and wreaked severe damage. There was increasing unrest among the slaves, and a bloody insurrection broke out in 1832 which was suppressed in even bloodier style. A year later the English Parliament emancipated the slaves, creating an interim five-year apprenticeship period for them, and providing £20 million compensation for their former owners. Edward Moulton Barrett 'was glad of it', although in his gloomy moments he saw emancipation as contributing to his own – and Jamaica's – ruin.

Edward's income fell below his requirements. It became clear that he would have to sell Hope End, which was his main asset and his greatest expense. Yet he could not bear even to contemplate the idea at first. He arranged a further mortgage on the house, but he continued to live as extravagantly as before. He gave no hint of these problems to his family. To have done so would have been a confession of weakness and failure, showing him to be as financially unreliable as his father. It was providential perhaps that his wife had died three years before the news of the sale of Hope End became public knowledge.

His children remained ignorant of these developments until around the time of their grandmother's death. Elizabeth, already alerted by gossip, described her first inklings of the disaster ahead, glimpsed seemingly through telepathy: 'How I remember the coming of that letter to apprize him of the loss of his fortune . . . and just one shadow past on his face when he read it . . . and then he broke away from the melancholy and

43

Elizabeth Barrett Browning

threw himself into the jests and laughter of his innocent boys . . .'.

Their father found it impossible to tell his children what was happening. Writing to his brother on 15 February 1831, he disclosed that he was about to return from London to Hope End, 'although it will be for a distressing object, the packing up of all my things for removing thence. God only knows where, but He knows best. I dread the effect on my dear children. . . .' And he added a postscript, 'say nothing on the subject of removal to the Girls. They must forget it.' One can only explain his silence over the sale as a form of cowardice; he could not bring himself to tell his family that he had become comparatively poor and must sell Hope End, for this to him meant that he had failed them.

Meanwhile Elizabeth listened to the gathering rumours from servants and tenants, and grew increasingly bewildered and anxious about the future. 'A fat gentlemen with rings' appeared and said that 'the place is to be sold . . . and that he had been appointed by a counsellor to take possession,' Elizabeth told Boyd. On another occasion she heard that 'all the servants are discharged except Mrs Robinson, because no one else will go with the family to the West Indies'.

It was a measure of the awe in which she and her siblings held their father that none of them could bring themselves to ask directly if Hope End was to be sold. They spoke about the possibility and the rumours in front of him at mealtimes, but he gave no sign either way. It was maddening, and yet at the same time Elizabeth admired her father's 'extraordinary powers of self-command'. But she resented his treating her like a child; 'It seems hard upon me that nothing of my childhood, except its tranquillity, should have passed away,' she complained.

Her difficulties were compounded by Boyd having to leave Woodland Lodge in May 1831 when his lease ran out. Boyd had promised Elizabeth that he would remain near by and only move when and to wherever the Barretts moved. 'You cannot think how it has relieved me,' she had told him, although it was a rash promise on Boyd's part and a measure of how involved with Elizabeth he had become. He found himself in a difficult situation, and with an irate and unhappy wife, because it was impossible to gain any idea of Edward Moulton Barrett's intentions. Eventually Boyd again took a year's lease on Ruby Cottage. Elizabeth was thankful. She ventured to tell her father about this at dinner – apprehensive that she might blush and give away her feelings – and was pathetically relieved when he seemed pleased. The one person who was definitely *not* pleased with the situation was Mrs Boyd. She had come to believe that Elizabeth's father disliked the idea of the Boyds living near by. Her belief may have been derived partly from a wish to see an end to Elizabeth's visits, for she was beginning to resent her intrusion, and the effect she had on her husband. But there was also real justification, for Edward Moulton Barrett was no longer willing to meet Boyd, and was increasingly concerned by the intensity of his daughter's friendship. Her collapse in January had greatly alarmed him, and he was worried by her thinness and hectic manner. That he himself might be partly to blame did not occur to him. He was convinced that the fault lay with Boyd, and he began to grow antagonistic towards Elizabeth's visits.

Her behaviour began to excite comment from people at home. On the day of a visit to Boyd she sometimes rose at dawn – when noon was her more usual time – and appeared on Boyd's doorstep at the unearthly hour of seven or eight in the morning. On more than one occasion she arrived when Mrs Boyd was still in bed, and sat talking to the unfortunate woman in the bedroom while her husband was being shaved and dressed. Naturally enough both Mrs Boyd and her daughter were incensed by this kind of behaviour and tensions inevitably developed between them all. Annie was led to cast aspersions on Elizabeth's poetry and compared one poem unfavourably to a popular ditty in a newspaper advertising boot polish. Mrs Boyd became so offhand in manner that even Elizabeth noticed and wrote in her diary, 'What a woman to be Mr Boyd's wife.' Yet she continued to end many of her letters with 'My love to Mrs Boyd and Annie'.

In May, Arabella Graham-Clarke, Aunt Bell or Bummy as she was known to the Barretts, who had looked after the household for a few months when her sister had died, now returned to Hope End at her brother-in-law's request. Elizabeth tried to pump her for information, but she was 'hermetically sealed' and fobbed her off with, 'Why should you make yourself uneasy, my dear, till your Papa tells you himself? Why should you not trust him with doing what is best?' 'It is not I who distrust, it is Papa who distrusts me,' Elizabeth was tempted to reply. Insult was added to injury when her father and Bummy were several times observed in close 'secret' meetings. All the children were shocked when Henry announced that he had unexpectedly entered the library and come across his father and his aunt crying together.

Silent she might be over the fate of Hope End, but Bummy had no hesitations about giving Elizabeth her opinion on the Boyds. She suggested that Elizabeth might not always be a welcome visitor and that the Boyds might be glad to see the back of her. In Bummy's view Boyd was old enough, and had been long enough married to know better; he should not encourage Elizabeth to behave so irresponsibly. She did not mince her words and one noisy scene ended with Bummy pointing an accusing finger at 'those nasty Boyds', and Elizabeth in tears of rage.

At last, on 10 August 1831, the sale of Hope End was advertised in the local and London papers, but while this finally ended one set of doubts it did nothing to ease their minds over when and to where they might move. The advertisement invited would-be buyers to view the house 'by ticket', an invitation seized on by every voyeur in the neighbourhood, and 'parties of pleasure' arrived in carriage-loads and toured the house and grounds. 'It is very painful,' Elizabeth reported to Boyd, 'to be exposed to such intrusions, so very painful, that I should long ago have wished myself away even from Hope End – if it were not for *you*.'

Her father, in London, was suddenly struck down by cholera, a victim of the epidemic which was sweeping the country that summer. Elizabeth was aghast that he might have died. 'What should we have done *then*?' she enquired after his recovery. Anything could be borne 'as long as he is left to us,' she told herself, and with her next breath she added despairingly, 'Papa says nothing about Hope End.' Indeed, to the very end, he never mentioned the sale.

Elizabeth worried helplessly about where the family might go, hoping for Brighton or somewhere near London, terrified that Jamaica was a possibility. She could not bear even to think of it. There would be no intellectual companionship, she would be isolated from books and literary magazines, and perhaps worst of all, she would be in contact with the slaves – or ex-slaves as they were about to become. She was ashamed that Barrett wealth was derived from 'blood of the slave' and felt, although not so strongly as she was later to do, that she was cursed because of it. From childhood she had heard talk of slavery, of her great-great Barrett grandfather who had 'flogged his slaves like a divinity', and of the punishments meted out to disobedient slaves. She shrank from entering that world.

By the spring of 1832 she was a wreck, thin and tired and easily upset. Bummy suggested they both went away for a rest, 'but *that*, I could not and would not do'. Her father was now at home and she feared to leave him, dreading lest he should return to London. She was on tenterhooks that 'something is impending'. In April her father was so alarmed by her ghostly look and unhappy demeanour that he put a stop to her visits to Boyd. When Elizabeth asked to spend a few days helping Boyd with his correspondence, her father gave her an emphatic no. He told her angrily that she was 'turning into a shadow, thinner and thinner every day, and that he knew perfectly well what would be the end of it – meaning I suppose, the end of *me* . . . I might commit suicide if I pleased, but he would not be party to it, by consenting to your proposal.'

The year's lease on Ruby Cottage was coming to an end. Elizabeth still had no clue as to where the family might move. Hope End was not yet sold (the price was in the region of £50,000, a considerable sum for that time). Mrs Boyd had reached the end of her tether and was intent on moving from Malvern, despite her husband's vacillations and his obvious distress at losing Elizabeth's company. They left in mid May.

Boyd wrote Elizabeth a kindly, comforting letter when he departed, looking back with pleasure on their meetings, and assuring her of his regard for her. But Elizabeth's nerves had temporarily cracked under the strain and she saw the separation as a punishment from God, well deserved because, 'I often looked too much for comfort to you – instead of looking higher than you. No help that is merely human, is stronger than a reed.' 'But . . . although I have deserved to be pained on your account, I have not deserved to be pained by *you*.' Never, she appealed, 'withdraw your friendship from me'. She sent a message to Mrs Boyd, her feelings thinly veiled, asking her

> to believe that I do not think of you unkindly from *any* cause. On the contrary I shall retain a grateful recollection of the kindness and attention you always showed me when I was at your house. . . . I am quite aware that in your late removal I had no right or shadow of a right, to be considered and I sincerely hope that both you and Annie may gain from it as much happiness as you expect and I have lost.

Boyd moved first to Frome, in Somerset, and then to Bathampton, outside Bath. He wrote to Elizabeth regularly, even suggesting that the Barretts, when they did move, should stop at Bath for several days en route, so that the two might meet. But Elizabeth had regained a sense of proportion – though

47

she was by now so emaciated, with a persistent cough, that her
father stopped her teaching Latin to her brothers Henry and
Alfred, and gave the work to Bro – and she not only pointed out
how impractical the plan was, but asked, 'What would be the
use of going to see you, only to wish you goodbye again.'

Boyd continued to press her to visit him, on her own if need
be. She reproved him. It was unreasonable to expect *her* to visit
him; only if he had rented a house near by would that have been
possible. Boyd could not expect her 'to displease the person,
who loves me better than any person in the world loves me, for
the sake of visiting you for a week or two'. She left no doubt as to
her priorities, her father was a clear winner. Boyd responded
touchily, but Elizabeth was not prepared to give ground.

> Papa . . . would make any sacrifice for what, *he* believed, may
> happen – but . . . he may think it better for me to remain
> quietly with him than to go to you or any other person. . . . I
> am not sure that he is not right . . . I would barter almost
> every kind of pleasure for the loss of every kind of pain, and
> consent to be only tranquil instead of pleased. For a long time
> my powers of feeling pleasure and pain have been clashing
> against each other – and neither my body nor mind can bear it
> any longer. . . .

Towards the end of July her father announced baldly that
Hope End had at last been sold. He immediately left for Devon-
shire. Within a week he was back, having rented the largest
vacant house in Sidmouth mainly, it seemed, for Elizabeth, 'the
warmth of the climate may do me good'.

Just before she left Hope End Elizabeth wrote sadly to Boyd:
'There is one thing – perhaps a foolish thing – but I cannot bear to
think of it. I cannot bear to think that the rooms and walls in
which we have not been for so long [her mother's], because they
have become to us too painfully dear – will be inhabited and
trodden and laughed in, by strangers.' It was of her mother that
she thought during her last days at Hope End, her mother's
voice echoing in the white rose garden, 'You will never find
another person who will love you as I love you.'

5

Sidmouth,
1832–1835

To the end Edward Moulton Barrett dithered over when to leave
Hope End. The children had expected 'to go every day for many
days', a day was actually fixed, then he changed his mind and,
'we are now dragging on day after day, not knowing how many
hours of Hope End are left to us'. But on 24 August 1832,
Elizabeth and Bummy, with servants, and all the family except
Mr Barrett, Bro and the ten-year-old Sette 'whom Papa *could not*
part with' – they remained behind to dispose of the last of their
possessions – were at last 'thrust out of our paradise', and set off
by carriage for Sidmouth.

They stayed the night at Bath, which was exactly half-way on
the 130-mile journey, and only three miles from where Boyd was
living. Elizabeth was not even tempted to see him. She was so
'exhausted by agitation and fatigue that [I] could scarcely *stand*
when the carriage stopped at the hotel – and the next morning I
was obliged to breakfast in my bedroom and go from it, into the
carriage'. She sent him an apologetic explanation, but in truth
she had little desire to meet under such trying circumstances.

She was no longer the infatuated and spellbound young
woman of earlier days. Three months had passed since the
Boyds had left Herefordshire, and during that time Elizabeth
had sunk back thankfully into family life and involved herself
closely with her father. He watched her protectively, for she still
had 'a disagreeable cough' which came on whenever she
attempted to walk or talk, and he supervised her activities,
insisting she must not tire herself. She wanted to know that he
was at hand and cared for her, and she basked in his concern,
although this did not improve her cough and may even have
encouraged it.

The party set off from Bath later than anticipated, and reached
Sidmouth after dark. They were all 'confused and frightened',
the more so as they had difficulty in locating their new home.
But once there Elizabeth slept well, 'lulled to sleep . . . by the

49

rolling reverberatory solemn sound' of the sea, and next morning awoke to welcome the new surroundings. She liked the house, which faced the sea and looked on to green sloping hills and trees at the back, and had myrtles and hydrangeas flowering in the garden. Above all she delighted in the 'warmth and softness of the air', a major reason why her father, with Elizabeth in mind, had chosen Sidmouth. The house had until recently been the official residence of the Grand Duchess Helena of Russia, but it was small for a family the size of the Barretts, and tiny compared to Hope End, and they were all 'squeezed in little rooms, two in a bed'; Elizabeth probably shared hers with Arabel. They stayed there for a year, until chimneys and lumps of masonry started to fall around them, and they were forced to move to new accommodation for safety's sake. Only Aunt Bell disliked Sidmouth, and she went home after a few weeks.

Elizabeth's health improved dramatically, as much from her new-found sense of tranquillity as the warm sea air. She ate well and with the rest of the family – meals alone in her room were no longer allowed – put on weight and her cough disappeared. She went on long walks and donkey rides up the cliffs and along the coast, sometimes walking the animal into the sea above its knees, on expeditions by boat, rowed by Bro or Sam, picnicked in the bay, and made excursions by steamer as far afield as Torquay. The smaller boys, Sette, Alfred and Occy, shrimped among the rocks, and even Elizabeth occasionally paddled and got herself wet, although she refused to emulate Arabel who swam regularly, even during winter. She resumed teaching her younger brothers and entered into all the family jollities.

It was striking how her social phobias lessened. Soon after arriving at Sidmouth Elizabeth had resolved that, 'although it may not be possible for me to live as secludedly as I have done, I will have no new acquaintance except by necessity. . . . Besides, Papa might not like my knowing people whom he does not know.' Compared to Henrietta and her older brothers, who entered enthusiastically into the social life of Sidmouth, 'so much quadrilling and cricketing', Elizabeth certainly led a quiet existence. But she responded to the dozen or so people who called on the family, and made numerous acquaintances through attending missionary and Bible meetings with Arabel, and her father when he was at Sidmouth.

Much of her time was taken up during the first eighteen months with seeing Hugh Boyd. Normally capable of showing little warmth of feeling or spontaneity outside the works of the Early Christian Fathers, his friendship with Elizabeth had transformed him into a man who, for want of a better phrase, was half in love with her. Unable to settle at Bathampton, he had moved purposelessly to Bath which he left after a few weeks to arrive unannounced in Sidmouth, accompanied only by his maid. There he took lodgings.

Elizabeth was astonished and indignant that Mrs Boyd had not accompanied her husband. She had, she said, intended to come but at the last moment Annie had been taken ill and she had stayed behind in Bathampton to take care of her. Annie was soon sufficiently recovered to attend a stream of parties and balls in Bath, and Mrs Boyd in turn now became too unwell to leave. It was almost five months before she and her daughter gathered themselves together and arrived at Sidmouth. Before then acrimonious letters passed between Elizabeth and Mrs Boyd. Elizabeth criticised her for leaving her husband to cope on his own and for 'his four months' want of comfort'. Mrs Boyd counterattacked by accusing Elizabeth of encouraging him to visit Sidmouth for her own selfish ends, and blamed her for the whole fiasco. 'Whatever pleasure I have received from Mr Boyd's being here,' Elizabeth replied with vigour, 'it has not prevented me from wishing more than once, that he had not come here.'

The Boyds now settled into a rented house, which they leased for a year, only five minutes' walk from the Barretts' home. Elizabeth called on Boyd almost every day, and they resumed their old routine of translation and reading aloud. She must have read him her translation of *Prometheus Bound* which she completed in 1833 and which was published that same year 'by the author of *An Essay on Mind*', but there is no record of Boyd's reaction. Elizabeth herself was subsequently greatly ashamed of the work, and went to some lengths to destroy the unsold copies.

During Elizabeth's visits to Boyd in Herefordshire he had never allowed her to walk out alone with him, and he continued to observe this taboo at Sidmouth. It was as though he was fearful of being seen with her in public, of what people might surmise – a fear perhaps of his unacceptable wishes being exposed. Elizabeth had minded this in the past, but now it was a matter of amusement or indifference. She still enjoyed reading with him. She admired his erudition and continued to learn from him, but she had begun to recognise that he was a 'man of slow mind', 'with a child's way of looking at things'. He was readily put out of humour and sometimes took offence for the most trivial of reasons, rarely considering that he might be in the wrong. It was a measure of Boyd's tolerance and affection for Elizabeth that she was able to chide him, to persuade him to reconsider a decision or opinion, and even to smile at himself. She no longer trembled that Boyd be displeased with her, or worried that she had not come up to his expectations. Hero worship had given way to a wider appreciation of his worth as well as his failings, sympathy for his difficulties and deepening affection. At heart, as she wrote after his death, he was 'one of the most simple and upright of human beings'.

Boyd came gradually if painfully to recognise the change in Elizabeth. He loved her as much as he could love anyone, and continued to do so until his death in 1848. Slowly the turbulence within him subsided and he came to terms with his emotions. He became a devoted substitute father to her, always interested in her life and ready to help whenever needed. He was far more concerned with her than his own daughter. To Elizabeth he was to prove a godsend.

While at Sidmouth her father showed no antagonism towards Boyd, for it was plain that he no longer represented a threat to her peace of mind and health. But he had no desire to meet him, and Elizabeth made no attempt to bring the two men together. The old imperative need for them to know and like one another was gone. Elizabeth had no conflict of emotions on that score.

When the lease on their house expired in the spring of 1834, it was almost axiomatic that the Boyds would leave Sidmouth. Mrs Boyd and her daughter were pining for the pleasures of Bath (although the former was already showing signs of the illness that was to end her life later that year). Boyd was ready to depart. Elizabeth, one suspects, was relieved.

Elizabeth's friendship with George Barrett Hunter[1] was already well established before Boyd left Sidmouth. 'Dear Mr Hunter' was the minister of the Marsh Independent Chapel, a fiery evangelist whose preaching set his congregation, including Elizabeth, afire and even aroused the enthusiasm of her father. In fact Edward Moulton Barrett extended an unusual degree of friendliness to the preacher, and he and his six-year-old daughter had free access to the Barrett home. Elizabeth listened closely to his orations on Sundays and was impressed, not only by his power of delivery, but by the literacy and intellectual strength of his sermons. Hunter was remarkably well educated and read considering his poor background, with a mind that Elizabeth respected and could 'look up to'. He introduced her to new ideas and theological works, and he became a valued teacher in her eyes; not as erudite as Boyd, but more alive and vital, and able to respond to her newly gained zest and curiosity. Like Boyd, he possessed a streak of restlessness which led him frequently to change his job and home, a querulous nature and a tendency to take offence easily. Hunter's wife had been confined to a mental asylum after the birth of her daughter, and Hunter led a lonely life, caring for his child without help, in addition to his many pastoral activities. Elizabeth admired his fortitude and saw him as a tragic and heroic figure. She took his daughter Mary under her wing, gave her lessons and encouraged her to join with the younger Barrett boys in their activities.

Elizabeth became fond of Hunter, but without the passion she had felt for Boyd. They walked and talked together on theological issues, and climbed the cliff to a favourite seat overlooking the sea where they were seldom disturbed. On one occasion, accompanied by Arabel and Mary, they took a round trip by steamer to Torquay. They encountered such a 'rough rolling sea' that seventy of the ninety passengers were prostrated by seasickness, and Elizabeth and Hunter 'had to nurse all our party – but, sad to relate, just within a mile of landing I lost my oceanic reputation too – and universal ruin swallowed all – except Mr Hunter'.

In 1834 Hunter gave up his post as minister at the Marsh Independent Chapel – the reason is obscure, but there may have been pressure from a dissatisfied congregation – to become an itinerant preacher to chapels in the surrounding towns and villages. Elizabeth would sometimes accompany him on comparatively long journeys, even as far as Exeter, in the company of one of her sisters or other enthusiastic followers, often not returning home until late at night; on one occasion at half past one in the morning.

She was happy and creative during the last two years at Sidmouth. Although she preferred solitude to social intercourse, she craved a close companion and guide, someone whom she could admire and trust; the teacher was naturally to be a man for Elizabeth regarded the male mind as intellectually superior to the female, although not morally, with greater power and depth. All her life she revered strong men and time and again she mistook inadequacy disguised as despotism for real strength. To be in love with a man on whom she could depend was her greatest wish, even surpassing her need to be a poet. Not that she was in love with Hunter; she was excited by the idea, no more.

> Art is much, but love is more,
> Oh Art, my Art, thou'rt much, but love is more!
> Art symbolises heaven, but love is God
> And makes heaven.[2]

George Hunter was greatly attracted to Elizabeth. She was stimulating, widely read and well informed, with wit and charm. He was in full agreement with Miss Mitford that she was 'one of the most interesting persons that I had ever seen. . . . a slight delicate figure and shower of dark curls falling over either side of a most expressive face, large tender eyes, richly fringed by dark eyelashes, a smile like a sunbeam and such a look of youthfulness . . . '. And in those days she was 'alive to the vanities of costume' and liked to dress in 'very simple but graceful and costly dresses, her favourite colour being green'. No wonder, when such a woman 'bent those big dark eyes' at him and interested herself in his life, that he fell deeply in love. He saw her increasingly as 'his', an attitude which could only have pleased Elizabeth. She encouraged his possessiveness by including their shared experiences in her poems, and writing of themes which she knew would please him.

> For tho' we never spoke
> Of the grey water and the shaded rock,
> Dark wave and stone unconsciously were fused
> Into the plaintive speaking that we used
> Of absent friends and memories unforsook;
> And, had we seen each other's face, we had
> Seen haply each was sad.[3]

Most of the poems she wrote at this time were later published, and Hunter proclaimed them to be, 'Mine, because you taught me to call them so'.

Bro was away in Jamaica from 1833 to the autumn of 1835,[4] and as her father spent much of his time in London, her relationship with Hunter came to form an important part of Elizabeth's life. It was a contented existence, involving no emotional strain for her, and she looked on Hunter as her teacher and companion. Only later did she perceive the pathetic, self-destructive side of his nature.

For Hunter the friendship must have been a frustrating one, adding to his habitual discontent and rancour. There was no question of marriage, for he was already married. Even if he had been free, the contrast between his own penurious state and unreliable income and the comparative luxury of Barrett life made the idea impossible.

Elizabeth was not perceptive when it came to recognising the feelings of others. She was too self-centred to take much notice of Hunter's discontent, or if she did so to attribute the cause to herself. She did not expect self-pity from the man she admired; she expected him to rise above all adversity, as her father had done. On this principle she would never compromise.

After the humiliation and upheaval of selling Hope End, Edward Moulton Barrett adapted remarkably quickly to his family living in Sidmouth. He was relieved that Elizabeth's health had improved and he encouraged her friendship with Hunter, no doubt calculating that the Evangelical preacher would have a better influence on his daughter than Boyd.

His main concern, however, was still with his finances, and he was intent on making himself and his family more secure. He had plenty to worry about although he was prone to exaggerate his difficulties. He was pessimistic about the outcome of the litigation with his cousin Richard Barrett in Jamaica, which continued to drag on seemingly without end. His brother's more sanguine view of the matter provoked him into saying peevishly that he, Edward, would have to bear the major brunt of the loss if judgment finally went against them: 'The demand on you will be small, whereas it makes me a beggar for life.'

In 1833 the bill to emancipate the slaves was passed, to take effect from 1 August 1834. An apprenticeship period was introduced, to ease the transition from slavery to freedom, and the slave owners received compensation amounting in all to £20 million. Edward Moulton Barrett's feelings were, as usual, mixed. His first reaction was that the West Indies was irreparably ruined: 'Nobody in his senses would think of even attempting the culture of sugar . . . they had better hang weights to the side of the island of Jamaica and sink it at once.' But he later told his brother that he was 'glad of it', although he feared what the outcome would be in Jamaica. 'Everything will . . . depend on what is done for the cultivation of the negro mind during their

55

apprenticeship and hence the next six years will be the most important, not only to the proprietors of the Estates but also to the happiness and comfort and peace of the negro himself.'

He decided in 1833, after much pushing from his brother, that Bro should go to Jamaica to assist during this difficult transitional period, and to bring back a first-hand account of events on the estates. He had feared Elizabeth would raise objections to her brother's departure, but there was remarkably little opposition: 'Our beloved Ba . . . has consented in a spirit that has if possible raised her still higher in my estimation,' her father declared. This was not altogether surprising, for Boyd was still at Sidmouth and Hunter was already beginning to provide a close companionship. For the moment it seemed as though she had outgrown the need for Bro.

Bro sailed for Jamaica in November, preceded by a letter which reflected his father's mixed sense of pride and distrust of his son, and betraying his conviction that, like all his children, Bro needed to be protected: 'I fear he will be too willing to expose himself and exert himself overmuch, but you will be a kind guardian and advise and restrain him from all excesses.' In fact Bro, now aged twenty-six, liked social life, had an eye for the ladies, and was bored by work, as his father well knew.

Edward Moulton Barrett kept a close eye on his son, not only from the reports that arrived regularly from his brother, but also through Hope Waddell, the leader of the Presbyterian Mission Station in Jamaica, who was closely connected with Sam Moulton Barrett, and kept an officious watch over the moral behaviour of his nephews. Bro in fact behaved with propriety in Jamaica and worked well enough to please his uncle. Apart from the odd peccadillo, he was basically too indolent to misbehave in a way likely to draw Presbyterian wrath down on his head. His brother Sam, who followed him to Jamaica in 1836, was a very different character, bursting with energy and independent spirit, and frequently criticised by Hope Waddell for his womanising and dissolute behaviour; more than once he was recalled home. But there was no such trouble with Bro and he returned in the autumn of 1835 apparently unchanged by his experiences.

Towards the end of 1834, while in London, Edward Moulton Barrett became ill with what he called a 'rheumatic' condition, but which evolved into a serious infection of the chest. He developed pleurisy and 'water in the lungs', and was sufficiently unwell to move to his mother's old house at 63 Baker Street, where Nanny Treppy had continued to live and who now cared for him. As was so often the case, the cure was worse than the disease, and he complained bitterly of the 'violent character' of the medicines he was given, which 'destroyed for the time all the energy of the body and mind'.

He returned to Sidmouth at the end of December to convalesce, but he remained physically weak and depressed during the first six months of 1835. At the end of June he wrote his brother a pathologically gloomy letter, foreseeing huge debts incurred through the litigation, which he could not possibly pay, but would 'defeat' through death. 'For I do not think I shall last long,' he explained, 'my late illness has left effects that plainly speak to me, this is not long to be my abiding place, when my successor will come into clear and undisputed possession of the Properties and stand free from all claims to which my life interest in them makes me liable.'

But gradually his spirits lifted and his energies returned. He felt secure as his family gathered round him. George returned to Sidmouth from Glasgow with a law degree, ready to join the Inner Temple. Charles came back without a degree, prevented by his crippling anxiety and stammer from taking the public examination. Bro arrived home from Jamaica in the autumn.

He decided that they must all move to London. He was dissatisfied with commuting between London and Sidmouth. His work suffered, he found the travelling tiring, especially since his illness, and perhaps most important of all, he did not want to be separated from his children for weeks at a time. He also had to consider George's future as a barrister.

He rented a furnished house in Gloucester Place, Marylebone, near where his mother had lived preparatory to finding a permanent home. But he showed his usual vacillation, dithering over this house and that, and it was two years before he eventually signed the lease for 50 Wimpole Street, at the end of 1837, 'whose walls', Elizabeth remarked with disdain, 'look so much like Newgate's turned inside out.' The house was newly decorated throughout, the furniture from Hope End was taken out of store and moved there and Elizabeth was at last reunited with her books.

6

London,
1835–1838

'Poor Sidmouth left afar. . . . Half my soul . . . seems to have stayed behind on the sea shore, which I love more than ever now that I cannot walk on it.' She felt claustrophobic at first in London, 'wrapped in a yellow mist'. The muddy, filthy streets contrasted starkly with the clean sands of Sidmouth, the air was raw and sooty, smelt of drains and irritated her chest, and offered her little incentive to go out. She did her best to like London, and to compensate for its awfulness by thinking that 'if you can't see even a leaf or a sparrow without soot on it, there are parrots in the Zoo, and the pictures at the Royal Academy, and real live poets above all'. But she found it hard work, and her thoughts kept returning to Sidmouth. During her first London Christmas she was 'frozen to the fender', her bedroom windows taped and the temperature of the room kept high by roaring fires, while at Sidmouth, she was informed, there was scarcely 'a little frost every day'.

Almost her only social activity at this time was to go with Arabel to see Boyd, now living in Hampstead with his daughter, a fifteen-minute carriage drive from Gloucester Place, or to attend the Paddington Chapel service with the rest of the family and afterwards meet with James Stratten, the preacher.

She was immensely proud of George when, in January 1836, he passed the classics exam for the Inner Temple with flying colours; 'I am so vain of my brother,' she told Boyd, clearly frustrated by the lack of stimulation of all kind in her own life. Where were all the live poets whose company she had anticipated? Even her own Muse had seemingly hibernated on encountering the London climate.

Her chest was affected by the polluted atmosphere, her lack of exercise, and the unhealthy life style she was pursuing. She developed a cough at the beginning of January which forced her to postpone a visit to Boyd. 'Will you be generous, and forgive

me for having a cough?' she wrote. 'When it goes I shall be very
happy indeed to go too.' And again in March she was so
disabled by a bad cold that she had to keep to her bedroom. But
she did not lose weight, nor did her spirits drop, despite
circumstances. She missed the company of Hunter – she continued to write to him – but she enjoyed seeing Boyd again and
cheering him up, particularly with Arabel or Henrietta. And
Bro, with whom she could freely discuss literature and her
writing, was back with the family. Just when, petulantly, she
announced that she would 'rather walk to shun than walk to
see', her social life began to enlarge.

That spring, John Kenyon, who lived near by, a distant cousin
and therefore allowed by Edward Moulton Barrett into the
magic circle of the family, called on Elizabeth. A year or two
older than her father, the two had been undergraduates
together at Cambridge, and both men had come down without
degrees. He was a charming character, large, portly, red-faced
and bald, whom everyone loved, 'full of sweetness and
sympathy'. He was 'a friend of the poets' and knew virtually
everyone in the London literary world. He had long admired
Elizabeth's work, and he wrote passable poetry himself.

In the autumn of 1835 Kenyon's second wife had unexpectedly died, and the sense of loss was still strong when he paid his
first call on the Barretts. He was immediately interested in
Elizabeth, her forthright views and independent opinions, and
her appearance and charm – for she could be delightful when
she chose, depending on her empathy with the other person.
She liked him at once, and felt that he understood and
sympathised with her. He continued to call, bringing her
presents of new books and magazines, amusing her with
scandalous gossip, and discussing literary ideas and authors.
He discerned that her extreme shyness and reluctance to meet
new people were due to social inadequacy and the fear of
making a fool of herself; at heart, he was convinced, she wanted
to mix with witty and talented people. Practice with parties
would soon change her outlook and reduce her social anxiety.
He suggested she should attend a small dinner party he was
planning to give for Wordsworth – an enormous carrot, for she
much admired the poet. She was thrown into a dither for a time,
but then, fearing that refusal would upset and disappoint
Kenyon whose good opinion was now important to her,
accepted. Still hoping for a way out she appealed to her father

for a plausible excuse, but he was also an admirer of Wordsworth and unhesitatingly gave her his blessing to go. There was no escape.

Bro accompanied her, which helped to reduce her anxiety while waiting, and once at the party she enjoyed herself. Wordsworth 'was very kind to me, and let me hear his conversation', and she met 'the brilliant Landor . . . in whose hands the ashes of antiquity burn again', who talked to her and recited for her benefit two Greek epigrams he had recently composed, one being upon Napoleon. Bro, typically exhibitionistic, kept his end up in front of his sister by 'abusing' Landor for 'ambitious singularity and affectation'.

The day before the dinner party she met Mary Mitford, who was to become her closest and dearest friend and confidante over the next ten years. Kenyon was right in believing that the two women would take to one another, but even he could not have foreseen the intensity of their future friendship. Miss Mitford, almost twenty years older than Elizabeth, was well known as the author of *Our Village* and several tragedies, and was editor of a number of albums and Christmas books. She lived near Reading with her invalid father, a selfish old man whose extravagant habits made it imperative that his daughter earn a sizeable income through her writings. She was short and plump and wholly unintimidating. Like Kenyon, she knew everyone in the literary world. Her talk was always interesting; she invariably knew the up-to-date gossip, was conversant with the latest book of poems or criticisms to cause a stir, and was as avid a reader of French novels as Elizabeth.

They met on a visit to the Zoo, Kenyon having arranged for himself and Miss Mitford to call at Gloucester Place in his carriage and collect Elizabeth. It was a painless meeting – Kenyon introduced Elizabeth to Miss Mitford as 'the hermitress in Gloucester Place' – and Elizabeth, after the usual misgivings, enjoyed the outing and found that she could talk about herself, and everything else, with the greatest of ease. Miss Mitford, in turn, was much attracted to her. She described the event to her father:

Mr Kenyon [took] me to the giraffes and the Diorama, with both of which I was delighted. A sweet young woman, whom we called for in Gloucester Place, went with us – a Miss Barrett – who reads Greek as I do French, and has published some translations from Aeschylus and some most striking poems. She is a delightful young creature; shy and timid and modest. Nothing but her desire to see me got her out at all. . . .'

She was present at Kenyon's dinner party the next day, and noticed how Elizabeth blossomed when at ease in stimulating company. Elizabeth would lose her shyness in no time, she declared, 'if once brought forward in the society she is so fitted to adorn'. But Elizabeth did not go out again to dine until after her elopement, and apart from a visit to Chiswick House with Wordsworth and Miss Mitford – during which she thought she 'must certainly be dreaming' – her life of 'adventure' came to a halt. It was as though, having discovered two such people as Miss Mitford and Kenyon, whom she could love and trust, and who provided her with a window on to the literary world, she had no need of anyone else – except, of course, for her old friend Boyd in the background.

She saw Miss Mitford frequently, and began a steady correspondence with her, and Kenyon continued to call. All desire for parties and occasions where she might meet literary celebrities went and she firmly repelled Kenyon's suggestions for further expeditions; she was, she explained, too busy composing articles and poetry.

Kenyon became extremely fond of Elizabeth. He was too realistic a man to contemplate anything beyond friendship, and in any case he knew Edward Moulton Barrett's quirks and his possessiveness towards his children, but he greatly enjoyed her company. Despite his gregarious nature and many friends, he was lonely and unhappy as a widower. With her dark, reserved and sensual looks, the mixture of a challenging mind and emotional warmth, and a talented poet to boot, she exerted a strong fascination on a man like Kenyon. Her sisters suspected his feelings, and enjoyed discussing him and speculating on his intentions. Henrietta even wrote to her brother Sam in Jamaica, 'How would you like him to be your brother-in-law? . . . You must know that he is a great admirer of our dearest Ba – we torment her most terribly about him.'

Elizabeth was unmoved. The love of poetry, as she put it, now dominated her mind and activities. 'I seem to live while I write,' she explained. 'It is life for me. Why, what is it to live? Not to eat and drink and breathe – but to feel the life in you down all the fibres of being, passionately and joyfully.'

She was working on a long poem *The Poet's Vow* which was completed and published, still anonymously, in the *New Monthly* magazine in the summer of 1836. The poem is obscure, and she was taken to task by the critics for this, and advised to aim for 'greater clearness of expression' in future work. The criticism went home, as she told Miss Mitford: 'My fear of it makes me sometimes feel quite nervous and thought-tied in composition.' Later, she was to urge Robert Browning to be less obscure. Then she composed *The Seraphim*, an ambitious poem about the Crucifixion which contains some marvellous lines but is overall an uneven work. She submitted it to the *New Monthly* but there followed a long silence, due, it turned out, to the magazine's new editor having lost the manuscript.

She continued to visit Boyd and she sent him copies of all her poems. On one occasion, when she wanted to refer to a manuscript in the British Museum, Boyd suggested that she contact a friend of his who could help. At once Elizabeth's phobias reappeared: '. . . but do you remember that she is a stranger to me, and that I have a xenophobia as strongly, and perhaps more so than, a bibliomania,' she warned; 'besides, even if I liked it, Papa might not like my troubling a person with whom I have no acquaintance.'

In August 1837 Annie Boyd was married in Marylebone Church, and all three Barrett sisters attended the wedding. Boyd was not there, he was suffering from rheumatism at the time, but a more potent reason for his absence may have been that the bridegroom was a Roman Catholic, a denomination which Boyd detested. Elizabeth was well aware of her friend's antipathy and had probably heard his views on the marriage beforehand. After the wedding she attempted to mollify him:

> The bride looked very lovely and behaved very well – I mean without demonstrating . . . the agitation evidently within her. It seemed to me that she had been shedding many tears, although not in church . . . I am sure that you have prayed for her and blessed her – and that none but affectionate thoughts and associations are between you at this moment. She must love you dearly as her father – and you must dearly love your child.

Henrietta was less satisfied with London life than her sisters. She liked her rôle in managing the house – 'I waived my right to the sceptre of dinner ordering' long ago, Elizabeth told Robert Browning – but as the one 'most caring for the Polka' Henrietta found the restrictions imposed by her father on the social lives of his children intolerable; no one unrelated to the family could be entertained at home, and invitations to parties had to be refused. Whenever her father was away from home or otherwise engaged she seized her opportunity, and had her friends to the house and went out and about freely. No one minded the deception, although Elizabeth grieved that it was necessary, since it was seen to be the unavoidable consequence of their father's unreasonableness. Bro followed suit, and Elizabeth and Arabel were often on tenterhooks, acting as watchdogs when their father's return home was uncertain.

Inevitably their father discovered misdemeanours, and scenes ensued when the whole family was lectured at and treated as a group of naughty children. Elizabeth was 'made to suffer in the sufferings of those by my side. . . . depressed by petty daily sadnesses and terrors . . . my friends used to say "You look broken spirited" – and it was true. In the midst came my illness . . . '.

In October 1837 Elizabeth developed a cold which progressed to a persistent cough. She took to her bed, weak and exhausted, and eventually, although reluctantly, let her father call in Dr William Chambers, physician-in-ordinary to King William and Queen Adelaide and later to Queen Victoria. Elizabeth liked Chambers, who came to understand her temperament and to sympathise with her difficulties and position in the house. She trusted him and was grateful 'for a feeling and a sympathy which are certainly rare in his profession . . . '. He did not at first find signs of serious disease. Elizabeth was run down and tired, and he treated her by rest and confined her to her room. It was now that she developed the habit of not rising from bed until the afternoon ('Very useful in enabling an invalid to get through a good deal of writing without fatigue,' she advised Miss Mitford).

At the end of January 1838 she heard that her uncle, Sam Moulton Barrett, had died in Jamaica. He had been 'more than an uncle' to her and she was grief-stricken. She was far and away his favourite Barrett child; he had no children of his own. She always wore a locket he had given her in her teens – which later held a lock of Robert Browning's hair. He was as proud of her literary achievements as her father was, and treasured the copy of *The Battle of Marathon* which she had presented to him at the time of publication. In the summer of 1837, with prescience, or because of illness, he had arranged to transfer to her name his

63

share, amounting to one eighth, of the Moulton Barrett trading ship *David Lyon*. Although he died before the transaction could be completed, it went through without a hitch.

'Dear Ba', wrote Edward Moulton Barrett to his son Sam, 'feels [his death] most severely, her weakened state was little calculated to bear up against the shock, but I trust in the Lord that she will get well, and that soon.' He himself was deeply upset and anxious. He had been very close to his brother who had been the one person in whom he had always been able to confide, whom he trusted implicitly, and whose judgement on his affairs in Jamaica he considered before making any important decisions. 'Alas the tears I have shed for days past, the agony of my feelings, and the house of mourning in which I am, all confirm it. . . . is this all that man is made for . . . ?' For a time even his religious belief failed to keep his anguish within bounds. Then, as ever, he began to regain control of himself. 'I trust what has been loss to us, has been greater gain to him,' he repeated. He helped himself through comforting Elizabeth. 'I trust he has gone to those who loved him here. . . .' They would all meet one day, he told her, 'to sing the triumph of redeeming love'.

The shock of this tragedy had a disastrous effect on Elizabeth's lungs and she 'broke a blood vessel' in her chest. All the signs and symptoms that now followed are suggestive of pulmonary tuberculosis, although she was repeatedly told by her doctors that she did not have the disease. Medical diagnosis at that time was limited – the stethoscope had only recently been introduced and was still a crude instrument – but the reassurance may have been for psychological reasons, since the condition, then known as consumption, was regarded as likely to end fatally. We know now that it is caused by the tubercle bacillus, but emotional factors often play a part in its genesis.

She coughed blood intermittently, although never profusely. Her condition fluctuated, and at times she seemed so much improved that she was allowed downstairs and took her customary place on the sitting-room sofa, but the overall trend was slowly downhill. Still Dr Chambers preserved his optimistic front. He examined her chest with his rod-like stethoscope and repeated that, although the lungs 'were affected', there was no sign of serious disease. None the less, she continued to spit blood, complained of pains in her chest, and was weak and often miserable. Bouts of anxiety came and went, adding breathlessness and palpitations to her misery. Leeches, blistering, and digitalis increased her discomfort. Only opium gave her any peace or comfort.

Meanwhile, Elizabeth was working hard on the proofs of *The Seraphim, and Other Poems,* which was published in June 1838, under her full name for the first time. Female writers did not disclose their identity in the early nineteenth century because to publish was regarded as assertive and unfeminine. The novelist Mrs Brunton told a friend that she would as soon write under her real name as 'exhibit as a rope dancer', while those women who did disclose their authorship often emphasised their 'helpless femininity'. Southey summed up the conventional view of female writers: 'Literature cannot be the business of a woman's life and it ought not to be.' Her father, however, had given his unreserved approval for Elizabeth's name to appear on the volume; not because he was worried about her health but because he wanted his daughter to be recognised. Indeed, if anything he felt she exaggerated her symptoms and that Dr Chambers pandered to her.

Dr Chambers, in fact, was becoming increasingly concerned about Elizabeth's condition. The fine summer had not brought the improvement he had anticipated, and he feared that another London winter could have serious consequences for his patient. He sounded a warning in August and recommended she spend the winter in a warm climate. There was 'not at present any ulceration of the lungs – only a too great fullness of the blood vessels upon them. . . . he hoped the affected lung would eventually recover'; but she should not remain in London.

Her father was not prepared to allow Elizabeth to go abroad. He refused to let his children become separated from him again, having just established a permanent home after six years in the wilderness. Torquay was suggested. He demurred. It required the full weight of Dr Chambers's authority, and pressure from all sides of the family, before he was finally persuaded to agree.

7

Torquay,
1838–1841

Elizabeth sailed for Plymouth en route to Torquay at the beginning of September, accompanied by Bro, George, Henrietta and her maid, Crow. At first they stayed with their relatives, the Hedleys.[1] Then Bummy arrived and took charge, and they moved into rented accommodation at 3 Beacon Terrace, overlooking the bay.

The excitement of the journey acted as a stimulant and Elizabeth seemed better for the first three weeks. Dr de Barry, her new physician, adopted a firm line from the beginning. She was made to get up at 10 a.m. instead of her customary hour of 2 p.m., and was pushed in a wheelchair along the sea-front, or taken out in a boat when the sea was calm. The spitting of blood lessened and the doctor congratulated himself and his patient on the progress made. But it was not sustained and before long Elizabeth began to complain of feeling worse. She had 'an oppressive sense of weakness, and such lowness of spirits that I could have cried all day if there were no exertion in crying'. She blamed the depression on the digitalis she had been given, but it was more likely to have come from the strain and tension of the last year in London: the death of Uncle Sam, and the disagreements and discord between her father and the older children. She hated deceiving him, forced 'into concealments from the heart naturally nearest to us'. She loathed rows and when they involved her father she was left 'broken spirited'.

There was another reason for her depression, and the anxiety symptoms which were now intruding. Bro and George were due soon to return to London, leaving Elizabeth with Henrietta. The prospect of losing Bro literally terrified her. In her debilitated and unhappy state he seemed the only secure prop she had, the one person she could wholly trust and depend on. She felt as she had eighteen years earlier, when Bro had left for Charterhouse School, helpless and lost without him, and she panicked.

She wept like a distressed child, crying that she loved Bro 'best in the world beyond comparison and rivalship', until her aunt came to her assistance and appealed to Elizabeth's father to reverse his decision to recall Bro home. George was expendable and could return to London at once, but, 'You will break her heart if you call Bro away,' she wrote. Edward Moulton Barrett relented enough for Bro to stay on, although he told Elizabeth that 'he considered it to be very wrong . . . to exact such a thing'.

Elizabeth seems to have perceived this as a half-victory only, not a firm guarantee that Bro would stay with her for as long as she remained at Torquay. She was fearful, as no doubt was Bro, that their father might decide that Bro was needed in Jamaica, and despatch him there without more ado. In consequence, the news of Bro's reprieve did nothing to alter her condition. She continued during the last two months of 1838 'to hang by a thread between life and death'.

She grew so weak she 'could barely suffer without fainting to be carried by Bro from bed to sofa downstairs'. She had violent and continuous headaches. Panic attacks brought on breathlessness and left her gasping for air, hardly able to whisper, her muscles convulsed in painful spasms. She refused solid food and could be persuaded to take only slops, as when she was fifteen, and she again became so emaciated and frail that everyone feared for her life.

She was by now causing her father great concern and he was in almost constant attendance. Nothing was too much trouble if it would benefit her. She was, he wrote, 'an handmaiden of the Lord. . . . the most beautiful of characters . . . possessed of the noblest mind'. Surely the Lord would spare her.

Elizabeth relaxed and visibly improved as she saw her father's distress, and his regard for her. 'He loves me too well,' she wrote after one of his visits. 'There was the cause of his grief in going. . . . I feel how dearly he loves me; there was the cause of my grief in seeing him go. One misses the presence of such as dearly love us. His tears fell almost as fast as mine when we parted.' She allowed herself to eat more, although she remained debilitated for months. The combination of anorexia nervosa and pulmonary tuberculosis is a dangerous one. Emaciation reduces the body's resistance and the bacillus may spread and firmly establish itself throughout the lungs, or other organs, with fatal outcome. There is little doubt that tuberculosis gained a permanent foothold in Elizabeth at this time. Its virulence was limited, but it was able to manifest itself openly in the future whenever she became very thin and run down.

She no longer worried about Bro. Her father's devotion to her was such that she felt Bro's position with her to be safe. Her behaviour continued to exhibit the childlike characteristics of anorexia nervosa: the making of excessive demands, helplessness, reluctance to eat unless encouraged, tearful histrionics and erratic moods.

In May 1839 she suddenly felt 'wonderfully better', although still weak and thin, 'not even able to stand up . . .'. Her father visited her 'again and again' and she clung touchingly to him, always protesting tearfully when the time came for his departure. She longed to be 'tied fast' to him and to be continually with him. The memory of her early illness came back repeatedly to her and she recalled herself waking from dreams, calling out, 'Papa, oh Papa!'

She begged to be allowed to return to London: she insisted she was better, she wanted to see Arabel, she missed the comfort of her room and her books, she needed to be near her father. She knew at heart that such a move was out of the question; she could barely stand, she continued to cough and faint, and she was still dreadfully thin. Her doctor declared that if he gave permission for her to go home it would be tantamount to his signing her death certificate. Her father was convinced and gave her a firm no, and gradually her pleas died away.

By the summer she was stronger, both mentally and physically, and 'a confusion of poems' now began to course through her mind. Miss Mitford asked her for a contribution, and she rapidly composed 'A Romance of the Ganges', where a father's love for his daughter proves to be the only love the female narrator can truly rely upon. The idea for 'The Lay of the Brown Rosary' probably came to her at about this time, although it was completed later. It is a poem, Elizabeth warned, that 'no one can read . . . by candlelight, far less by sunlight', and is remarkable not for its poetic merit so much as for the way it seems to reveal Elizabeth's feelings for her father.

The narrator is addressing her dead father:

I wish I were a young dead child and had thy company!
I wish I lay beside thy feet, a buried three-year child,
And wearing only a kiss of thine upon my lips that smiled!

She was beginning to regain the real world. Bro, who spent his time riding and fishing, going to 'agreeable soirées' with Henrietta, and painting in water-colours, had grown his hair long and fallen in love deeply enough to contemplate marriage.

He discussed the issue with Elizabeth, particularly the key question of how their father would react when told. Bro was wholly dependent financially on his father, and since it was most unlikely that his father would approve, the affair seemed doomed from the beginning. We do not know who the young woman was, and whether she had money of her own, but even if she had it is unlikely, given Bro's weak character, that he would have challenged his father and chosen his independence.

However, Elizabeth's imagination was fired. She put herself in his place and urged him to marry the woman he loved. To make this possible she offered Bro all her own money (she was the only Barrett child who possessed any; she had inherited from her grandmother and Uncle Sam capital which produced about £300 a year). Bro refused the offer, but he at least had the courage to raise the question with his father, who predictably swept the matter aside, with no more concern than if he had been swatting a fly.

Perhaps Elizabeth was disappointed in Bro. More likely, she was relieved that she would not be involved in a confrontation with her father, nor lose Bro. Whatever she thought, the incident seemed to have a beneficial effect and helped her to feel more alive and part of her surroundings. She took a greater interest in Dr de Barry, who called at Beacon Terrace every day and encouraged her to talk about herself. He was a keen young doctor, well qualified, with a daughter and a wife again pregnant. He was a sympathetic listener and Elizabeth looked forward to his visits. Whether he was a bibliophile and knowledgeable or interested in Elizabeth's poetry is conjecture, but most practitioners of that date had at least some interest in literature. Admittedly, he seemed to follow the accepted medical wisdom of the day, that mental activity should be kept to a minimum, and he forbade her to read or write. Despite this ban, which she must have heard numerous times before, and which no doubt amused rather than irritated her, she liked de Barry and for the most part obeyed his instructions.

As she grew stronger he planned outings and easy expeditions for her. At first he had difficulty in persuading her to leave her bedroom. She had been closeted there for almost six months and had grown used to 'the air and the silence' of the sickroom, and was at first fearful of having to mix with others, even though they included Bro and her sister. The idea of new surroundings transformed everyone temporarily into objects of terror. 'I did most emphatically abominate and nauseate the going

69

downstairs yesterday,' she wrote to Arabel. But she managed it with Dr de Barry's encouragement, and she recommenced the wheelchair rides.

Then in October 1839 Dr de Barry died suddenly after a brief illness. He had grown fond of Elizabeth – this was more than mere professional warmth – and asked after her repeatedly during his own illness, more than once demanding, unreasonably, that she call in another doctor, 'which I can't and won't do,' she replied emphatically. Imagine 'my sending for a substitute. . . . if you know how I shrink from a stranger in the shape of another physician'. It was worthy of a scene from one of her French novels. Gratified, Dr de Barry rose from his sick-bed too soon and, despite a rainstorm, immediately called on his patient – with fatal consequences. 'The physician was taken and the patient left – and left . . . deeply affected and shaken.' Elizabeth relapsed, 'was ill, and had my old attack of fever and imperviousness to sleep, and have not left my bed for longer than three quarters of an hour for the past three weeks'. She held herself responsible for de Barry's death. Had it not been for her he would have stayed in bed and lived. 'I am a useless, helpless person,' she told Miss Mitford.

For weeks she continued to lie despondently in bed. Life seemed pointless. Even God's will was hard to follow. She retreated to her old ways, and refused to eat anything but a few mouthfuls of food at a time, and then only after much picking and persuasion, wept frequently and tossed restlessly at night despite large doses of opium.

Early in April news arrived that her second brother Sam had died in Jamaica, a victim of yellow fever. 'It was a heavy blow for all of us,' she wrote, 'and I, being weak you see, was struck down by a *bodily* blow, in a moment, without time for tears.'

Sam had returned from Jamaica in December 1838, partly to give his father a first-hand description of the problems on the estates, and the difficulties that had followed the death of Uncle Sam at the end of 1837. He had also to explain away the complaints made against him by the Presbyterian missionary preacher, Hope Waddell, who had written to his father that not only was Sam paying his ex-slaves a miserable pittance of a wage, but worse, he had a Creole mistress and was in grave moral danger. In fact Edward Moulton Barrett had not been put out by the news, perhaps because Sam was working responsibly on the estates and his moral behaviour in Jamaica had no bearing on the life of the Moulton Barrett family in London, and there was no question of a marriage. Sam had returned to Jamaica in 1839, forgiven, with his father's blessing.

He had paid only a brief visit to Torquay during his stay in England, but Elizabeth had taken him to task for his escapades in Jamaica and urged him to change his ways. According to Hope Waddell, Sam did become a reformed character during the last four months of his life, which may have given Elizabeth some small comfort, although the change was more likely to have resulted from the increased responsibilities he had been given rather than any prayers and entreaties from Elizabeth, or his father.

She collapsed, 'so ill as to believe it utterly improbable, speaking humanly, that I should ever be any better'. Palpitations, fever, breathlessness, bouts of coughing and spitting of blood, and her extreme thinness roused everyone's anxieties. A second opinion was sought and an Exeter physician was called in to consult with Dr Scully, de Barry's replacement. Both firmly agreed that she did not have consumption, and that she would recover and be capable of an active independent life, 'although I can never be fit again for anything like exertion'. She cheered up after this news, although only to the extent of hoping for the best, 'the best meaning one sight more of London'. She remained weak and confined to bed, but was able to compose poetry at this time, including a short poem on 'Napoleon's Bones', a subject suggested by Dr Scully who seems to have recognised the therapeutic benefit of her writing.

Her father was with her continuously. He had urgent business in London, but he was fearful of leaving her. 'How to leave my beloved Ba, I know not. I fear the very mention of it, for she is indeed lamentably weak, and yet it is absolutely necessary I should go; I really know not how to act,' he informed Sette. He held her hand and prayed, and 'grew gentler', and Elizabeth felt very close. 'He let me draw nearer than ever I had done.'

The death of his son Sam shocked and saddened him, but did not lead to the emotional upheaval that had followed his brother's death. He loved Sam and grieved for him. But he was not an essential cog in his father's life. Only one of his children was that, his beloved Ba, who was becoming idealised in his mind and more and more 'perfect' and whose death he dreaded. Edward was a man who needed an ideal for his sense of security. His wife had replaced his mother to that end. Now Elizabeth took her mother's place. Elizabeth was in a privileged position and could do little wrong in her father's eyes; she won praise and escaped criticism. He prayed steadily for God's mercy. He was still with her in July, immediately before Bro died in the boating disaster.

Bro had become less essential to Elizabeth during the years that she was seeing so much of Hugh Boyd and Hunter, and Bro himself had been away in Jamaica for eighteen months. But Torquay had recreated their old intimacy and dependency. Elizabeth clung to Bro and loved him 'best in the world' – just as she had done in childhood – far better than she did her father, she told Robert Browning five years later, 'as he knew . . . and everyone who knew *me* could not choose but know what was my first and chiefest affection . . . '.

Her love for her brother had been passionate and open. They shared everything, had no secrets from one another and understood each other's feelings as though of one mind. They complemented one another. Bro's good-natured tolerance, sociability and lack of ambition paired with Elizabeth's passionate drive, intolerance and xenophobia. In the sickroom atmosphere of Torquay, the childhood nursery attitudes and atmosphere came back and she again felt inseparable from and at one with Bro. Bro responded, reaching out for her hand as he said that, 'he loved me better than them all and that he *would not* leave me . . . until I was well'.

It was a very different love from the one she had for her father. She loved him, but she was always his child. There was always a nagging fear that she might lose his love if she failed to do what he commanded and follow the path he wanted his children to pursue. His love demanded perfect obedience. She and Bro were equal and loved one another equally and without qualification. It was impossible to imagine anything else.

On 11 July Bro went sailing with two friends and a seaman in Tor Bay. The sea was calm and the wind light and there appeared to be no danger from any quarter. But at some point there was a squall, the boat capsized and they were all drowned – 'and he *had* left me! gone!' The tragedy was heightened by no one having seen the accident, although an unlikely claim was made, and Elizabeth and her father waited for several days before finally giving up hope. 'For three days we waited – and I hoped while I could – oh – that agony of three days.' Hope was eventually abandoned, although Bro's body was not washed up in Babbacombe Bay for a further three weeks. He was buried in Tor churchyard; no stone was put above his grave.

Elizabeth was too distraught to speak or to cry. Tears never came when she was grief-stricken, but within her mind 'tears ran scalding hot'. She described her feelings later in 'The Mask'.

> Ye weep for those who weep? she said –
> Ah fools! I bid you pass them by.
> Go, weep for those whose hearts have bled
> What time their eyes were dry.
> Whom sadder can I say? she said.

She was 'scarcely conscious', and her mind wandered in a semi-delirium, almost as though she were sleepwalking. Everyone at Torquay was shocked. Henrietta could scarcely comprehend what had happened. She roamed from room to room calling for her brother, sinking on to a chair in floods of tears, rolling and shaking on the floor, grasping and pleading with anyone to hand. Arabel was the most practical and down to earth, thinking of how to help others despite her flow of tears, 'her mind having stayed on God'. Edward Moulton Barrett reacted with his customary calm, more concerned with Elizabeth's state of mind than with the loss of his son. She 'has felt it to the very core, and what may be the result with her I know not, but considering everything she is wonderful', he wrote to Sette. And, he added, 'the Lord will eventually bring her out as gold, fine gold'.

Although he had been overwhelmed by his brother's death, those of his two sons were met with a more robust resignation: '. . . sometimes I can scarcely credit my loss, still I remember nothing happeneth of chance, neither in earth or heaven. . . . God has thought fit to afflict us, it would seem the one blow has not produced its effect, and He has in Judgment repeated it'. The lesson must be learnt, he reiterated, the family had to purify itself or God would afflict them all with a third blow – Elizabeth's death. He would promise anything to avert that tragedy. 'For myself,' he assured his children, 'I am supported, blessed be the Lord, and as billow upon billow pass over me, I desire to praise Him in the midst of it all.'

Supported he might be but the continued fear of harm coming to his one perfect child kept him at Torquay until the end of 1840. Admittedly there was no longer quite so much pressure for him to be back in London. Richard Barrett, who had been responsible for much of his recent financial troubles and worry over litigation, had died in 1839, probably poisoned, and by October 1840 Edward was able to accept that his 'pecuniary difficulties' were over.

Elizabeth Barrett Browning

Elizabeth continued to lie in bed for months. Her thoughts centred on Bro and her part in his death. She had kept him at Torquay. She had sinned by loving him too much and relied on him when she should have trusted God. So it had been with Boyd. When Boyd had suddenly left Herefordshire she had realised then that she had too often sought comfort from him instead of through prayer. She had deserved the 'heavy afflictions' with which God had 'been pleased to afflict me'. Boyd himself had warned her, when she first went to Torquay, not to become too dependent on Bro, 'of not suffering my natural affections to find me down too closely to the earth'. 'It is a foul sin, to sin *by* love, against Love,' she had answered, and assured him that she would be on her guard. Now she recognised how greatly she had sinned by clinging so much to Bro; that was why 'the Divine Hand cast me down in the place of graves and struck me terribly in the very life of my heart'. Her fear that she was cursed was revived. 'Cursed we are from generation to generation! – I seem to hear the "Commination Service".' Of all the Barretts, Elizabeth saw herself as the most cursed. Whenever upset she revived the idea that she had inherited the sins of her slave-owning ancestors, and was thereby doomed. If only, she maintained, she had 'some pure lineage' in place of 'the blood of the slave', she might have been protected from divine retribution.

For a long time she wanted to die. 'Only an unnatural tenacity to life prevented my following my beloved.' But suicide not only required more exertion than she possessed, but a loss of faith in God; and this she never lost. She was so weak at first that she could not 'sleep for five minutes together without fainting. For weeks they watched me . . . night after night . . . only ascertaining the transition [between sleep and death] by a sigh, or the sudden coldness of cheek and forehead. And now [in the autumn] I can sleep for an hour or more at a time – and the faintings are almost gone.' She became grossly emaciated, not simply because she refused to eat, but from vomiting 'from the simplest causes . . . even speaking a little too much provoked the most violent vomiting which of course increased the weakness in which it originated'. But this too eventually began to abate, and although still unhappy Elizabeth began slowly to take an interest in her surroundings. In the autumn she forced herself to work, 'otherwise I would be mad', and by November was starting to read again and to write several sonnets, including 'De Profundis' on the subject of sorrow. In 'The Mask' she revealed the grief she was to keep so well hidden over the next five years.

Her father stayed with her until December and then returned to London. She pleaded to return with him but Dr Scully was adamant that she was not fit enough to travel. Her father talked of moving her away to Clifton, or even Wales, which shocked and upset her. 'All that remains to me of earthly happiness seems to me dependent on my return to Wimpole Street,' she told her brother George, and urged him to convince their father of this.

She and her father rarely exchanged any ideas touching on their deeper emotions. Neither ever referred again to Bro. She was grateful that he had never reproached her, as her own conscience continued to do, for keeping Bro at Torquay. He never once said 'that if it had not been for *me*, the crown of his house would not have fallen. He *never did* . . . and he might have said it and more . . . and I could have answered nothing – except that I had paid my own price – and that the price I paid was greater than his *loss* . . . his!'

There was a bitterness in her gratitude which she was unable to disguise. Her loss was irreparable. No one could take Bro's place but she resigned herself to being patient. She now had a companion who spent much of his time on her bed, a six-month-old cocker spaniel, Flush.[2] He arrived in January, a present from Miss Mitford, the offspring of her own spaniel. He gave her hours of enjoyment. 'Flush amuses me sometimes when I am inclined to be amused by nothing else,' she told George.

On 1 September 1841, she was well enough to set out for London in a carriage which contained a bed fitted with myriad springs. She arrived home ten days later, exhausted but with a sense of peace; 'no more partings – nor meetings which were worse – almost much worse, sometimes'.

8

London,
1841–1845

She was exhausted when she returned to London, and thankful to be home at last. 'I will never leave my family for health's sake any more,' she resolved. Physically she was better, although extremely thin, but she still coughed blood, was easily fatigued and needed large doses of laudanum to sleep at night and remain calm during the day. Her mind was preoccupied with memories of Bro and her part in his death, and of her father's tenderness and affection.

Depression and apathy rested heavily on her, the latter magnified perhaps by opium. Even poetry failed to move her. It was Boyd who, more than anyone else, helped to bring her back to life. A letter and carefully chosen books from his library were awaiting her arrival. Just as, thirteen years earlier, he had encouraged her, when she was grieving for her mother, to read and study Greek, so he now urged her to translate recommended passages from the Early Christian Fathers, and to read again the Greek poets. She did as she was told and gradually her mind sharpened and opened up. 'The poetical part – that is the love of poetry – is growing in me as fully and strongly as if it were watered every day,' she told Boyd a month after her return.

The translations aroused her interest, and when Boyd announced himself satisfied she offered them to the *Athenaeum*, whose editor, Charles Dilke, accepted them. He also took up her proposal of an article on the Greek Christian Fathers – provided, since the *Athenaeum* was a strictly secular magazine, she limited the use of the words God and Christ!

Both John Kenyon and Miss Mitford thought she was wasting her talents on such subjects. But they were an invaluable stepping stone to the creative period of the next three years. A review of an anthology of poetry led to her writing several articles on English poetry from Chaucer to Wordsworth which were well received and brought her praise and constructive criticism from a wide range of people. Boyd was so impressed by her article on Shakespeare – where she linked the Bard to Homer – he told her that no one would have guessed it was written 'by a female'!

All her energies now went into her writing; poetry, criticisms and an increasingly large correspondence. She was so busy, and so much better in spirit, that by July she had decided to reduce or even give up book reviewing and concentrate on her poetry. But time-consuming as reviewing was, it had its credits, for when she gave Tennyson's 1842 volume of poems a good notice he sent her an appreciative thank-you note. She was flattered to hear from one of her poet heroes. 'I am sensible to the honour of being written to by Mr Tennyson, and am ready to kiss his shoe ties any day. This is not in joke . . . ,' she assured her brother George.

Her correspondence expanded to include almost everyone of note in the literary world of London and America, as well as numerous unknown admirers. Although she met many of them after her marriage, during the years spent at Wimpole Street she consistently refused to allow anyone to visit her outside the favoured few: Miss Mitford, Kenyon and his literary friend Miss Bayley, Hunter, and later Mrs Jameson. Many of her correspondents made valiant efforts to call, but she was invariably indisposed and 'too unwell' to receive them. But her letters were sparkling and full of interest and humour, qualities which many people found lacking when they came to meet her in person.

Her growing reputation as a poet, the widespread rumours that she was a bedridden invalid, half-paralysed, as beautiful as she was intelligent, captured the imagination of some men, and women, and they half fell in love with the picture they created in their minds. The painter Benjamin Haydon was one of them. She began to correspond with him in 1842 and by December Haydon was addressing her as his 'little darling invisible'. But all his requests to see her were refused, and when he tried calling in person at Wimpole Street he met with the same blank refusal. Elizabeth felt safe in her room, and she had no intention of allowing any stranger to invade her privacy, and possibly disturb her peace of mind. 'I *can't* see people,' she told Boyd, 'and if I could it would be very bad for me . . . although I would see *you*, dear Mr Boyd,' she added. She feared that the image people had of her would be shattered if they met her face to face. What would she say to them? What would they expect? She was very conscious of the way she had aged, of the sea change wrought by Torquay.

Miss Mitford's 1836 description of an enchantingly youthful-looking Elizabeth had been replaced in 1842 by a very different one. 'She has totally lost the rich, bright colouring which certainly made the greater part of her beauty. She is dark and pallid; the hair is almost hidden; the look of youth gone (I think she now looks as much beyond her actual age as, formerly, she looked behind it). . . . The expression too, is completely changed, the sweetness remains, but it is accompanied with more shrewdness, more gaiety. . . . '

Elizabeth gave a rather different, if jokey, verbal sketch of herself to Haydon in January 1843, after turning down a suggestion that they exchange portraits.

> I am little and black like Sappho – five feet one high – straight – eyes of various colours as the sun shines – called blue and black – affidavited for grey, sworn at for hazel – and set down by myself as dark green brown – grounded with brown, and green otherwise . . . not much nose of any kind; certes, no superfluity of nose – but to make up for it, a mouth suitable to a larger personality – oh, and a very very little nose – dark hair and complexion. Small face and sundries.

Haydon remained obsessed with Elizabeth and sent her his valuables for safe-keeping when threatened with debt collectors. After his suicide in June 1845, he requested, in his farewell letter, that she should be his executor, and edit his diaries.[1] Elizabeth was distressed but not thrown by the tragedy. They had never met and their correspondence contained none of the personal details she sent to Boyd. Above all, she was already involved with Robert Browning and had no emotional reserves to waste on grief. When, out of habit, she wondered aloud if she were responsible for Haydon's death, Robert dismissed the idea in no uncertain terms and she ceased to worry.

Boyd did not visit her. He was plagued by rheumatism, and the prospect of travelling to Wimpole Street was too daunting for him to face. Elizabeth was probably relieved, and she never pressed him to call. But she did see another male friend from the past. George Hunter, who was now living in Brighton, called in April 1842 and 'spent an hour or two with us', and came again in October. The former fascination and charm of his company had gone, although Hunter still looked on her as his 'angel of heaven', and behaved as though the friendship of the Sidmouth years had given him the right to dictate to her. He objected to her recent publications, on the grounds that 'the criticisms are not given with either sufficient seriousness or diffidence, that there is a painful sense of effort through the whole'. But she was not upset as she would have been four years earlier. There was now no involvement and excitement on her side. She recognised him as a resentful, disappointed man, limited by his personality, and she was both sad and sorry for him. The closeness was gone, in contrast to her friendship with Boyd which had deepened despite the lack of direct contact. It was two years before she saw Hunter again, but he wrote regularly during this time. He then came to live in London, and resumed regular visits.

Despite the irritation he aroused in her, she remained friendly and tolerated his boorish behaviour. But she became alarmed by his ill-tempered outbursts and eventually terminated his visits. It must have occurred to her at some point, as she listened to his angry outpourings, that in some ways he was a parody of her father. But if it did she never referred to it.

Her love for her father sustained her. Anticipating the sound of his footsteps on the stairs when he returned from work was a delight. Sometimes he brought her flowers, and the new edition of the *Athenaeum* or the *Pall Mall Gazette*. They talked, and she showed him a letter from Miss Mitford containing news of her father or some piece of literary gossip. But the most pleasurable and comforting event was at night, between eleven and twelve, before she went to bed. He came through the communicating door between their rooms and they sat and talked together for some time before praying. She described what happened then to Miss Mitford: 'Papa is my chaplain – prays with me every night – not out of a book, but simply and warmly at once – with one of my hands held in his and nobody beside him and me in the room. That is dear in him – is it not?'

It was a moving experience for them both. For her father the ceremony was much more than simply kneeling beside Elizabeth. He prayed with her and for her, and became united with her as he gave thanks for her survival and her returning health. He was gentle and affectionate and no outburst ever disturbed the calm. He kissed her goodnight. When he left she was at peace with herself – as he was. It seemed a perfect union.

Afterwards she lay peacefully in bed, Flush asleep beside her, his head on her shoulder until Arabel came at midnight, shook out her pillows and drew the curtains, and removed Flush. Then came her dose of laudanum and she was asleep 'in a red hood of poppies'.

It was a fairy-tale existence, unreal and unstable. Her greatest

pleasure was to please her father. His smile or a sign of appro-
bation was her reward. His flowers were the more welcome as
they signalled that he had earlier thought of her – alas, that they
perished so rapidly in the hot-house atmosphere of the room.
His love permeated her existence and gave meaning to her life.
She wished only to live for him; she was 'pure of wishes' for
herself. Day succeeded day without change in her routine.

But her emotions were slowly unthawing and developing,
and she began to take a more lively interest in some of her male
correspondents. In the past she would have discussed them
with Bro. Now she had Miss Mitford as a confidante, and the
two women, although separated by a generation, exchanged
views on those men they found interesting. Miss Mitford 'had
no sympathy with love', and had had no experience of it – which
added zest to her often witty and malicious descriptions of men.

Elizabeth had corresponded with Richard Hengist Horne –
writer, poet, critic and adventurer – since 1839 and co-operated
with him in several literary undertakings. Horne was a ladies'
man, and delighted in Elizabeth's letters. She had set the tone by
promising to be discreet over any 'literary secrets' he might tell
her; in turn she would be 'secret beyond womanity, if you are
frank beyond discretion'.

Horne was keen to see her, but as usual she stonewalled all his
requests.[2] When his pleas failed he tried a new approach and
threatened to come to Wimpole Street with his guitar and play
for her sisters, leaving the door open for her to hear. She was
increasingly intrigued by him and his reputation, until one day
she saw his picture; bald, with long curly ringlets at the side of
his head, 'like an assassin', she exclaimed, dismayed. Miss
Mitford gave the *coup de grâce* by describing his behaviour during
a brief stay at her home; he was 'disagreeable' and lacked
'refinement'; he asked to be called at four in the morning and did
not get up until eight; he poured water out of his glass over his
head at dinner; he wanted three baths a day; he giggled; was
astoundingly ignorant; had a mania for heiresses; and so on.

Then there was gossip about Henry Chorley, the critic of the
Athenaeum, who for a time was much attracted to the idea of
Elizabeth. Miss Mitford liked him, and felt warmly towards him
until he too came to stay with her. Afterwards she grew 'quite
cold about Mr Chorley' and reported to Elizabeth that, 'he is
very much changed and grown to be "a presumptuous cox-
comb" '. Clearly, when with Miss Mitford, a man had to be on
more than his best behaviour.

But tittle-tattle of this kind about men was of limited interest, and did not hold the imagination for long. More exciting and stimulating for Elizabeth were the French novels she devoured, a passion she shared with Miss Mitford; they constantly discussed what they had read and recommended new works to one another. Lying in bed or on her sofa, increasingly dissatisfied with her life, she was drawn to the people and events described in the books and shocked by what she read. Most of her knowledge – or rather her ideas – of physical love was derived from this literature. ' "Don Juan" or "La Nouvelle Héloïse" are mere Hannah Moore and Wilberforce [both staid evangelists] by the side of certain books that we wot of,' she joked with Miss Mitford. As for Crébillon fils, 'It is the most disgusting sensual book I ever *tried* to read – but didn't read, I do assure you' – a nice giveaway remark. Certain books were so lurid they should be burnt, she maintained, although what she was surely saying was that she felt burned by them.

She greatly admired George Sand, but was sometimes embarrassed by the frankness of her writings. 'The danger point about George Sand appears to me to lie in the irresistible power she attributes to human passion . . . guilty love cannot be resisted by the strongest will and most virtuous individuality. Then the disgusting tendency she has towards representing the passion of love under its physical aspect!' she complained. Sand's *Lélia* made her blush and she could not read through the novel

for its vileness. . . . Three blushes in one . . . for *Her* who could be so shameless – for her sex, whose purity is so disgraced – and for myself in particular who could hold such a book for five minutes in one hand while a coal fire burnt within reach of the other. . . . the whole lot looks like a conflagration. . . . my whole being aches with the sight.

One suspects that she both desired and was horrified by passionate involvement with a 'strong man', a passion that would embrace every aspect of her life. Such a relationship was impossible because she was a useless invalid who saw no man outside her family apart from Kenyon, and from 1844 onwards Hunter; and horrifying because of the conflict that would inevitably arise with her father were it to develop. Trying to lessen her disquiet she made a joke about the matter to Miss Mitford: 'How astonished [father] would be if I had Horne and Robert Browning upstairs in my bedroom!' – this was 1842, only a year after returning home from Torquay – 'He would certainly open his eyes and set me down among the inclined-to-be 'good for nothing' poetesses. . . .' Fortunately for Elizabeth her father had no inkling of these thoughts. For him she remained 'the purest woman', free of sensuality and misguided ideas of marriage, as devoted to him as he was to her. Miss Mitford, in fact, took the idea more seriously, and used it as a reason for persuading Elizabeth to develop a wider social life, so that she might meet some men. Such visits should be a normal part of her day, for they 'would not only be innocent but . . . proper'.

She poured her passion into love poems, but even this failed to stave off the despair that had begun to grip her mind. Depression worsened when she heard in October 1842 that her Torquay physician, Dr Scully, was seriously ill and, a month later, had died. She was 'overpowered' by sadness, and incapacitated by headache. 'And there has broken the last thread which connected me with that fatal place. . . . Think of living for two years in a place [actually she was there for three years] and of gathering nothing from it but grief.'

Memories and thoughts of Bro and their closeness tormented her again and magnified her sense of isolation and loss. She compared herself in her room to Mariana in the moated grange. It was not quite the same in 50 Wimpole Street, but:

> . . . 'My life is dreary
> He cometh not,' she said;
> She said, 'I am aweary, aweary,
> I would that I were dead!'[3]

What was the point of fame and praise and crowds of correspondents if she dwelt in silence? The answer was simple. She had only to open the door and people would enter, there need be no more silence. But her fears were too great, she had no one to help her and the barriers remained. Every new caller was turned away. Her sense of depression grew, the more so as she recognised that the fault lay within herself. In a moment of insight she wrote of herself, 'I belong to that pitiful order of weak women who cannot command their bodies with their souls at every moment and who sink down in hysterical disorder when they ought to act and resist.' But this did not prevent her from complaining, 'Do you think I was born to lead the life of an oyster, such as I do live here? . . . The prison doors are shut fast. . . .'

Still, she allowed no one to glimpse the distress that lay below the surface. She laughed and joked with her brothers and sisters; they were so accustomed to her 'imprisoned invalid misery' that they never perceived she was eating her heart out; they assumed she was content. Everybody, Elizabeth later assured Robert Browning, 'would tell you that the cheerfulness . . . was the remarkable thing in me – certainly it has been remarked about me again and again'. She was genuinely happy only in her father's presence. Then she felt at peace with herself. But when she was alone she wept and bemoaned her empty future. Yet her fear of altering the status quo was too enormous to permit any change.

If she could not satisfy her growing desires she could at least try to appease them. She attempted to push the clock back and deny her sexuality, as she had done sixteen years ago, by starving herself. She avoided fattening foods. She ate only small amounts, and never between meals. She ate alone in her room, and Flush was always present; he waxed fat on the titbits as she grew thin. Robert Browning, in one of his more witty asides, remarked that Elizabeth could 'eat so much of a chicken as Flush refuses'. Her maid, Crow, shook her head disapprovingly but could not persuade her to finish the meal. Her father admonished her for eating dry toast in place of dinner. That was why she was so thin, 'obstinacy and dry toast' had brought her to her present condition. 'If I pleased to have porter and beefsteak instead, I should be as well as ever I was, in a month,' Elizabeth reported to Robert. In the summer of 1843 she told Miss Mitford, seemingly unconcerned, that she had 'lost strength and grew to have two romantic dark caves for eyes, and white cheeks beneath – looking "horrible" as Papa said. . .'.

Emaciation would have diminished Elizabeth's sexual feelings and stopped menstruation, or caused it to become infrequent. Her thinness pushed her backwards and protected her from adult instincts. It also helped her to feel that, since she was in control of her body, she controlled her life, which reassured and calmed her. She became fatigued easily when very thin, but was otherwise unaffected by the weight loss. She was able to continue the tiny amount of exercise she undertook, and there was no falling off in her reading and writing.

Her family were concerned but not worried; they had long become accustomed to her eating habits and emaciated appearance. In truth, they regarded much of her sick behaviour as malingering. Her father had no doubts about why she was so thin; she made herself so by deliberately dieting.

From 1842 onwards Elizabeth's health slowly and steadily

improved. Within a few months of returning to Wimpole Street from Torquay she had begun to stagger haltingly from bed to sofa, which she viewed as a creditable feat. By July she was rising from bed at twelve in the morning and walking across the room with assistance from her maid. She was even able to 'stand alone' holding on to Crow's finger, despite wobbling back and fro. 'This new pedestal of mine is . . . far more glorious than safe,' she proclaimed. From there she progressed to being carried downstairs by one of her brothers – usually Stormie – and taken out for short rides in the wheelchair. By midsummer she had ceased to cough blood and her voice was normal. She had a temporary setback in the autumn when 'my dear friend Dr Scully' died, but despite her gloom her overall progress continued. 'Those hysterics', when she was 'convulsed' and lost 'the power of swallowing', were symptoms of the past.

Her recovery was helped by the unusually mild winter of 1842, and during the next summer she went out regularly in her chair on warm days, for ten or fifteen minutes at a time. Her spirits improved and she accepted Kenyon's challenge to visit him at his home in Regent's Park 'and stay there lying on the sofa for two or three hours, safe and silent and looking on the trees, with Flush as a sister'. 'If I can get used to the motion of the chair I will do it before the end of the summer – or at any rate dream of it,' she promised him.

She became irate when anyone offered her medical advice or talked of having new opinions. Earlier on she had rebuked Boyd on this account: 'I shall dread being annoyed by more medical speculation and consultations. Pray do not suggest any,' she told him – although, in fact, Dr Jago, the practitioner Boyd wanted Elizabeth to see, later became her trusted physician.

Miss Mitford's suggestion that she should move to the country met with a similar snub: 'I think that what is called "London unhealthiness" is rather a sentiment than an opinion.' (This was a time when cholera was rife in the towns!) 'If we were bricked up in the city we might talk of thick airs or no airs – but here, on the very verge of the country, some 200 yards from Regent's Park which opens onto "Hampstead's breeze heath". . . . ' Then, revealingly, she added, 'If I went away . . . I must give up a good deal – my evenings with papa for instance. . . .'

A regular supply of opium was essential to Elizabeth's tranquillity and evenness of spirits. She had had her first experience with the drug at fifteen, when she was ill with anorexia nervosa and hysteria. There is no reason to suppose that she continued it after her recovery, although she may have resorted to it occasionally if unwell or upset. It was not until 1838 that she began taking opium regularly and in increasing amounts. She continued the habit except for a year, from the last month of her pregnancy in 1849 to her fourth and final miscarriage, until her death. She usually had a preparation of morphine and ether – she called the mixture her 'amreeta draught', 'because the tranquillising power has been wonderful' – which, from the Torquay period onwards, she took in comparatively large quantities.

Opium has been used for centuries as a painkiller and tranquilliser. Although the symptoms of intoxication and withdrawal were well known in the seventeenth century, it was only in the nineteenth century that addiction to opium began to be recognised as a growing social problem and to attract public censure. Medical practitioners were the main culprits in starting people on the habit and all too often in causing them to abuse the drug. Elizabeth reported an occasion when the doctor 'made me take it . . . before the right hour and when I was talking quite cheerfully, just for the need he observed in my pulse. . . '. And she assured Mrs Martin[4] that at another time the doctor had told her that she could not do with less than forty drops of laudanum a day. It was understandable. No other drug could equal the power of opium.

It was usually given in the form of laudanum, an alcoholic tincture of opium, measured in drops; twenty-five drops contained about one grain (60 mg) of opium, a heavy dose for anyone unused to it; for inexperienced adults as little as four grains of opium could be fatal. But those who became tolerant to it, Coleridge for instance, could safely consume much greater quantities. De Quincey, although known to exaggerate, claimed that by 1816 his dose was 320 grains (19·2 grams) or 8000 drops a day! An established heroin addict today takes the equivalent of about twenty grains (1200 mg) of opium a day.

Opium dependency became more of a problem after morphine, the main active ingredient, was isolated from opium and produced commercially from 1827 onwards. A gram of opium contains 100 milligrams of morphine, and a solution of morphine is therefore ten times more potent than the same quantity of laudanum. How potent Elizabeth's daily amreeta mixture was is difficult to gauge. She said she took between forty and sixty

85

Elizabeth Barrett Browning

drops, but on occasions she took more, probably much more
during bouts of hysteria. She described how restless she was at
one period during her stay at Torquay, and how even two
draughts of opium failed to bring sleep. 'Opium – opium – night
after night!' she complained, but she loved the drug's effects.
After she left Torquay she probably averaged between three and
four grains (180–240 mg) of morphine, or thirty to forty grains of
opium a day.

The beneficial effects of opium are relaxation and tranquillity,
cheerfulness, even gaiety, and loss of pain. As a sleeping
draught it is invaluable for the tense insomniac. In large dosage
it may occasionally cause excitement, visions, and hysterical
behaviour. It can prevent nausea and vomiting, but also cause it
in those without tolerance, and it reduces or even abolishes
hunger. Elizabeth described her drug's main value as, to 'keep
the pulse from fluttering and fainting . . . to give the right
composure and point of balance to the nervous system. . . . It
quiets my mind, calms my pulse – warms my feet – relieves my
chest – I take life and heart and sleep and calm from opium, and
praise it gratefully.'

She was adamant that she did not simply take it for 'my
spirits', as de Quincey mostly did, and that she did not have
unpleasant side effects. But in fact it was largely in order to keep
up her spirits and appear outwardly cheerful, as well as to
ensure she slept well at night, that she needed her elixir so
desperately. Without it she was sure she could not cope
adequately with her life, or even write as well as she did. In 1843
she told her brother George that she was 'writing such poems – I
am in a fit of writing . . . long to live by myself for three months
in a forest of chestnuts and cedars, in a holy succession of
poetical paragraphs and morphine draughts.' Despite suspicions, there is no convincing evidence in her poetry of morphine inspired imagery.[5]

The amount of opium she was regularly taking was great
enough to cause withdrawal symptoms when the dosage was
reduced too low, too quickly. The strength of individual
preparations varied considerably between chemists, and mis-
takes in making up preparations inevitably occurred. Elizabeth's
occasional complaints of muscle restlessness, aching limbs,
headache and insomnia could sometimes have been symptoms
of withdrawal rather than the result of increased nervousness.
On at least two occasions chemists gave her understrength
solutions of opium and she became restless and upset, and was

on the point of developing 'paralysis' before a stronger potion rescued her.

Aside from keeping up her spirits opium reduced her hunger and made it easier for her to diet. She claimed, in fact, that the drug improved her appetite; in so far as it relaxed her mind and stomach muscles, it could have done so, without appreciably increasing hunger. It was the craving for starchy foods and sweets, liable to develop during rigorous dieting, that was so effectively abolished by morphine. The drug also countered any sexual feelings that had survived the emaciation.

The expense of the morphine was not inconsiderable. She received nearly £50 a quarter from her investments, and almost all that went on buying morphine. She was embarrassed by this extravagance and excused herself in various ways; that doctors insisted she had the drug, and that it was necessary for the good of her lungs 'by equalising the general circulation'. She was insistent that she was not dependent on it.

She did not want her father to know her opium habit, or its extent and warned her brother George not to mention the subject when he wrote to her (since family letters were usually read by her father). Later, she was very much on the defensive with Robert Browning, who battled long and unsuccessfully to persuade her to reduce, if not stop opium. He attempted to make a joke of the drug habit by comparing his dependence on Elizabeth with her addiction. 'How do you suppose I feel . . . without my proper quantity of morphine? May I call you my morphine?' he asked, heavyhandedly. But Elizabeth was not over-amused by the topic. 'Can I be as good for you as morphine is for me . . . ?' she replied. 'Even at the cost of being as bad also. Can't you leave me off without risking your life, – nor go on with me without running the hazards of all poison? Ah! – it will not do, so . . . I may not be your morphine, even if I shall be your Ba.'

Only with Miss Mitford – who apparently took opium in moderation, perhaps to allow her to cope with her father, and the trials of male house guests – could she joke and write naturally about the subject. 'Vivat opium! And may you and I live by its means! Moderation . . . being very particularly good in this . . .' she proclaimed. And when she learned that Miss Mitford was about to go on a journey she offered the advice, 'Did you ever try . . . on the [travel] sickness beginning to threaten – brandy and water and a little opium? Do try it.'

Elizabeth herself was not averse, at particularly trying

moments or when the wind was in the east, to adding a spoonful of brandy to her glass of opium; a potent mixture, which would have had the additional advantage of reducing the unpleasant smell of ether, but this was not usual. By and large her intake of opium was well controlled by her personal maid, Crow, who had been with her throughout the three years at Torquay, and cared for her in London until May 1844 when she left, having secretly married the butler and become pregnant.

Elizabeth was painfully vexed by this event. She stayed awake at nights, wept, and had a continuous headache at the prospect of losing Crow. 'I am much attached to her . . . and the idea of a stranger is scarcely tolerable to me . . . ' she informed Kenyon. She had trusted Crow, and allowed herself to be firmly organised by her; it was 'an affectionate, gentle (always respectful) control. . . . You must not have the window open in an east wind, – and the like . . . '. She measured out the exact amount of opium or amreeta mixture prescribed by the doctor, and no extra was normally allowed.

When the new maid, Wilson, arrived, Elizabeth behaved at first as a spoilt, indulged child, continually testing her reactions; 'I may have the window open all day, if it blows a hurricane. . . . I may take double morphine draughts if I like. I may go to bed as late as I please – and talk as long. It is a liberty I am not grown strong enough for – ', she admitted. In time she acclimatised herself to Wilson and the opium draughts resumed their even flow. Only when Robert Browning voiced his concern of the habit did Elizabeth even consider reducing 'the calming remedy' – 'slowly and gradually something *may* be done'. It never was.

9

The Courtship,
1845–1846

Elizabeth had long admired Robert Browning's poetry, but far from uncritically: 'Much I wish away – impotent attempts at humour – the vain jangling with rhymes . . . '. She looked on him as 'a true original poet'. Writing in the *Athenaeum* in 1842 she had linked him with Tennyson as the most promising of the younger English poets. Her friend Miss Mitford had never been an enthusiast despite Elizabeth's persistent propaganda: 'I mean to make you value more Mr Browning,' she declared. She was unsuccessful, for in 1847 Miss Mitford still thought of his poetry as 'one heap of obscurity, confusion and weakness'. Both women agreed however that Robert ought to give up writing plays, which 'is like reading a riddle book right through without stopping to guess the answer'.

Miss Mitford had first encountered Robert Browning at a dinner party in May 1836, the day before Kenyon introduced her to Elizabeth, and seems never to have taken to him. Her acerbic comment, when she heard of the Brownings' marriage was, 'a strange sort of person to carry such a person as Elizabeth Barrett off her feet'. She was downright rude about his appearance, although she had met him only once before: 'He seemed to me about the height and size of a boy of twelve years old – Femmelette – is a word made for him.' Elizabeth was amused by some of her more outrageous stories and prejudices, but continued to argue strongly in Browning's defence. It was 'not effeminacy for him to give up riding for his family's sake – rather "affectionateness", not wanting to give them cause for anxiety,' she maintained.

She heard very different accounts of Robert from Kenyon, for whom the poet was 'a great favourite' and recommended for 'his high cultivation and attainments and similar humility of bearing'. Kenyon had known Browning for some years. They had met at a party where Kenyon learnt he had been a schoolfellow of Robert's father. He had called at Hatch End to renew the acquaintance and there began a close friendship with Robert. He liked and admired his work, and gave him valuable encouragement and help, including financial, after his marriage; and when he died he bequeathed Robert a large sum.

Kenyon often spoke warmly of Robert to Elizabeth on his visits; Elizabeth told Robert later during their courtship, 'You are and always have been, a chief favourite – appreciated, praised, loved . . . '. Kenyon's ambition was to introduce the two people he so loved to one another, and he tried to engineer a meeting in March 1842. But although pleased by the idea of Browning wishing to see her, she said a firm no, and Robert was turned away. 'It was my blind dislike of strangers,' she explained.

They continued to hear of one another and take an active interest in each other's work, despite not meeting. Kenyon never lost an opportunity to praise the one to the other, and to keep an interest going. Without his machinations Robert's eventual success in reaching Elizabeth's sofa side might have been much more difficult. On the other hand, Elizabeth's gloom after the publication of her poems in June 1844 was such that any distraction was better than none. Even her terror of strangers lessened. When Horne, about to go abroad for an indefinite time, begged to be received, her instant, reflex reaction was to cry, ' "No", like a wild Indian' – whereupon he wrote 'a letter expressive of mortification and vexation – that I grew ashamed of myself and told him to come any day . . . '. It was a notable departure from habit, although in the end he never came and she clapped her hands 'for joy when I felt my danger to be passed'.

The 1844 poems included a piece written at great speed, 'Lady Geraldine's Courtship' – celebrating the love of the wealthy highborn lady for a poor humble poet – which contained a reference to Browning.

Or at times a modern volume, Wordsworth's solemn-
    thoughted idyll,
Howitt's ballad-verse, or Tennyson's enchanted reverie, –
Or from Browning some 'Pomegranate', which, if cut deep
    down the middle,
Shows a heart within blood-tinctured, of a veined humanity.

Browning read the poem when he returned home from Italy in December 1844. He spoke to Kenyon, who agreed it was proper for him to write to Elizabeth, and that she would 'be even pleased to hear' from him. He wrote his famous first letter, he claimed, 'on account of my purely personal obligation', with no hidden intent and 'on the whole, *unwillingly*'. The courtship was under way.

Robert Browning was nearly thirty-three when he met Elizabeth Barrett. He was six years younger than her, and came from a very different background, although his family were well enough off to be able to support their son until his marriage. His mother Sarah, born in Scotland, of German extraction, was thirty-eight when she married, and ten years older than her husband. She was pregnant soon after marriage, miscarried and quickly became pregnant again; Robert was born on 7 May 1812. A daughter, Sarianna, followed in 1814.

Sarah Browning was a quiet, strong personality, usually calm and controlled, very much the dominant influence in the family, on whom everyone relied. She was devoted to her son. She was forty when he was born and had half expected another miscarriage, so that his safe arrival had left her marvelling and thankful, but anxious for his healthy survival. All her life she fussed over him and pandered to his needs. She loved her daughter, but it was Robert she treasured, the more so as she came to recognise his exceptional qualities and mental powers. She and her husband looked on Robert as a genius, certainly from his early teens. It caused little serious concern to his parents, therefore, when he declared at sixteen that he intended to devote his life to being a poet and nothing else, although other members of the family raised objections, and Robert had to fight 'many good battles to preserve' his 'absolute independence'.

His mother was a deeply religious woman, Church of Scotland turned Congregationalist – she converted her husband to that sect soon after their marriage – and the strength of Robert's faith caused her almost as much concern as his health. He had been 'passionately religious' in childhood, but when in his teens he rebelled and became a 'freethinker' she was saddened; she redoubled her prayers, and Robert's faith, if not religious practice, returned.

They were extraordinarily close. Robert was receptive to her state of mind and feelings in the way that a child tightly bonded to his mother often is. He always was, he told Elizabeth, 'ill and well with her . . . '. When his mother had a pain or felt uncomfortable, so did Robert. Once, when Robert complained of headache, and wondered about its cause, his doctor pointed to his mother sitting beside him – there, he said, is 'the cause. . . . there sits your mother . . . whom you absolutely resemble . . . '. She slept in the room next to his, with her door always open in case he should need her. However late he returned home his mother would be lying awake for him, and he would go to her bedside for a goodnight kiss. She packed his bags if he went away and bought him his clothes. 'I have been accustomed by pure chance, to have another will lead mine in the little daily matters of life,' he told Elizabeth before the marriage. Elizabeth soon discovered that he hated shopping, that 'he would rather leap down among the lions after your glove as the knight of old, than walk into a shop for you'.

Sarah Browning developed 'tic douloureux', or trigeminal neuralgia, in middle life. It is a most upsetting, painful affliction. Spasms of agonising pain grip one side of the face or head, often so severely that the sufferer is totally incapacitated. Attacks may be precipitated by eating, talking, change of temperature, a light touch on the cheek, a psychological stress. In the beginning there are prolonged periods of freedom from pain, but these gradually become shorter and eventually the pain is almost continuous. Often there is a change of temperament and the individual becomes solitary and moody. This happened in some degree with Sarah Browning. A friend of the family recalled seeing her 'bowed with pain' and hardly able to speak as she and her husband took a slow walk. Her daughter praised her 'immense courage'. It was a painful sight for Robert to endure and a frustration that he could do so little to help.

Robert was tormented by head pains (Sarianna was also affected, although not to the same degree) during her bad periods; the pain seemed to transmit itself to him from his mother in the same way a husband can experience labour pains during his wife's confinement. Through habit, perhaps, his head had now become his vulnerable 'organ', and troubled him whenever he was seriously frustrated or worried.

Robert Browning senior was an unusual man. Outwardly he was gentle, unworldly and kind-hearted; his son admired his 'strange sweetness of soul'. He had a childlike nature, his head usually buried in a book, was impractical in the house and content to be organised by Sarah.

He had been sent to St Kitts to work on a sugar plantation by his father when nineteen – through his dead mother, a Creole, he stood to inherit the plantation. He had quickly 'conceived such a hatred to the slave system' that 'he relinquished every prospect', gave up the job and returned home, 'to his father's profound astonishment and rage'. While in St Kitts he had 'some abominable early experience', which he was never able to disclose; if questioned 'he shuts his eyes involuntarily and shows exactly the same mask of loathing that may be noticed while a piece of cruelty is mentioned . . . and the word "blood", even, makes him change colour'.

He had a large library, collected mostly from second-hand bookstalls over the years; among the books were a number dealing with torture and sadomasochism, which his son read avidly. Browning senior's interest in crimes of violence verged on the morbid and was at variance with his squeamishness over blood and cruelty. The only time he was late for work at the Bank, it is reported, was on the morning of the execution of the Mannings – murderers in a notorious, widely reported crime – the implication being that he had stopped to watch the hanging. One suspects that, beneath his benign exterior, lurked sadistic fantasies which he kept under tight control and which were only able to express themselves indirectly.

When he returned from the West Indies he had hoped to study as a painter, but his father refused to assist him – virtually threw him out of the family home – and he was forced to take a clerkship in the Bank of England. He 'always detested' his work, and never troubled to deny that he continued at the Bank solely for the money. He was a clever caricaturist – perhaps allowing cruelty an outlet – and could catch the essence of his sitter's nature with a few pen strokes; he was much in demand among his fellow clerks and neighbours. He also wrote poetry, some tolerably good, often amusing and cutting. He was a mine of information on almost any conceivable subject, and if he did not have the answer at his fingertips he had the ability to discover it rapidly on his bookshelves.

He wholeheartedly backed Robert's intention of becoming a poet, and supported him financially without protest, paying for the printing of his early works. He tried his best to understand and like his son's poetry, but it was not really his style, and at times he was frankly out of his depth. But he delighted in illustrating the poems and he greatly amused the family and pleased his son by his efforts.

Until the end of his life Robert sought his father's help whenever he needed information, especially of an arcane nature. He loved his father, but far less deeply than he did his mother. His father was too childish a character for Robert to confide in or rely on emotionally. It was to his mother that he went to discuss his problems and share his worries; his father only heard of them at second hand.

Robert's sister Sarianna was almost slavishly devoted to her brother. She copied out his poems – indeed, 'She was my amanuensis in those days', went to theatres with him, read his work, and discussed ideas with him. She was intelligent, humorous, and strong-minded, well read, and an amusing storyteller and raconteur. She had a lisp, but this did little to reduce her talkativeness, which at times verged on the verbose. She had a mass of ebony hair, white skin, and quick, sharp intelligent eyes and, when young, she attracted a number of suitors. Like all the family she was short, barely five feet. Early in life she decided to dedicate her life to her family, perhaps influenced by her mother's chronic illness and her father's impractical nature, as well as Robert's continuing presence at home.

They were a self-contained, happy family: 'Father, mother, only son and only daughter formed a most suited, harmonious, and intellectual family.'[2]

Robert Browning decided to be a poet when he was seventeen. He had entered London University the year before, to read German and classical languages, but had never adapted to the routine. His teachers appeared to be both dull and foolish – in those early years he had a habit of calling people 'fools', which aroused his mother's biblical concern: 'Whoever calleth his brother a fool . . . ' she warned – and the lectures bored him. He left before the end of the first year; his father, whose habitual calmness was disturbed, found the event 'as painful as it was unexpected'. One suspects that Robert Browning senior had hoped his brilliant son would more than compensate for the frustrations and humiliations he had had to endure from his own father. Robert's closest friends had opted for law, and this was his father's choice for him, but he rejected all the professions and the Church, briefly considered painting, and finally and decisively opted for poetry. He knew that he would have no trouble from his parents: 'Since I was a child I never worked for the least or greatest thing within the compass of their means to give, but given it was, – nor for liberty but it was conceded, nor confidence but it was bestowed.' To be a poet, Robert was convinced, 'requires the whole man', and there was no room for extraneous activities. The question of how he was to support himself never bothered him, although other members of his family, outside his immediate relations, looked on him as a lazy parasite.

But he was no layabout when it came to literary work. *Pauline* was published anonymously in 1833, when he was twenty-one, the cost borne by his aunt. It rapidly sank from sight and, perhaps because it contained revealing autobiographical material, Browning tried later to keep his authorship secret and the poem out of print, and succeeded for many years. For a long time he resisted Elizabeth's pleas to see a copy. 'Must you see *Pauline*?' he asked. 'If I could pray you to revoke that decision! For it is altogether foolish and not boyish.'

Paracelsus had appeared in 1835. He received good reviews on the whole, and his reputation and self-confidence rose. Elizabeth had been much impressed by the poem. Then came the fiasco of *Sordello*, which had taken him seven years to compose. Browning was accused of obscurantism and affectation, and widely ridiculed. Jane Carlyle, after reading the poem, asked whether Sordello was a man, a city, or a book. And the actor/manager Macready claimed that he tried to read it before and after dinner and both times found it 'not readable'. Browning's reputation and pride suffered badly, and the charge of obscurity stuck to him for years to come, colouring future reviews of his work.

Pippa Passes – an early favourite of Elizabeth's – was published in 1841 as the first number of the pamphlet series, *Bells and Pomegranates*. In addition during this period he wrote five plays, hoping to make some money, although only two were staged and these were short-lived.

Robert travelled abroad on three occasions before his elopement. The first time was to St Petersburg in 1834, which took him away from home for some three months. He had become friends with the Russian Consul General in London, and when the latter was summoned to St Petersburg and suggested he might accompany him as his secretary, Robert accepted with alacrity. In 1838 he had his first taste of Italy, going by sea to Venice, thence to Asolo and then slowly home. The third occasion was in August 1844 when he sailed for Naples for a longer tour of Italy. He returned to London in December, shortly after the publication of Elizabeth's next collection of *Poems*.

Browning was a handsome man, slim and dark, with long, thick hair. He dressed elegantly, and one young lady described him as 'a trifle of a dandy'. Carlyle's first opinion of him was influenced by his 'smart green riding coat' which suggested 'proclivities for the turf and a scamphood'. Later, after Carlyle had become a good friend, he altered the description to 'a dainty Leigh Huntish kind of fellow, with much ingenuity, vivacity and comely gracefulness'.

He was a brilliant conversationalist, sometimes compulsively so, and by the time he met Elizabeth he had a wide circle of literary friends and acquaintances. Despite his lack of height – he was about five foot six – he was attractive to women. He confided to Elizabeth that he had never previously loved a woman, only 'had likings' which 'used to come and go'.

During his teens he had been enamoured of the Flower sisters, Eliza and Sarah, especially Eliza (who was reported to have been the prototype for Pauline). Eliza was nearly ten years older, and 'the finest religious composer of her time'. Fanny Haworth, who was eleven years older, attracted his admiration for a time, but the relationship never progressed beyond warm friendship. These women were all intelligent and talented in different ways with passable looks, but his interest in them waned as he came to know them better. He had a 'kind of male prudery with respect of "young ladies" ', and feared that with the least encouragement on his part 'something would be sure to follow'. He was also convinced that 'there must be this disproportionateness in a beloved object'. He told Elizabeth: '. . . Before I knew you women seemed not so much better than myself therefore no love for them . . . There is no love but from beneath, far beneath . . . '.

Having failed to find a woman who fitted his needs, Robert had finally concluded, at the ripe age of thirty-two, that it was impossible for him to love any woman: '. . . having wondered at this in the beginning, and fought not a little against it, having acquiesced in it at last, and accounted for it all to myself, and become, if anything, rather proud of it than sorry . . .'.

Robert Browning first wrote to Elizabeth on 10 January 1845.

I love your verses with all my heart, my dear Miss Barrett. – and this is no offhand complimentary letter that I shall write – whatever else, no prompt matter of course recognition of your genius, and there a grateful and natural end of the thing. Since the day last week when I first read your poems, I quite laugh to remember how I have been turning and turning again in my mind what I should be able to tell you of their effect upon me, for in first flush of delight I thought I would this once get out of my habit of purely passive enjoyment, when I do really enjoy, and thoroughly justify my admiration – perhaps even, as a loyal fellow craftsman should, try and find fault and do you some little good to be proud of hereafter! – But nothing comes of it all – so in to me has it gone, and part of me has it become, this great living poetry of yours, not a flower of which but took root and grew – Oh, how different this is from lying to be dried and pressed flat and prized highly, and put in a book with a proper account at top and bottom, and shut up and put away. . . . Of the book called a 'Flora' besides! After all, I need not give up a thought of doing that too, in time; because even now, talking with whoever is worthy, I can give a reason for my faith in one and another excellence, the fresh strange music, the affluent language, the exquisite pathos and true brave new thoughts – but in thus addressing myself to you – your own self, and for the first time, my feeling rises altogether. I do, as I say, love these books with all my heart – and I love you too.

This famous letter amused, even delighted her. She knew and admired Browning's work. She was both flattered and pleased to read his fulsome praise, and she was particularly struck by his passionate intensity. To be told: 'I do . . . love these books with all my heart – and I love you too' by a stranger (although its meaning was plainly not impertinent) was exciting, especially for someone who lived entirely in books and dreams. No one had ever before spoken in such language to her. She was sufficiently affected to joke with Miss Mitford – which she later regretted – that she had had 'a real letter' from Robert Browning which said he loved her, adding, 'You are not to mistake this, not to repeat it – for of course it is simply the purest of philanthropies.'

Elizabeth's reply was sent next day, not a simple thank-you letter, but taking up his suggeston that he might criticise her poems – she had high respect for 'your power in your Art'. Enticingly, she told him that she knew a good deal about him: 'Mr Kenyon often speaks of you', and reversing her usual phobic stance, she virtually invited him to call on her 'in the Spring' – a measure of her loneliness and how his letter had stirred her. It was totally unlike those 'heaps of letters which go into the fire one after another', written to her by men whose aim was largely to see 'what will come of it'.

The correspondence flowed backwards and forwards. Each praised the other's poetry. Elizabeth told Robert that she was a devout admirer and student of his works. Robert returned the compliment:

> Your poetry must be . . . infinitely more to me than mine to you – for you *do* what I always wanted, hope to do, and only now seem likely to do for the first time. You speak out, *you* , – I only make men and women speak – give you truth broken into prismatic hues, and fear the pure white light, even if it is in me, but I am going to try; so it will be no small comfort to have your company just now. . . .

From the beginning each poet looked at the other with idealistic eyes, and set about creating the image each desired. Elizabeth wanted a teacher, a man she might look up to who could follow in Boyd's footsteps; a strong man whom she might cast into the heroic mould and admire, and beyond that she wanted a passionate relationship – not in a sexual sense but the kind she had experienced with Bro. She sent him her analysis of his poetic character:

> You can deal both with abstract thought and with human passion in the most passionate sense. . . . You have an immense grasp in Art; and no one at all accustomed to consider the usual form of it, could help regarding with reverence and gladness the gradual expansion of your powers. Then you are 'masculine' to the height – and I, as a woman, have studied some of your gestures of language and intonation wistfully, as a thing beyond me far!

What did Robert Browning want from Elizabeth? He sought a woman whose intellect as well as goodness would be far above his. He had to look up to a woman before he could love her. Only then could he trust himself to her care and affection: 'It is pleasanter to lie back on the cushions inside the carriage and let another drive – but if you suspect he cannot drive?' From the start he seemed to have no doubts about Elizabeth.

Very soon in their correspondence Robert began to tell Elizabeth about his plans and current work, and to discuss working problems. She radiated interest: 'Your greatest works are to come. . . . Need I assure you that I shall always hear with the deepest interest every word you will say to me of what you are doing or about to do.' This was no mere flattery, for Elizabeth had long ago seen through the patchy obtuseness of his writing and recognised his great qualities.

Robert took a lively interest in Elizabeth's health: 'Always [give me] a little official bulletin line that shall say "I am better" or "Still better".' The interest verged on the morbid and began early in the correspondence, before they had met. This may have followed naturally from his habit of always enquiring about his mother's health but it also reflected his growing impatience to meet with Elizabeth, and his irritation at her procrastination, and use of ill health as the excuse. 'Real warm Spring,' he announced at the end of February, 'and the birds know it; and in Spring I shall see you . . . for when did I once fail to get whatever I had set my heart upon?' The boast excited Elizabeth but failed to put a stop to her delaying tactics. Her spring, she maintained, came later, 'the new style'.

As Robert's frustrations grew so did his headaches. 'I have been surprised', he wrote on 3 May, 'with something not unlike illness of late – I have had a constant pain in the head for these two months, which only very rough exercise gets rid of. . . . I thought I never could be unwell.' Then he added, as though to point to her part in the symptom, 'Just now it is gone, thanks to polking all night and walking home by broad daylight. . . . And do you know I said "this must *go*, cannot mean to stay, so I will not tell Miss Barrett . . ." – but I mean to tell you all, or more of the truth. . . .'

Still Elizabeth made no move. Robert entreated, demanded, pleaded by turn. 'You shall laugh at the East Winds yet, . . . if my truest heart's wishes avail, as they have hitherto done.' When Elizabeth responded vaguely that she was 'essentially better' and 'it is well to fly towards the light', he asked, 'Do you think I shall see you in two months, three months? I may travel perhaps.'

Elizabeth's complacency was shaken. She did not want Robert to go away. She admitted that she was apprehensive of meeting him. 'This implacable weather! This East wind that seems to blow through the sun and moon! Who can be well in such a wind? . . . April is coming. There will be both a May and a June if we live to see such things, and perhaps after all, we may. And as to seeing *you* besides . . . you distrust me . . . penetrate my morbidity and guess that when the moment comes to see a living human face to which I am not accustomed, I shrink and grow pale in spirit.' Then, taking courage, she asked, 'Do you really mean [to travel]? If you do, I shall have to miss you.'

Robert assured her that he had no intention of going abroad, and that she need have no fear of *him*. The idea was laughable, he told her; '. . . the thin white face . . . is laughing at me in the glass yonder at the fancy of making anyone afraid'. Robert could have been describing Elizabeth's rather than his own face reflected in the mirror, which was perhaps an indication that he was already in close empathy with her. His ability to identify with others and see their problems and experiences through *their* minds was one of Robert's remarkable gifts and accounts for the insights he shows in so much of his poetry, particularly the dramatic monologues. 'Here is the bad wind back again,' he declared. 'And do you know . . . I cannot help fancying the East wind does my head harm too.'

On 12 May Robert was invited by Kenyon to dinner with his sister together with Elizabeth's brother and sister, probably George and Henrietta. Elizabeth was agog to see Robert through their eyes and told him so. He was upset at the idea. He thought it very wrong that Elizabeth, albeit at second hand, should observe him, while he continued to remain on the outside. He became so angry at the idea that he made himself ill and cancelled the dinner: 'My head took to ringing such a literal alarm that I wondered what was to come of it,' he explained. He sent a long account of himself in response to her concerned enquiry and ended it, 'Oh the day, I shall see you with my own, own eyes. For how little you understand me; or rather yourself – if you think I would dare see you, without your leave, that way!' So agitated was he that he despatched a second letter that same day, 'I ask you *not* to see me so long as you are unwell, or mistrustful of –

'No, no, that is being too grand! Do see me when you can, and let me not be only writing myself.'

Elizabeth at last realised that, if the friendship was to continue, she must allow him to call. She wrote, flustered, that he might come on 'any day after two, or before six'; but, she added,

Here is nothing to see in me; nor to hear in me. . . . If my poetry is worth anything to any eye, it is the flower of me. . . . I feel ashamed of having made a fuss. . . . I am deeply touched by your caring. You are not well now and must be quiet. I entreat you not to think of coming until the head is better.

Nothing could cause Robert to delay. 'I will call at two on Tuesday', he replied by return of post; 'thank you . . . for the infinite kindness.

'Now, if I do not seem grateful enough to you, am I so much to blame? You see it is high time you *saw* me, for I have clearly written myself *out!*'

It had taken eighteen weeks and twenty-seven letters to achieve the meeting on 20 May, and the relationship was already far advanced. Elizabeth knew for certain that Robert could combine the rôles of teacher and companion, and become the person for whom she had long held 'blind hopes', who could stand in place of Bro, and provide the mental stimulation she so much lacked. It was, she told him, 'delightful to be broad awake and think of you as a friend'.

Everyone at 50 Wimpole Street was surprised when Elizabeth agreed to see Robert Browning. She had been in a flurry of nerves ever since she had written the letter of invitation; as she had composed it 'tears ran down my cheek: I could not tell why: partly it might be mere nervousness'. She was 'vexed' with Robert 'for wishing to come as other people did, and vexed with myself with not being able to refuse you as I did them'.

Elizabeth's room was at the back of the house on the third floor, directly below Henrietta's. The walls were green – always her favourite colour; her sisters claimed it disguised her complexion – and the room was usually dark or shadowy except on the sunniest summer days. She disliked brightly lit rooms. Heavy, green damask curtains hung at the windows and restricted the light, for she preferred them to be drawn. 'I do hate white dimity curtains. . . .' she wrote, '. . . it is the white light which comes through the dimity which is so hateful to me.' The darkness matched her phobic character, hid her from full exposure, and disguised her looks. The gloom was increased by the massive ivy (a present from Kenyon) planted outside in the window box, which grew across the windows and up to Henrietta's room. 'I should like not to be able to see out of any of my three windows for the thickness of the ivy,' she wrote. In the one clear window she had fitted a transparent blind on which was stencilled a castle and gateway, outlined when there was sunshine.

During winter and spring the windows remained shut and all cracks and crevices were carefully papered over. A fire burned continuously and the temperature of the room kept constantly at 65°F or more. The room was never properly cleaned during this 'close season' and dust accumulated everywhere in heaps – even Flush was reluctant to go beneath the bed from the size of the spiders there! The atmosphere was dry, airless and claustrophobic.

Elizabeth had never, since Bro's death, varied her dress; a black silk one in the summer, a black velvet one, fully lined, during the winter. Not far from her bed was the sofa on which she lay during the day and wrote or received a guest. There was also an armchair, a table and dressing table, wardrobe, wash-basin, perhaps a commode and bookshelves. Decorations included busts of poets and philosophers – a present from her father – and on her walls were prints and sketches, including a portrait of Miss Mitford and a chalk sketch of her father. Normally, prints of Browning and Tennyson hung below one another on the wall, but these were removed by Elizabeth just before Robert called.

The first meeting lasted an hour. Elizabeth was so excited that afterwards she was unable to rid her mind of Robert. 'I had a sense of your presence constantly,' she told him later. Next morning she felt impelled to describe to her father the impact her visitor had made, surely a clear hint of the feelings Robert had aroused. 'It is most extraordinary how the idea of Mr Browning does beset me – I suppose it is not being used to see strangers, in some degree, – but it haunts me . . . it is a persecution.' She acknowledged that she was no longer fully in control of her emotions, 'Do you know,' she confessed, 'that I was frightened of you? frightened in this way. I felt as if you had a power over me and meant to use it, and that I could not breathe or speak very differently from what you chose to make me. As to my thoughts, I had it in my head somehow that you read *them* as you read the newspapers.'

Elizabeth did not even consider the possibility that she might be in love. For years she had been convinced that no man, especially one she respected, could love her. 'I never thought that any man whom I could love, would stoop to love *me*, even if I attained so far as the sight of such.' She understood that men were attracted by the idea of a female poet, especially one as well known as she and mysteriously hidden from the public eye; she received plenty of 'empty written gallantries . . . all the more perhaps from my peculiar position' – but this was 'without consequence'. She believed that any man rash enough to be attracted to her would soon lose his enthusiasm and go away. She had confidence in herself as a poet, but little as a woman. People liked her for her achievements; Boyd had responded to her intellect; her father loved her because she pleased him. No one had ever loved her for herself as Bro or her mother had. She recalled her mother's words: 'You will never find another person, who will love you as I love you.' At fourteen she had turned from her mother, and a life of domesticity and childbearing, and chosen the masculine world of intellectual achievement for the power and freedom it seemed to offer. She was very conscious of her femininity, yet having rejected the conventional female rôle, she felt only half a woman, and compensated by pointing out the unsatisfactory lives of most married women, and the humiliations they endured at the hands of their husbands. But underneath her scorn of marriage was her sense of inadequacy as a woman, and the consequent fear that she could never please a man and fulfil his expectations.

Elizabeth had loved an ideal for years, 'seen sometimes in a dream and sometimes in a book', who 'must be above one . . . as far as one can reach with one's eyes (soul-eyes), not reach to touch.' Her ideal man always had heroic qualities; all her life she had made the ones she loved and admired heroes; her father was one, and in the future, Napoleon III and Cavour were to become such. George Sand – for her masculine and feminine qualities – was already in her pantheon and now Robert Browning was to join her. When she looked back after a year she came to feel that she had loved Robert Browning, 'all my life unawares, that is, the idea of you'.

But her mind was not tuned to such thoughts on that Monday afternoon. She had no conscious fancy that she would love Robert Browning. 'My ambition when we began our correspondence,' she told him, 'was simply that you should forget I was a woman . . . and let us be friends, and consent to teach me. . . .' She looked him full in the eye, without embarrassment on that occasion. She was not able to repeat that for many weeks to come because of what followed.

The impact on Robert Browning of their meeting was enormous. Although he strongly denied Elizabeth's accusation that he 'came with the intention of loving whomever' he should find, he admitted having a presentiment, amounting to more than a hope, that he might encounter the woman he could love. He had believed at first, from common rumours, that Elizabeth suffered from an incurable injury of the spine, and 'that he never could hope to see [her] stand up before his face'. The manner in which she received him on her own, for Henrietta who had shown him up quickly disappeared, lying on her sofa, wrapped in shawls and rugs, emaciated, pale and drawn, would have created a striking effect. There was clearly an immediate rapport. Robert was attracted to her in every way, even to the 'dear pale cheek and the thin hand'. She was all that her letters and Kenyon had promised. Despite her emaciation she exerted an irresistible charm when she was interested in her companion, and Robert was drawn to her. When he left the house he was already in love, although a day or two would have to pass before his racing thoughts slowed to a crystal-clear conviction. The 'utterly impossible . . . the finding such a one as you', had come to pass.

He did not believe at first that Elizabeth would ever return his love, a natural corollary one might suppose to falling in love with a comparative stranger. But he knew that he had loved the notion of her all his life, and that she was his ideal. He would be happy to serve her in every way possible, and be her friend and companion, he assured himself.

After their first meeting Robert returned home and wrote a short thank-you note, which although unexceptional in content showed signs of his agitation; thanks jumbled with did I do 'wrong in anything, did I stay too long, speak very loud, can we meet again?' But nothing in the letter prepared Elizabeth for the one that came two days later. Robert, overwhelmed by his emotions, had written a passionate letter declaring that he loved her 'from my soul', and offered her his life, 'as much of it as she would take', and so on. We have to guess, since the actual letter does not exist – he obediently burnt it (crying 'serve it right') after Elizabeth returned it to him at his request – but it probably contained eulogies and sentiments similar to those he composed from the end of August 1845 onwards, when he began to break 'the silence' imposed on him by Elizabeth.

Elizabeth was surprised and irritated, as much by Robert's lack of self-control as by what he wrote. 'You do not know what pain you give in speaking so wildly,' she told him.

> You have said some intemperate things . . . fancies, – which you will not say over again, nor unsay, but *forget at once* and *for ever, having said* at all. . . . Now, if there should be one word of answer attempted to this; or of reference; *I must not* . . . *I will not see you again*. . . . So for my sake you will not say it – I think you will not – and spare me the sadness of having to break through an intercourse just as it is promising pleasure to me; to me who have so many sadnesses and so few pleasures.

Robert retreated like an alarmed prawn, continuing to fix his eyes on her. He had, he told her, 'been soundly frightened'. In defence he offered her an understanding of his nature: '. . . for every poor speck of a Vesuvius or a Stromboli in my microcosm there are huge layers of ice and pits of black cold water'. He normally kept his passionate nature under strict control, but occasionally the control went awry, the ice melted, and violent emotions erupted. That was what caused him to write his intemperate letter, 'in an unwise moment'. He begged her pardon and 'blushingly assured [her] *that* was only a slip of the tongue, . . . your friendship I am sure I have not lost —'

Nor had he. Elizabeth was so anxious to ensure that Robert had not been too upset by her reaction that she immediately composed

> the most humble apologies dear Mr Browning, for having spent so much solemnity on so simple a matter. . . . You will find it difficult to believe me perhaps when I assure you that I never made such a mistake (I mean of overseriousness to indefinite compliments), no never in my life before . . . – I wrote what I wrote so unfortunately, *through reverence for you*, and not at all from vanity on my own account. . . . Now we will shuffle the cards and take patience, and begin the game again if you please.

They met on an average at seven- to ten-day intervals, and exchanged letters every few days. Once the pattern had become established, and she sensed her deeper affection for Robert, Elizabeth began to grow increasingly apprehensive lest her father discover the extent of their friendship and end it. She was fearful that he would guess her secret. She was certain that he would never tolerate an intimate relationship between her and Robert, and she felt guilty about her new feelings. The last thing she wanted was to upset her father, but at the same time she was determined to continue her friendship. She went sometimes to absurd lengths to ensure secrecy. Robert called usually between 2 and 3 p.m., on any day except Sunday, when Elizabeth did not have a visitor. If there was any danger, a message would be given to him at the door on his arrival and he would at once depart. He normally stayed for between one and two hours or more, and left well before 6 p.m., when Edward Moulton Barrett returned from the City.

Elizabeth's brothers and sisters were continually in and out of the house and knew about the visits. Their only concern was that Elizabeth should enjoy herself and she had no fears that they might give away her secret. Indeed, they were all well versed in deceiving their father, which was the only way they had of combating his more unreasonable prejudices and prohibitions.

Elizabeth was reticent when Kenyon, who called regularly, asked about Robert's visits, and was almost silent on the subject to Miss Mitford, from whom she had formerly had no secrets. She cautioned Robert 'to say just as little about your visits here and of me as you find possible . . . even to Mr Kenyon . . . as to every other person whatever – You must trust me'. She attempted without success to explain her attitude: 'It does not follow that you should be ashamed of my friendship or that I should not be proud of yours, if we avoid making it a subject of conversation in high places, or low places.' Robert calmed her fears; no hint of the visits could 'ooze out'; he had spoken of Elizabeth to three people only, his father, mother and sister 'whom I made comprehend exactly your position and the necessity for the absolute silence I enjoined respecting the permission to see you. You may depend on them.'

So the secret friendship developed. Her father believed that Robert called every fortnight or so and discussed poetry and related matters with his daughter and since the visits gave her pleasure, he raised no objections. The idea that Elizabeth could be attracted to Robert was, at this stage, outside his comprehension, for he saw her as wholly 'pure' and asexual; she could not conceivably step outside the rôle of being his daughter.

Elizabeth asked Robert to comment on her new translation of *Prometheus Bound,* and he took immense pains over it. She was duly grateful, and pleaded to see his new poetry. He showed her 'The Bishop Orders his Tomb at St Praxed's' and 'The Guardian Angel', already published, which she had not read. She was delighted and impressed. Then Robert gave her 'The Flight of the Duchess' – he had written the first nine sections earlier and they had been published in April 1845 in *Hood's* magazine and admired by Elizabeth – which he was in the process of completing. He asked for criticism, then provoked Elizabeth by warning her not to be 'tempted by that pleasure of pleasing which I think is your besetting sin . . . and so cut me off from the other pleasure of being profited.' Indignantly she refuted the accusation: 'if you had spoken of my sister Henrietta . . . you would have been right – so right! But for *me.* . . '.

She was at first diffident of criticising his work.

I can tell you truly what I think of . . . your Duchess – but I must of necessity hesitate and fall into misgiving of the adequacy of my truth. To judge at all of a work of yours, I must *look up to it*, and *far up*. And thus, it is not at all from an overpleasure in pleasing *you*, not at all from an inclination to depreciate myself, that I speak and feel as I do . . . ; it is simply the consequence of a true comprehension of you and of me.

She was intrigued by the tale of the Duchess – understandably allying herself with the heroine – which concerns an attractive young woman who becomes ill and wasted through the loveless behaviour of her gauche, insensitive husband. The lady was small, like Elizabeth, and not unlike her on one of her good days.

> She was the smallest lady alive,
> Made in a piece of nature's madness
> Too small, almost, for the life and gladness
> That overfilled her, as some hive
> Out of the bears' reach on the high trees
> Is crowded with its safe merry bees.

A mysterious old gypsy crone arrives just as the husband is setting forth to hunt, and closets herself with the Duchess. She offers her freedom and love, although with plenty of hardship,

> And many and long must the trials be.

But if she accepts

> And thou shalt know, those arms once curled
> About thee, what we knew before,
> How love is the only good in the world.
> Henceforth be loved as heart can love,
> Or brain devise, or hand approve!

The Duchess chooses freedom and departs with the gypsy.

> I pushed the gate wide, she shook the bridge,
> And the palfrey bounded – and so we lost her.

Robert did not of course have Elizabeth in mind when he began the poem – for this was prior to meeting her – but she must have been in the forefront of his thoughts when he completed the second half. Elizabeth's criticisms were detailed and Robert adopted all her suggestions – none of which altered the story.

Elizabeth was moved by the poem and frequently referred to it in her letters. She could hardly fail to make the connection between her father and the Duke husband, even if she failed to put it into words. She, like the Duchess, was no better than a prisoner. Her father, no more than the Duke, was not a cruel man, but unable to see her as she really was, and provide nourishment. Until Robert arrived, bearing as much promise as the old gypsy woman, she had been pining away. Now there was hope. The possibility of her own flight was still in the far distance, but the *idea* of freedom and love struck a vibrant chord for her.

Their co-operation on the Duchess undoubtedly brought them closer together; even to discuss a fellow poet's work, let alone alter and improve it, is an intimate act, demanding considerable trust on both sides. Elizabeth learnt much about Robert, and in the process, one may at least surmise, Robert planted the possibility of flight in her mind.

Robert initially planned the poem around a description of the life the Duchess was to have with her future gypsy lover; her dreary life with the Duke would not have been given in detail, as it is, but simply have been deduced by the reader, whereas in the final version of the poem it is the other way round; the Duchess's unhappy married life is recounted and the life-to-be with the lover is left to the imagination. 'Of course it comes to the same thing, for one would have show half by half like a cut orange,' Robert opined. Elizabeth's reply was revealing: 'Orange is orange – but *which half* of the orange is not predestinated from all eternity – ; is it *so*?' Surely she was asking whether her own escape was written in the cards. This was quite early in the courtship, before the possibility had been seriously raised by Robert and indicated the direction her thoughts and fantasies were taking.

However much, during the summer of 1845, Elizabeth tried to push Robert away his devotion never weakened. For months she tried to persuade herself that it was 'a sort of *infatuation*, . . . a bare impulse', that would evaporate. But Robert continued to visit her with the same regularity and enthusiasm. From his sixth visit he always brought her flowers from his garden at New Cross, usually roses and carnations. Elizabeth was not only appreciative but positively encouraged the practice: '. . . the roses do not die' (most flowers wilted and died on the spot when they encountered the atmosphere of Elizabeth's room) 'and their buds are coming out. . . . Now that the windows may be open [it was June 30th], the flowers take heart to live a little in this room.' Robert responded as a grateful lover, 'How good you are to my roses . . .'.

Elizabeth's sisters were equally loud in their praise – 'they never saw such flowers anywhere – anywhere here in London'. It became important for Robert, almost a matter of honour, that her room should always contain his blooms. On one occasion he sent them by messenger, but failed to include a note with them. She bantered with him,

It is very kind to send these flowers – too kind – why are they sent? and without a single word . . . which is not too kind certainly. I looked down into the heart of the roses and turned the carnations over and over to the peril of their leaves, and in vain. Not a word do I deserve today, I suppose! But I do thank you for these flowers . . . they are beautiful, and they came . . . just when I wanted them . . . only you ought not to give away all the flowers of your garden to *me*.

Robert rarely failed to ask after her health, and to urge her to exercise. 'I thank God you are better: do pray make fresh endeavours to profit by this partial respite in the weather! All about you must urge that – but even from my distance, the effect might come of such wishes. But you *are* better – look so and speak so.' She responded to his encouragement and pleasure in her bodily achievements. 'I am behaving very well in going out into the noise; not quite out of doors yet, on account of the heat – and I am better as you say, without any doubt at all, and stronger – only my looks are a little deceitful.' She had put on weight, and her chest was trouble free. On 7 July she went out in a carriage for the first time; 'no fainting nor anything very wrong'. Robert congratulated her: 'You are all that is good and kind: I am happy and thankful the beginning (and worst of it) is over and so well.' He was determined that there should be no slackening. Although in those early months he did not know her father's nature, he was realistic enough to recognise that his future with Elizabeth depended largely on her becoming physically active. 'Your health – that before all! . . . as assuring all eventually . . . and on the other accounts you must know. Never pray, *pray*, never lose one sunny day or propitious hour to go out or walk about.'

In turn Elizabeth worried about Robert's health. Her oft-repeated 'How is your head? May I be hoping the best for it?', was not simply a measure of her affection, but also perhaps of her concern that Robert might not be a strong enough man to cope with the strain of caring for her. Robert had headaches almost continuously through the courtship, together with noises in the head (tinnitus) and dizziness. He never failed to keep Elizabeth posted on his symptoms, and sometimes she asked anxiously,

> You *will* have advice (will you not?) if that pain does not grow better directly? It cannot be prudent or even *safe* to let a pain in the head go on for so long, and no remedy be attempted for it . . . and you cannot be sure that it is merely a nervous pain and that it may not have consequences. So you will see someone with an opinion to give, and take it? *Do*, I beseech you.

Both Robert and Elizabeth intuitively understood that his symptoms were related to his emotions. He was by nature passionate, inhibited and impatient, a difficult mix at the best of times, a combination which was liable to provoke psychosomatic symptoms in the frustrating circumstances of the courtship, the more so because of 'the power I have over myself'. But like most sufferers, Robert also employed his symptoms to good use, to communicate thoughts and feelings that he was not always permitted to express, or believed to be tactless; above all to signal to Elizabeth just how frustrated he was. It was, for instance, intensely irritating for Robert, at the end of July, to read, 'As long as I live and to the last moment of my life, I shall remember . . . all the generous interest and feeling you have spent on me – wasted on me I was going to write –' Robert immediately replied, in a brief note, 'I will not hide from you that my head aches now; and I have let the hours go by one after one. . . . Am I better you ask!' His patience had begun to run out. A week earlier he had blurted out, 'I cannot write this morning – I should say too much and have to be sorry and afraid – let me be safely yours ever. . . . '
Elizabeth became concerned. On 25 August, she told him,

> I must speak off my mind. . . . How can it be that you are unwell again . . . and that you should talk . . . of being 'weary in your soul' . . . you? What should make *you*, dearest friend, weary in your soul; or out of spirits in any way? – Do tell me . . . or is it (which I am inclined to think most probable) that you are tired of a same life and want change? . . . Would it not therefore be wise of you in that case to fold your life new again and go abroad at once? What can make you weary in your soul, is a problem to me. . . .

The letter contained several messages. It invited him to explode and speak his mind, 'Do tell me.' It offered him an opening to leave her – the letter had begun with, 'I am always expecting to hear or to see how tired you are at last of me!' – which she knew full well he would not take. And she was raising the issue of leaving home and going abroad; it was not only Robert who needed a change, for her too it was 'a problem'. As though attempting to make her meaning clearer, she continued with a description of her father, which Robert may have found more confusing than enlightening, and then an account of Bro and his death. At the end she confessed, 'I have never said so much to a living being. I never *could* speak or write of it.' With this letter Elizabeth opened her heart and exposed her deeper needs. It was a clear invitation to Robert to share her life.

Robert had no doubts about himself, and he believed in her, 'Absolutely utterly.' For the first time since writing his reckless letter he felt free to express himself to Elizabeth: 'I loved you from my soul and gave you my life, so much of it as you would take . . . the assurance of your friendship, the intimacy to which you admit me, *now*, make the truest, deepest joy of my life –' This was the medicine for which he had been waiting, 'I am much better, with a little headache . . . and fast going –'

Robert did not yet fully comprehend the complexity of Elizabeth's situation. So far he had seen almost nothing of her family. Henrietta had met him on his first visit, he may have caught a glimpse of Arabel, and he had spoken with George at a literary party. Her father remained unseen, only occasionally mentioned by Elizabeth.

On 12 July there was a violent thunderstorm, and Elizabeth, terrified, was cowering in a corner when her father entered the room. He was scornful and 'called it disgraceful to anybody who had ever learnt the alphabet – to which I answered humbly that "I knew it was" – but if I had been impertinent I *might* have added that wisdom does not come by the alphabet but because of it'. Telling Robert this, she added, 'Dr Chambers, part of whose office it is, Papa says, to reconcile foolish women to their follies, [explained] – that some nervous systems are especially sensitive to the effects of electricity.'

Robert sprang to her defence, 'Your father must pardon me for holding most firmly with Dr Chambers – his theory is quite borne out by my own experience . . .'. But this was scarcely an account of unreasonable behaviour on her father's part. Nor was her father's irritation when, surprising her, he found her eating dry toast only for dinner. That was why she was ill, he complained; let her regularly consume porter and beef steaks and she could be well within a month. Robert took her father's side on this last occasion. 'Get well,' he urged her, and 'let me send porter instead of flowers – and beefsteak too!'

Elizabeth's confidence in Robert was such that she relaxed her guard and strongly criticised her father. But afterwards she was uneasy, especially when she recalled how indignant Robert had been.

> You must not, make an unjust opinion out of what I said today. I have been uncomfortable since, lest you should – and perhaps it would have been better if I had not said it. . . . only that you could not long be a friend of mine without knowing and seeing what so lies on the surface. . . . one would rather be crossed and vexed a little than vex a person one loves. . . . it is possible to get used to the harness and run easily in it at last; . . . it has happened . . . that my own sense of right and happiness on any important point of *overt* action, has never run contrariwise to the way of obedience required of me . . . while in things not exactly *overt*, I and all of us are apt to act sometimes up to the limit of our means of acting . . . and no waiting for cognisance or permission. Ah – and that last is the worst of it all perhaps! To be forced into concealments from the heart naturally nearest to us . . . and then the disingenuousness – the cowardice – the 'vices of slaves'! and . . . all my brothers, . . . constrained *bodily* into submission . . . that worst and most dishonouring of necessities, the necessity of *living*, everyone of them all, except myself, being dependent in money matters on the inflexible will.

Suddenly, aghast at what she had disclosed, she performed a quick volte-face, and praised her father's

> deep, tender affection behind and below all those patriarchal ideas of governing grown up children 'in the way they must go'. . . . there never was a truer affection in a father's heart . . . nor a worthier heart itself . . . a heart loyaller and purer, and more compelling to gratitude and reverence than his. . . . The evil is in the system . . . he simply takes it to be his duty to rule, and to make happy according to his own views. . . . He loves us through and through – and I, for one, *love* him.

Robert was understandably confused – although pleased to share such confidences – and unsure how to reply. He had been indignant at what he had been told and called her father a tyrant, and Elizabeth had become upset. It was clear to him that he had to be extremely careful over the matter of her father, and this was reflected in the brevity and tact of his next letters.

Elizabeth was thoroughly muddled. She was uneasy over her feelings for Robert and fearful her father would guess and be angry. She wanted to keep Robert at arm's length for safety's sake, yet she longed to disclose her passion. The mental conflict distorted her perception of her father and she no longer saw him in a reasonable light. Now, he was either a heartless tyrant, as Robert said, or a loving protector, a devil or a god. There seemed no middle position.

In July Elizabeth learnt that her father and aunt (Mrs Hedley), had been overheard discussing the question of her being sent to Alexandria or Malta for the winter. The subject had probably been raised by her aunt, and Elizabeth's initial reaction was a casual one: 'a passing talk and thought, I dare say! and it would not *be* in any case, until September or October; though . . . I suppose I should not be much consulted . . . '.

In previous years, when she had been less well, Dr Chambers and her father had both suggested wintering in Madeira or Malta, and she had flatly turned down the proposal, adamant that she would never leave home again for health reasons. But since then her views on her life and its future had changed dramatically. She wanted to be well. Illness held no advantage for her; it was a positive drawback to her ambitions. She dreaded the winter for the threat it posed to her health. Everyone, Kenyon, her family, Robert, was urging her to go abroad and escape the cold and damp fog. That she was so much stronger was an additional reason for going away, for if she did she might be completely cured. Only her father was silent on the subject. Robert urged her to speak to him, but she dithered and time became short. Eventually she approached him and he suggested getting Dr Chambers's opinion, which she did at the end of August. He recommended that she spend the winter in Pisa. 'I wanted simply a warm climate and air; I might be well if I pleased.' Her father's initial reaction was 'dead silence'. Then he wrote a 'hard cold letter', surely a sign of disapproval. What it said is not known, but surprisingly Elizabeth understood it to give grudging consent to her Pisa plan and she began enquiring of the sailing dates of steamers to the Mediterranean.

Decisions by Edward Moulton Barrett concerning his family were traditionally unreliable and liable to be reversed, but on this occasion it does seem likely that Elizabeth's wish to go caused her to misread the letter. She made plans and then 'spoke face to face and quite firmly' with her father – 'so as to pass with my sisters for the "bravest person in the house" '. He told her bluntly that he did not approve of her going and when Elizabeth, understandably upset, asked him to say that 'he was not displeased with me – he *wouldn't*'. Brothers, sisters and aunt were indignant, and Kenyon was sufficiently upset to stay in town in the hope of being able to help, but to no avail.

A week later she had a second confrontation with precisely the same result, leaving Elizabeth with bitter feelings. 'Words have been said,' she told Robert, 'that I cannot easily forget, nor remember without pain.' All her pleas fell on deaf ears. 'I might do my own way, he said – *he* would not speak – *he* would not say that he was not displeased with me, nor the contrary: – I had better do what I liked: – for his part he washed his hands of me altogether.'

On the advice of her brother George she continued preparations for the voyage, without much hope. Her father had immediately shown his displeasure by ceasing his nightly visits to Elizabeth's room – 'he could not well throw me further from him than by ceasing to pay them – the thing is quite expressively significant'. George made a last ineffectual attempt to get his father to change his mind. 'I might go if I pleased,' Elizabeth reported, 'but that going it would be under his heaviest displeasure.' She decided to abandon the idea of going to Italy.

Elizabeth was angry and upset: '. . . . the pain of it was acutely felt by me; for never had I doubted but that Papa would catch at any human chance of restoring my health.' 'The bitterest "fact" of all is, that I had believed Papa to have loved me more than he obviously does': she turned to Robert for comfort.

Robert had kept quiet about her father's behaviour until now, aware that outspoken criticism was likely to do his cause more harm than good. But his mounting indignation finally got the better of him. 'I truly wish,' he wrote, '*you* may never feel what I have to bear in looking on, quite powerless, and silent, while you are subjected to this treatment.' It was intolerable that her father should make such unreasonable decisions. It was not right that Elizabeth should obey them, 'the jewel is not being guarded over, but ruined, cast away'. He advocated disobedience: '. . . . in your case I do think you are called upon to do your duty to yourself; . . . . Your own reason should examine the whole matter in dispute by every light which can be put in requisition.' It was wrong of Elizabeth 'to blindly adopt his pleasure, and die under it'. She must act on her 'own best conviction – not to abjure it and accept another will, and say "*there* is my plain duty" '.

Robert was passionately aroused by these events. He suffered to see Elizabeth suffer. His blood boiled to encounter such despotism. Like his father he hated tyranny, but while his father had had the courage to say so and return home from the West Indies, Robert could act only through Elizabeth. Had he had his way he would have faced her father, spoken his mind, and accepted the consequences; if need be he would have taken Elizabeth away despite the risks to her health. 'You are in what I should wonder at as the veriest slavery,' he told her, 'and I who *could* free you from it, I am here scarcely daring to write . . . though I know you must feel for me and forgive what forces itself from me. . . .' At this point he threw caution to the wind. 'Now while I *dream*, let me once dream! I would marry you now and thus – I would come when you let me and go when you bade me – I would be no more than one of your brothers "no more" – . . . when your head ached I should be here.'

Elizabeth's spirits rose. 'Your words have done me good and made me happy. . . . I thank and bless you for them, . . . to receive such a proof of attachment from *you*, not only over-powers every present evil—' Her bitterness lessened. 'The tearmarks went away [replaced by] the moisture of new, happy tears.'

She responded unreservedly and for the first time allowed herself to express what she really felt.

> You have touched me more profoundly than I thought even *you* could have touched me – my heart was full when you came here today. Henceforward I am yours for everything but to do you harm . . . none, except God and your will, shall interpose between you and me. . . . I mean, that if He should free me within a moderate time from the trailing chain of this weakness, I will then be to you whatever at that hour you shall choose . . . whether friend or more than friend. . . .

Robert was overjoyed. He had, it seemed, almost won the prize. But next day he was told by Elizabeth, 'Don't think too hardly of poor Papa. You have his wrong side . . . his side of peculiar wrongness . . . to you just now. When you have walked round him you will have other thoughts of him.' Openly declaring her allegiance to Robert had provided an antidote to the anger set off by her father, rather as an attempted suicide will relieve depression.

But this time she did not withdraw her commitment to Robert. 'I feel myself bound to you as one human being cannot be more bound to another; . . . you are more to me at this moment than all the rest of the world. . . . I trust you *implicitly* – and am not too proud to owe all things to you. But now let us wait and see what the winter does or undoes.' She promised that if she survived the winter she would marry him – if he still wanted her!

This was a momentous decision and it was not long before she began to have doubts and look back to her father. 'He is naturally stern and has exaggerated notions of authority,' she admitted; 'but these things go with high and noble qualities . . . Always he has the greatest power over my heart. . . .' Then, aware of Robert's puzzlement and irritation, she asked,

> Do you ever wonder at me . . . that I should write such things, and have written others so different? *I have thought that in myself very often.* Insincerity and injustice may seem the two ends, while I occupy the straight betwixt two. But there has been no insincerity – nor is there injustice. I believe, I am certain, I have loved him better than the rest of his children. I have heard the fountain within the rock, and my heart has struggled in towards him through the stones of the rock! Knowing what is excellent in him well. . . . With such high qualities . . . so upright and honourable – you would esteem him, you would like him, I think. . . .

Robert was not prepared to like him. On the contrary he now felt hostile and ready to fight for Elizabeth. His natural impulse was to act openly, to ask for an interview with her father and settle the issue. But Elizabeth was aghast at the idea and urged caution. She *knew*, she told him, that if he did he would be forbidden the house,

> without a moment's scruple. . . . We should be separated from *that moment* [of speaking to him] . . . hindered from writing, hindered from meeting . . . and I could evade nothing, as I am – not to say that I should have fainting fits at every lifting of his voice. . . . Then . . . the positive disobedience might be a greater offence than the unauthorised act. I shut my eyes in terror sometimes.

She persuaded Robert that he was powerless to influence her

father, and that he should stay in the background. Her father was totally unreasonable to any argument. None of his children 'will ever marry without a breach . . . . You might as well think to sweep off a third of the stars of Heaven with the motion of your eyelashes,' she warned him.

Robert found the subterfuges he was forced to practise increasingly irksome. Elizabeth was forever imagining that her father was on the brink of discovering their secret. His protests were to no avail. Elizabeth waxed hot and cold by turn. One moment she assured him that 'there is no sort of risk *for the present* – and if I ran the risk of making you uncomfortable about *that*, I did foolishly'. At another time she admonished him for wanting to call more often; if he did 'and it was *observed*, difficulties and vexations would follow'.

There was, in fact, no reason why her father should seriously suspect they were lovers. He was away from the house at his work in the City every weekday, including Saturday, and neither his children nor the servants were likely to inform him of what was going on. True, Robert had once called unusually early, before he had left for work, when 'it was plain to see, that he was not altogether pleased at finding you here in the morning. There was no pretext for objecting gravely – but it was plain that he was not pleased.' Seeing his concerned look she hastened to reassure him. 'Do not let this make you uncomfortable, he will forget all about it.' It sometimes seemed as if Elizabeth wanted to make Robert uneasy, as though she needed his anxiety to balance her own. When he took up Henrietta's comment that her father's anger, 'would not be so formidable after all', if Robert spoke to him about their engagement, Elizabeth poured scorn on the idea and on her sister. 'Poor dearest Henrietta, who trembles at the least trembling of the brows . . . who has less courage than I, and the same views of the future. "Why was I afraid?" she said – "where was the danger? Who would be the *informer*?" Well! I will not say any more.' Robert must listen to her for she knew best. 'I see, I know.' The result of her father discovering their secret would be 'the end of all . . . '.

She reiterated that no one, outside her brothers and sisters, must know about the frequency of Robert's visits. Even their friend Kenyon must be kept in the dark. It was absurd, as Robert pointed out. Kenyon had encouraged their liaison and suspected that they were at least close friends; Elizabeth was prone to blush bright red when he asked about Robert. But she was not prepared to give an inch: '. . . it is most inadvisable, both for his sake and ours. . . . We should involve him in ever so many fears for us, and force him to have his share of the odium at last. Papa would not speak to him again while he lived. And people might say, "Mr Kenyon did it all." ' Then in a rush she added, to Robert's amazement, 'It is a matter of feeling with me after all, that as I *cannot* give my confidence to my father, I should refuse it to others.'

It was hard on Robert not to be able to speak freely of his love. Elizabeth was able to share her confidences with her sisters but Robert had no one other than his mother and sister and his cousin James Silverthorne. To him, the 'silence' was the saddest aspect of their engagement, and added to his frustration and impatience. He had begun to dream:

> I never used to dream unless indisposed, and rarely then . . . nightmare dreams . . . invariable – of one sort. I stand (powerless to interpose by a word ever) and see the infliction of tyranny on the unresisting man or beast – and I wake just in time not to die: let no one try this kind of experiment on me or mine!

The nightmare was obviously related to Robert's frustrations. The sensation of terror, of being about to die, came from his pent-up anger which, threatening to get out of control, jerked him awake. There was a violent side to Robert's character which normally he kept under a tight rein – 'my two or three fire eyes' – which sometimes alarmed Elizabeth; it was too close to her father's thunder. Perhaps it was her awareness of this which made her say, 'I am Cassandra you know, and smell the slaughter in the bathroom.' But who was to be Agamemnon?

Robert was in a high state of tension by the spring of 1846, with headaches and dizzy spells. His mother was in no better shape, with agonising neuralgia. Robert kept no secrets from her and recounted the despotic behaviour of Elizabeth's father and the way he treated his children. The strain on the old lady, who was in her seventies, was considerable and must have added to the worry of having her son commit himself to a sick woman she had never met. Elizabeth was politely concerned for Robert's mother and worried extravagantly over him. 'I am uneasy about your head – that pain in it – what can it mean? I do beseech you to think of me just so much as will lead you to take regular exercise every day . . . ', and so on.

Eventually Robert exploded and said what he really thought

The poetess. I too have my vocation, – my work to do [from *Aurora Leigh*].

Facsimile of Elizabeth's diary entry
of 8 January 1832

Papa and I talked about predestination
this evening. The first time I have
ventured on the subject these two
years – I mean with *him*.
Dreamt about Adolphe & Endymion,
& a lady who was by turns Emily &
Amalthaea, & of her murdering
Endymion whose soul was infused
into Adolphe. Papa reproached her.
But she held up her beautiful face, &
said, 'I am yet very fair'. 'Clay Walls'
said Papa! –
A funny dream! –

Hope End (*below*), the Barretts'
home: '. . . out of the Arabian
nights . . .'

Elizabeth's father, Edward Moulton-Barrett: '. . . only one person holds the thunder . . .'

Her mother, Mary: '. . . a sweet gentle nature . . .'

Her beloved brother Bro: '. . . the heart too tender for energy'.

Her sister, Henrietta: '. . . most caring for the Polka . . .'

Elizabeth and Robert Browning during their protracted courtship by letter.

From Robert to Elizabeth, 28 January 1846

Wednesday

Ever dearest – I will say, as you desire, nothing on the subject – but strictly for myself: you engaged me to consult my own good in the keeping or breaking our engagement; not *your* good as it might even seem to me; much less seem to another. My only good in this world – that against which all the world goes for nothing – is to spend my life with you, and be yours. You know that

From Elizabeth to Robert, 15 July 1846

Wednesday morning

And is it true of today as you said it would be, ever dearest, that you wish to be with me? Let me have the comfort, or luxury rather, of the thought of it, before tomorrow takes you a step further off.

At dinner my aunt said to Papa . . . 'I have not seen Ba all day – and when I went to her room, to my astonishment a gentleman was sitting there.' 'Who was *that*?' said Papa's eyes to Arabel – 'Mr. Browning called here today,' she answered – 'And Ba bowed her head,' continued my aunt, 'as if she meant to signify to me that I was not to come' – 'Oh,' cried Henrietta, '*that* must have been a mistake of yours. Perhaps she meant just the contrary.' 'You should have gone it,' Papa said, 'and seen the *poet*.' Now if she really were to do that the next time!

Robert Browning's father *(opposite)*; his son admired his 'strange sweetness of soul'.

Robert's sister, Sarianna *(below left)*: 'She was my amanuensis in those days.'

John Kenyon *(below right)*, Robert and Elizabeth's good friend and sympathiser in their liaison: '. . . people might say, "Mr Kenyon did it all."'

Robert and Elizabeth in Italy in the 1850s.

Casa Guidi, their house in Florence, much loved by Elizabeth: 'the dark retreat'.

Facsimile of Elizabeth's last poem, 'The North and the South',
handwritten by Robert at the end of May 1861.

[facsimile of handwritten poem]

The North and the South

'Now give us lands where the olives grow',
   Cried the North to the South,
'Where the sun with a golden mouth can blow
Blue bubbles of grapes down a vineyard-row!.'
   Cried the North to the South.

'Now give us men from the sunless plain,'
   Cried the South to the North,
'By need of work in the snow and the rain,
Made strong, and brave by familiar pain!'
   Cried the South to the North.

Elizabeth and their son Penini: 'A
neutral creature . . .'.

Robert and Penini in 1870, nine years
after Elizabeth's death. Robert was
'. . . determined to make an English
boy . . .'.

Elizabeth in Rome, May 1861, a month before her death.

of her father. He was 'wicked', his conduct was 'intolerable'. It was 'shocking' that he should show himself 'not pleased' at Robert's coming 'to chat with and amuse a little that invalid daughter, once a month, so far as is known'.

This time Elizabeth did not rush to her father's defence. She joined forces with him and replied,

> The root of the evil is the miserable misconception of the limits and character of parental rights . . . it is a mistake of the intellect rather than of the heart . . . after using one's children as one's chattels for a time, the children drop lower and lower toward the level of the chattels, and the duties of human sympathy to them become difficult in proportion. And . . . *love*, he does not conceive of at all. He has feeling, he can be moved deeply, he is capable of affection in a peculiar way, but *that*, he does not understand. . . .

Robert was heartened. He gave a final growl: 'I very much fear that you would soon discover what one fault of mine is, if you were to hear anyone assert such a right in my presence.'

Elizabeth's dilemma was steadily increasing. She wanted to leave home and live with Robert. She knew her father would never agree to this, and that sooner or later she must take the law into her own hands. 'Papa seems to have no more idea of my living beyond these four walls than a journey to Lapland,' she admitted to Robert. But part of her still clung to her four walls, and feared losing her father. The solution to intractable problems in the past had been through anorexia nervosa, to attract her father's attention and concern, and point to a suitable end. But the last thing she wanted now was to attract her father's attention by appearing ill. This would arouse his concern, and he would immediately forbid Robert calling, just as he had stopped her visits to Boyd when she became anorexic in 1832. There was another factor to take into consideration. If she made herself ill, she would not be well enough to leave Wimpole Street with Robert when the time came. She was realistic enough to reject anorexia and follow Robert's advice; to eat more, take lots of exercise, and never miss a chance to walk up and down the stairs and go into the fresh air.

The winter of 1844–5 was unusually mild and Elizabeth continued to gain strength; she walked, went for rides, and visited exhibitions. Not only the weather but her psychological state contributed to her health. She felt sure of Robert and loved for her own sake, and she had a future to which she could look forward. In a word, she was happy. But a shadow still hung over her. Her father was never far from her mind, and the thought of his anger still upset her. Despite the pleasure and comfort that Robert gave her, there were moments when she missed her father and was saddened by his absence. The smallest gesture of affection, or hint of reconciliation, both gladdened her and made her feel guilty. She wanted to be loved by him in the old way. But she also wanted Robert, and the two were incompatible. She copied her father's habit of looking the other way when faced with painful decisions; she pushed the question of marriage from her mind.

Robert was not prepared to allow that for long. In early January he disturbed her calm. 'This living without you is too tormenting now. So begin thinking, – as for Spring, as for a New Year, as for a new life.' She fobbed him off with, 'the weather is as miraculous as the rest', but he returned to the attack a fortnight later. 'I claim your promise's fulfilment [the promise she had made in September that if she remained well she would marry him] – say, at the summer's end: it cannot be for your good that this state of things should continue. We can go to Italy for a year or two. . . .'

She agreed at length that, '. . . If in the time of fine weather, I am not ill . . . *then* . . . *not now* . . . you shall decide . . .'. There was still plenty of time and she did not intend to be tied down to a date; when the time should come, 'I will make no difficulties.'

Robert restrained himself until April, then resumed the pressure. 'Oh, dearest, let us marry soon, very soon, and end all this [subterfuge].' The strain was again building in him, and 'all yesterday I was very unwell'. A few weeks later, Elizabeth suggested, without warning, that it might

> be wiser and better for me to go to Italy with Miss Bayley [a literary friend of Kenyon's], or with any other person who may be willing to take me . . . and that you should follow . . . leaving other thoughts for another year . . . or . . . shall we gain anything . . . by remaining quietly as we are, you at New Cross and I here, until next year's summer or autumn?

Robert controlled himself at first. 'Your good is my good, and your will mine,' he answered. 'If you were convinced *that* good would be promoted by our remaining as we are for twenty years instead of one, I should endeavour to submit in the end.' Then he exploded, 'Every day that passes before *that day* is one the more of hardly endurable anxiety and irritation, to say the least; and the thought of another year's intervention of hope deferred – altogether intolerable!'

They discussed possible places where they might live – Sardinia, Pisa, Florence, southern Italy, even Greece, though the latter was more in jest than serious. Much of it was like playing a game to Elizabeth; she could indulge her fantasies and progress indulgently through the classical world. But Robert took such matters seriously, and carefully weighed the pros and cons of each suggested place. In the end the consensus was for Pisa.

Other people were taking an interest in Elizabeth's future. In June 1846 Mrs Jameson,[3] now a close friend of both of them, suggested taking Elizabeth to Italy, but Kenyon advised her that Elizabeth's father would never give his consent. Mrs Jameson had been indignant. '*Can* nothing be done to rescue her from this? *Ought* it to continue?'

Next month her uncle and aunt advised her to be decisive and, willy-nilly, pack her bags and go to Italy, that 'to live on in this fashion, in this room was lamentable to contemplate'.

Perhaps the most significant exchange was with her old friend Boyd whom she visited for the first time in early July. 'Something in a note' led to his asking 'if I were going to be a nun'. On the next visit in August, 'he put his question precisely right', and Elizabeth admitted that she was engaged to Robert.[4] Boyd, to her satisfaction, 'approved highly of the whole, and exhorted me . . . to keep to my purpose'. She was amused to discover that much of his pleasure was derived from anger he still felt towards her father. 'I am sure he triumphs inwardly in the idea of a chain being broken which he has so often denounced in words that pained and vexed me. . . .'

The question of how the couple would live when abroad concerned Robert increasingly. He had lived entirely off his father so far and never seriously considered paid work; had not bothered himself 'beyond considering the lilies how they grow'. His 'careless sweet habitude of living – this absolute independence of mine' was vitally important to him; without it 'my heart would starve and die'. The possibility of life with Elizabeth changed that outlook. If need be he would give up his independence. 'I am sure that whenever I make up my mind I can be rich enough and to spare.' He would set about obtaining employment, write a play, or 'a novel on the subject of

Napoleon'. Elizabeth dismissed the idea out of hand. 'You cannot despise the gold and gauds of the world more than I do. . . . And if I *wished* to be very poor, – I *could not*, with three or four hundred a year of which no living will can dispossess me. And is not the chief good of money, the being free from the need of thinking of it?' In fact, like Robert, she believed that a poet needed to devote his life totally to his writing and not be distracted by other activities.

Robert did not in the least mind living off Elizabeth's money, any more than Elizabeth was concerned about it. But he did worry over what the Moulton Barrett family might say about it. The Victorian middle class believed strongly that a man should earn enough to support his wife adequately, and disapproved of anyone not doing so. Robert was used to members of his family, other than his parents, criticising him and was not oversensitive on that score, but he did mind being regarded as a fortune hunter who was marrying Elizabeth for her money.

Why should it matter where the money came from, 'from you or me?' Elizabeth demanded. 'It will be as much mine as yours when we are together. What is anybody to do with us?' She could hardly be called 'too rich'. Far from people accusing Robert of marrying her for money, they were more likely 'to say that I have *taken you in*'.

Robert remained uneasy and continued to return to the subject. In August he asked the exact amount she had. 'I want to know, being your possible husband. My notion of the perfection of money arrangements is that of a fairy purse which every day should hold *so* much, and there an end of trouble.'

Elizabeth had 'eight thousand pounds in the funds, of which the interest comes to me quarterly . . . from forty pounds to forty-five pounds . . . every three months . . . and there is the ship money . . . a little under two hundred pounds a year on an average.' This was more than enough for two people to live comfortably, if carefully on in Italy; Robert himself had mentioned a sum of a hundred pounds as being sufficient. A minor matter was how to obtain sufficient cash to pay for their journey to Italy; Elizabeth would have difficulty in obtaining money from her father, who looked after her finances and would be highly suspicious of a request for a hundred pounds or so. In the event Robert borrowed the money from his father. Robert remained uneasy, and eventually Elizabeth, half mocking, told him he was at liberty 'to arrange that after the deaths of us the money should return to my family'. He refused to let the matter drop and in the end, Elizabeth drafted and signed a 'document' for his approval.

> In compliance with the request of Robert Browning, who may possibly become my husband, that I would express in writing my wishes respecting the ultimate disposal of whatever property I possess at this time, whether in the funds or elsewhere. . . . I hereby declare my wishes to be . . . that, Robert Browning . . . having, of course, as it is his right to do, first held and used the property in question for the term of his natural life . . . should bequeath the same, by an equal division to my two sisters, or in the case of the previous death of either or both of them, to such of my surviving brothers as most shall need it by the judgment of my eldest surviving brother.
>
> Elizabeth Barrett

'That is sufficient,' Robert agreed, and added, 'There may even be a *claimant*, instead of a recipient.' He was raising the possibility, for the first time, that he and Elizabeth might have a child. Nowhere else in their correspondence is the matter touched on. But Elizabeth was by now either bored by the subject of money, or did not want to consider such an eventuality. 'We will not carry on this discussion any further.'

One sign of Elizabeth's hesitancy to commit herself to marriage was her refusal to meet any of the Browning family before she eloped. She even raised objections to Robert confiding in them, which amazed him. And he was hurt, although he never said so directly, when she squashed his proposals that she and they might meet.

Sarianna was avid to see Elizabeth. It was she who usually picked the flowers Robert brought to Elizabeth's room. Elizabeth invariably thanked her through Robert, and did not, it seems, write to her at this time. When Kenyon, no doubt with Robert's connivance, suggested that Sarianna should call on her, the very idea made her 'tremble'. 'Do you imagine that I am not afraid of your family?' she asked. She made a flurry of excuses and then appealed to Robert not to misunderstand her reasons.

> I was afraid of not being liked enough . . . and I felt it to be impossible to receive so near a relative of yours . . . as I should a stranger. There would be the need in me of being affectionate to your sister! How could I not? Yet how could I?

Elizabeth Barrett Browning

> Everything is at once too near and too far. . . . I would rather, ten times over, receive Queen Victoria and all her court. . . .

Robert's suggestion that she drive to New Cross to meet his family met with the same brickwall response. 'It was not from a mere motive of shyness,' she assured him. She did not want to seem lacking in respect or affection but it would be socially wrong for her to call. (The excuse was like the one she gave repeatedly for not calling on Boyd in 1828.) For good measure she added that the less his parents knew about their relationship, the less likely they were to be blamed by her father and others, and hurt. Robert ridiculed the idea, but came to recognise that it was useless to go on trying, and restricted himself to passing affectionate messages between Elizabeth and his mother.

Robert's hope that Elizabeth would make up her mind and stick to it rose momentarily when she remarked about her father, 'I hope he will try to forgive me, as I have forgiven him, long ago.' But within a few days she was backsliding, and apologising for creating 'unnecessary delays'. She made much of her distress over her father and the difficulty she had in meeting his eye. 'How I can look and sleep as well as I do, is a miracle. . . . I think nothing of Italy now, though I shall enjoy it of course when the time comes. I think only that you love me, that you are the angel of my life. . . .' This was not what Robert wanted to hear at this late stage. His headache was almost unbearable.

> Show me one good reason why we gain anything by deferring our departure till next week instead of tomorrow. . . . If the cold plunge *must* be taken, all this shivering delay on the bank is hurtful as well as fruitless. I *do* understand your anxieties . . . but if . . . you really determine to act as we propose in spite of them . . . a new leaf is turned over in our journal. . . . You tell me you have decided to go [to Italy] . . . you will be prepared to go . . . by the end of September at the very latest.

Then, afraid he might have sounded too harsh, he added,

> If you find yourself unable, or unwilling to make this effort, tell me so – I will not offer a word in objection – I will continue our present life . . . and wait till next autumn, and the next and the next, till providence end our waiting. . . . If, on the other hand, you make up your mind to leave England now, you will be prepared by the end of September. . . . forgive

whatever you shall judge to need forgiveness here – I am not too well this morning and write with an aching head. My mother's suffering continues too!

It was Elizabeth's father who finally forced the issue. On 10 September he decided to move the family to Kent, for at least one month, while the Wimpole Street house was cleaned. ('If I had been considered at all . . . we should have been taken away earlier,' was Elizabeth's comment.) There was no time to be lost. 'I will do as you wish,' she told Robert. He acted rapidly and decisively. 'We must be married *directly* and go to Italy. . . . Your words, first and last, have been that "you would not fail me" – you will not.'

'I shall not fail to you – I do not, I will not, I will act by your decision, and I wish you to decide.'

On Saturday 12 September at 11 a.m. they were married in Marylebone Church, a few hundred yards from Wimpole Street, with her maid, Wilson, and Robert's cousin, James Silverthorne, in attendance. They parted immediately after the service, and Elizabeth drove to Boyd's house, where she was persuaded to drink a glass of Cyprus wine and eat some bread and butter while waiting for her sisters to join her. They had not been told about the wedding, to protect them from the wrath of their father, but Arabel for one guessed, and Henrietta must have had a strong inkling. Boyd of course knew, and his delight, if silently expressed, perhaps helped to raise Elizabeth's courage. It was the last time she saw him. He died eighteen months later after a stroke, on 10 May 1848.[5]

Elizabeth had a week to wait before leaving for Paris, en route to Pisa. She was terrified of discovery. The conflicts in her mind over her father returned tenfold. She was 'paralysed' at the thought of telling him,

Papa I am married; I hope you will be not too displeased. Ah, poor Papa! . . . he will be angry – he will cast me off as far from him.

We will submit. . . . I will put myself under his feet, to be forgiven a little . . . enough to be taken up again into his arms. I love him – he is my father *above* all. And *you*, because you are so generous and tender to me, will let me . . . and help me to try to win back the alienated affection. . . . Surely I may say to him . . . 'with the exception of this act, I have submitted to the least of your wishes all my life long. Set the life against the act, and forgive me, for the sake of the daughter you once loved.'

Surely I may say *that* – and entreat him to pardon the happiness that has come at last.

And *he* will wish in return, that I had died years ago – For the storm will come and endure. And at last, perhaps, he will forgive us, it is my hope.

She cried for her father's forgiveness, but she could also proclaim wholeheartedly that she was Robert's. 'I have a right now openly to love you, and to hear the people call it a duty, when I do. . . .'

The strain was immense. She became so thin and ill-looking that everyone noticed, which only increased her terror. She raised her dose of opium to sleep and remain calm. She kept her head, and on Saturday afternoon, 19 September, she, Wilson and Flush left Wimpole Street, while the rest of the family were at dinner.

Robert was a changed man after the marriage. 'Dearest,' he wrote next day, 'I woke this morning *quite well* – quite free from the sensation in the head. I have not woken so, for two years perhaps – what have you been doing to me?' His anger towards her father had largely gone, and he tried to ease her distress and grief at leaving him. 'I shall always have "the utmost respect" for him,' he told her, and 'I will do my utmost to conciliate your father.' Had he been able to do so life would have been very different for them both.

Edward Moulton Barrett had been vexed with his eldest daughter for almost a year. He had withdrawn from her company, but had made no direct criticism of her or Robert. One may ask why this state of affairs continued for so long.

One reason, perhaps, was Elizabeth's changed attitude towards her father. Previously happy and relaxed with him, she was now anxious and embarrassed in his presence, fearful of betraying herself by some revealing word or look, and therefore stiff and offputting in her manner. Her father must have been hurt and puzzled by this, and driven to keep his distance.

On the other hand he had been much put out by Elizabeth's – and her brother George's – attempts to persuade him to change his mind over her spending the winter in Italy, and his obstinate pride required Elizabeth to give some recognisable sign of repentance. Was he perhaps waiting for her to fall ill, which would bring him post-haste to her bedside, as in the past? He knew that she could make herself ill through starvation. In the event the opposite happened; she put on weight and grew healthier until the last month.

It is impossible to know how much he associated her improved health with Robert Browning. He tolerated the friendship, believing the visits to be no more than one or two a month, but he may well have grown increasingly incensed with Robert's presence, and the continuous supply of fresh flowers that appeared in Elizabeth's room. One suspects that, sooner or later, he would have denounced Robert as *persona non grata* and prohibited all communication between him and Elizabeth.

When Elizabeth eloped her father was at first stunned, then enraged. He wrote her a condemnatory letter, severing all connection with him. Had she died he would have preserved her memory for ever, as he did with his wife. As it was, he wiped her from his life. Yet his anguish must have been enormous.

Anger temporarily hid his grief and resulted in his behaving with uncharacteristic abandon. He threw himself into a round of dinner parties, 'frothing over with high spirits', and denying his angst; a process similar to the 'manic defence' which had succeeded his wife's death. The enormous mental energy expended on suppressing his unhappiness overflowed into these unusual channels. But in time this ceased, and the artificial euphoria was replaced by melancholia. He had lost his last prop.

10

Flight to Pisa and Florence, 1846–1851

The flight of the Duchess was child's play compared to the Brownings' escape. They crossed to Le Havre from Southampton at night. The weather was foul. Elizabeth was exhausted on arrival and had to rest the next day. As though fearful of delay they took the night diligence to Rouen and travelled thence by rail to Paris.

For Elizabeth the journey was a nightmare. Whether she actually slept at Le Havre is unrecorded, but she seemed to be in a dreamlike state in the diligence. She lay cradled in Robert's arms, like a baby, sometimes babbling excitedly at the sight of the horses in the moonlight, a scene made for Fuseli. 'Now five horses, now seven . . . all looking wild, some of them white, some brown, some black, with manes leaping . . . a fantastic scene.'

Robert feared for her life and as soon as they reached Paris sought out Mrs Jameson, whom he knew to be at the Hôtel de Ville, and sent her a terse note: 'Come and see your friend and my wife Elizabeth Barrett Browning.' She came at once, astonished to learn of their marriage, 'wise people, wild poets or not', brought them to her hotel and organised them. She found Elizabeth to be 'nervous, frightened, ashamed, agitated, happy, miserable', and horribly weak, 'in a most feeble state'. She insisted that the couple stay in her hotel for at least a week, so that Elizabeth could regain her strength.

Paris was for Elizabeth blurred and indistinct. 'Such a strange week it was, altogether like a vision. Whether in body or out of body I cannot tell scarcely.' It was too soon to comprehend that she was married and free. She was homesick for her 'big room' and her family. She longed and dreaded to read their letters and learn what they thought of her.

Weak, exhausted, and emaciated she was barely able to swallow at first. With rest and food, and Robert's 'infinite tenderness', aided by Mrs Jameson, Elizabeth began to improve and respond to Robert's 'wit and wisdom'. She went with Robert and Mrs Jameson to restaurants – an event previously unimaginable – and once to the Louvre, but for the most part she 'kept very still . . . and was satisfied with the idea of Paris'.

After a week she was strong enough to continue the journey to Orléans, where her mail was waiting. When she reached her hotel room she could barely stand or catch her breath for dread of what she was to learn. Robert fetched the mail, a large bundle which included congratulations from friends like Kenyon and Carlyle, as well as those from all her relatives. She sat trembling on the bed at first, unable to bring herself 'to open one and growing paler and colder every moment'. Robert urged her to begin but she pushed him away and told him to leave; she had 'to meet the agony alone'.

Her father's response was as she had feared. He had cast her out of the family and declared that she no longer existed for him. She had committed an unforgivable sin and 'sold her soul for genius' – a Faustian concept which made her smile wanly but did nothing to lift her spirit.

It was the unexpected antipathy of her brothers, and especially George, which angered her. She had believed that George, above all the men in the family, would understand and sympathise with her actions. He had, after all, helped her over the Pisa affair and done his best to persuade their father to give way. He was the one brother who had met Robert, and liked him. It was to George that she had entrusted the delivery of her explanatory letter to her father – which, in the event, George declined to effect, and it was left to Henrietta. She was shocked that he had assumed the rôle of prosecuting counsel; he arraigned her for absconding from home and leaving 'the weight of shame and sorrow to be borne by the family', as though, Elizabeth complained, 'I was not even married'. But what really touched her on the raw was the implication – it was more like a statement, Elizabeth considered – that Robert was penniless and had married her for her money. 'Those insinuations about money and Mr Browning being reiterated, are really de trop altogether.'

Her relief to find her sisters were on her side was enormous, and allowed her to cry, 'from the balm of your tender words', she told them.

Robert dealt with her like a sick child, 'laid me down on the bed and sat by me for hours, pouring out floods of tenderness and goodness and promising to win back for me the affection of father and brothers'. She had acted correctly and been true to her firmest convictions, he assured her, for did she not believe that, as she had put it, 'the most strictly personal act of one's life' was the sole responsibility of the person concerned?

He soothed her and she became calm and even optimistic. 'With time and patience my poor dearest Papa will be melted into opening his arms to us . . .' she repeated, like a prayer. 'I cannot believe that he will forget me, as he says he will, and go on thinking me dead rather than alive and happy.' Robert's patience was infinite. He rarely left her side and kept up a flow of encouragement, interspersed with stories which made her laugh.

They resumed their journey, through Bourges, where Elizabeth was persuaded to visit the cathedral and admire the stained-glass windows, to Roanne and Lyon. Elizabeth's emaciation and bodily discomfort worried her companions, but the distress helped to divert her thoughts from her father. Mrs Jameson wrote, 'Not only we have had to carry her fainting from the carriage but from her extreme thinness and weakness, every few hours' journey has bruised her all over, till movement becomes almost unbearable . . . all this has been endured with *patience* . . . unselfish sweetness of the temper . . . unfailing consideration for others.'

From Lyon they travelled down the Rhône to Avignon through a torrential rainstorm. It had taken them ten days from Paris, far longer than they had anticipated, but the slowness was necessary to preserve Elizabeth's strength and she revived quickly after each day's rest. She was even strong enough to visit Vaucluse, and see the fountain 'where Petrarch lives still . . . '.

They reached Pisa in mid October. Elizabeth was worn out and 'almost helpless' although 'wonderfully well considering'. Pisa looked a haven of peace: 'A majestic silent city, built of marble and backed by purple mountains . . . so beautiful and so full of repose, yet not desolate: it is rather the repose of sleep than of death'.

They took rooms for six months in Vasari's Collegio Ferdinando, overlooking the Duomo and leaning tower, avoiding 'the warm orthodox position by the Arno' on the advice of the leading Pisan physician – 'Better to have cool rooms to live in and warm walks to go out along'. But the rooms proved rather too cold for comfort, and they were obliged to have fires morning and evening.

It rained solidly for the first ten days, but then came 'a divine sunshine' and warmth. Elizabeth and Robert walked by the river every day and went for drives into the hills, and when she was tired they sat in the sun and watched the lizards, and once Robert caught her 'a giant grasshopper'. She slept soundly, ate well and thrived. Mrs Jameson, before she left for Rome at the beginning of November, proclaimed, 'You are not *improved*, you are *transformed*.'

She had put on weight with Robert's choice of menu, protesting only mildly when she considered he was exceeding the reasonable; the 'greatest quarrel' they had at Pisa was when Elizabeth would not eat as much as Robert expected. Their tastes in food were similar, although one suspects that Robert adjusted his to cater for Elizabeth's fads and fancies. 'A little chicken and plenty of cayenne, and above all things, pudding, will satisfy us both,' she wrote to Henrietta.

Never once did Elizabeth cook a meal; making toast comprised her own culinary accomplishment and that, Robert teased her, was usually burnt. All their food was bought in from a nearby trattoria, and always chosen by Robert. 'It is a privilege on my part and an advantage on my husband's,' she said in later years, 'that I have never ordered a dinner once since my marriage. . . . what would become of me (and of the house) I wonder, if I had a house to manage. . . .' They had eggs for breakfast, dinner came at 2 p.m., at 6 p.m. coffee and rolls made with milk appeared, and for supper they ate roast chestnuts and grapes. Robert plied her with Chianti. 'Fancy me,' she told her sister, 'drinking claret out of tumblers. . . . Robert aspires to make me take more of this claret than he would himself, pouring it into the glass when I am looking another way, and entreating me by ever so much invocation when I look and refuse! And then, I never being famous for resisting his invocations, am at the end of dinner too giddy to see his face. . . .' Perhaps to emphasise the additional benefits of love, she added, '. . . this process never gives me a headache, as two spoonfuls of your port used to do, and never makes me feverish'. Robert was immensely pleased. 'We are as happy as two owls in a hole, two toads under a tree stump; or any other queer two poking creatures that we let live, after the fashion of their black hearts, only Ba is fat and rosy.'

After Mrs Jameson left they kept to their own company. Elizabeth wrote, 'We like our seclusion here in Pisa, though rather extreme, perhaps, for people who want to see Italy and the Italians – for I might as well almost . . . be shut up in my big

room . . . so very, very quiet we are . . . knowing not a creature.'
Robert encouraged their isolation and was determined that none
of the English residents of Pisa should call. To an outsider
looking in, the scene was of almost claustrophobic narrowness,
and Elizabeth's old doubts about herself momentarily surfaced.
'To talk for four and twenty hours together was surely a strain,'
she observed, and it might be profitable to encourage the
occasional visitor. But at heart she was happy to have Robert all
to herself.

Robert was rarely away from Elizabeth's side. If she stood up
and walked to the window, Robert did the same. At night time,
when Wilson said it was time to prepare for bed, he
accompanied her to the bedroom door. For one hour only in the
daytime was he separated, when he went, protesting, for an
energetic walk with Flush. Amused, she described to Mrs
Jameson Robert's 'dreary walk on Lung' Arno . . . in ever such
an imprecative humour'. Their days seemed to be full, 'what
with music and books and writing and talking'.

While at Pisa she wrote 'The Runaway Slave at Pilgrim's
Point', an anti-slavery poem commissioned by an American
magazine as far back as 1845. It is about a girl whose black lover
is killed, and who is then raped by a white 'master'. She
strangles the child which is born, then runs away, is pursued,
captured, whipped and killed. There are obvious similarities
between Elizabeth and the slave girl, and her father's treatment
of her must have been in her mind as she was composing the
poem. When Mrs Jameson raised an eyebrow over the subject of
the poem she wrote indignantly, 'Is it possible that you think a
woman has no business with questions like the question of
slavery? Then she had better use a pen no more. She had better
subside into slavery and concubinage herself. . . .'

She insisted, at times almost shrilly, that she had no regrets
over her own escape from Wimpole Street. 'Ask me again if I
enjoy my liberty. . . . my head goes round sometimes. . . . I
never was happy before in my life. Ah, but, of course the painful
thoughts recur!' She could not be 'better or happier' with Robert,
yet she missed her family. 'There are some I love too tenderly to
be easy under their displeasure, or . . . injustice.' She could not
accept a life permanently divorced from her father. 'I cannot
believe that he will forget me, as he says he will, and go on
thinking me to be dead rather than alive and happy. So I manage
to hope for the best, and all that remains, all my life here, *is* best
already. . . .'

She wrote frequently to her sisters, demanding to be told about everything that happened at home, and above all about her father's health and activities. She was distressed to hear that Arabel had suffered because of her; '. . . the injustice is rampant,' she cried when she learnt that Arabel had been moved to a smaller bedroom (understandable surely, since she used to share Elizabeth's room for sleeping),[1] and an uncomfortable bed. 'Do write to me soon,' she pleaded, 'and let me know whether . . . Papa is kinder to her.' She wanted up-to-date information on her brothers, and even the behaviour of the domestics concerned her.

Her spirits rose as her brothers gradually came round and 'forgave her'. George made amends in the New Year, although he continued to maintain for a time that Robert had led her astray, and full friendship was only restored after their London visit in 1851.

She wrote regularly to her father, and although she had no reply she convinced herself that he read the letters and thought of her, as she thought of him.

It would have been remarkable had Robert written poetry during these early years of marriage. He alone was responsible for Elizabeth's happiness and health, and he made her feel 'completely spoilt and happy'. He took charge of everything, including their finances. He entertained her, shared the same novels, took her for walks and expeditions, and revered her. He was, at different times, a husband, lover and nurse. Whenever unhappy or ill, she clung to him. 'He is my compensation for the bitterness of life,' she proclaimed at low moments.

Sexual intercourse probably first began in Pisa. During the courtship they had kissed and made love as much as was possible in the circumstances. Robert's letters at that time convey a sense of physical passion: 'I kiss your hand, and your eyes, and now your lips. . . . No words can tell how I am your own.' Elizabeth, on the other hand, is more circumspect, perhaps because of convention – although she was prepared to discuss the more passionate scenes in French novels with Miss Mitford with spirit and disinhibition – but more, one suspects, because she was not a sensual woman. Her letters during the engagement bear this out. 'I love you with my soul,' committed her to Robert more deeply than any wish to kiss or touch him.

It is unlikely they did anything more than hold one another and kiss during the journey to Pisa. Elizabeth was exhausted,

Elizabeth Barrett Browning

emaciated, and her body was bruised and sore from the carriage rides. But once installed in their rooms and rested, they began to make love. There is no reason to suppose that Elizabeth was alarmed by the prospect of intercourse. It was Robert who was prudish and uneasy initially. Having brashly told Elizabeth that he knew 'what most of the pleasures of this world are', he then confessed that he was daunted by the prospect of undressing and washing in front of her. Would she mind, he asked, if he had a separate dressing room on account of this modesty? She did not. In her social world not to have had one would have been exceptional.

Mrs Jameson remarked of Elizabeth that, '. . .there is not a trace of animal spirits, though evidently a sense [of] deep happiness, gratitude and love'. But these spirits must have been at least stirred by lovemaking. In *Aurora Leigh*, Elizabeth makes no bones of her belief that a woman has as much right to sexual pleasure as a man. Both partners join

> With all that strain
> of sexual passion, which devours the flesh
> in a sacrament of souls.[2]

A good sexual life enhances the closeness of two people. This thought was in her mind perhaps when she celebrated her second month of marriage. 'Every hour has bound me to him more and more; if the beginning was well, still better it is now – that is what he says to me, and I say back again day by day.'

Robert, one feels, was a sympathetic lover, and exactly caught Elizabeth's feelings:

> Be a god and hold me
> With a charm!
> Be a man and fold me
> With thine arm.[3]

Their rooms at Pisa overlooked the route funeral processions took to and from the cathedral.

The monks, sometimes all in black and sometimes all in white . . . chant in a train, carrying torches . . . and on the bier comes the corpse . . . openfaced . . . except just a veil. At first we both used to wish to see the sight . . . but the horror . . .

134

grew too strong for me soon . . . and he feels it too, and attends to me often when I say, 'Oh, *don't* go to the window'. But sometimes he cries out . . . 'I can't help it, Ba – it *draws* me.' Such horrible, hoarse chanting, it is – like the croaking of death itself.

Robert was drawn to stories and scenes of death and suffering. It was a side of her husband that Elizabeth did not altogether like. For this reason, in the last year of her life, she refused to take an interest in *The Old Yellow Book* which Robert so excitedly brought home from the market. One wonders what she thought of 'The Confessional', that poem written by Robert before they met – to which she suggested minor alterations – which tells the gruesome story of a young woman whose lover is burnt at the stake and who is tortured by the Inquisition because of their love. Sexual passion and agony are disturbingly intertwined in the poem.

> I had a lover – shame avaunt!
> This poor wrenched body, grim and gaunt,
> Was kissed all over till it burned,
> By lips the truest, love e'er turned
> His heart's own tint: one night they kissed
> My soul out in a burning mist.[4]

Partly because of the dullness of Pisa, they planned moving to Florence. But in January 1847 Wilson suddenly complained of stomach pains, and alarmed Elizabeth so much that a doctor was summoned. It proved to be a minor disorder, but Wilson spent ten days in bed, and during this time Elizabeth not only helped to look after her, and made her toast, but learned to dress herself, 'lace one's very own stays, and cause hook and eyes to meet behind one's very own back', and 'to comb out and twist one's own hair'.

No sooner was Wilson back on her feet than Elizabeth started to complain of 'sudden violent pains which come on in the night, relieved by friction and a few spoonfuls of brandy, and going off as suddenly as they come'.

Wilson guessed and feared that Elizabeth was having a miscarriage, and blamed it on the amount of opium she was consuming. Despite Robert's urging she had continued the drug. 'I have not left off my draughts – oh no! – I have not been

"charmed" up to that point, though gradually I can diminish it,'
she told Henrietta. Elizabeth panicked at the idea of being
pregnant and denied the possibility. She refused to send for Dr
Cook, and Robert, for once, was out of his depth. She confessed
she was 'frightened out of my wits by the suggestion about the
morphine, and out of my *wit* about the entreaty about Dr Cook'.

The pains stopped as suddenly as they had begun and an
uneasy calm followed. Six weeks later, at the end of March, the
pains returned, and this time were severe enough for Elizabeth
to agree to Dr Cook being summoned. He confirmed that she
was pregnant, and that it was too late to prevent the miscarriage.
She must have conceived about a fortnight after her arrival in
Pisa.

Remarkably, no depression followed the miscarriage, but
although she was soon out of bed, she was exhausted. 'I lie here
flat on the sofa. . . . I rest and take port wine by wineglasses,'
she wrote to Mrs Martin. She was exultant at having been
pregnant. To discover that she *could* conceive and be a mother
was enormously exciting, and she felt complete, a woman in
every sense. Her pride in herself more than compensated for the
disappointment of miscarrying, and showed in her high spirits.

The fact that she did not know she was pregnant was probably
because she was accustomed to her periods stopping when she
was very thin or stressed. By twenty weeks one might have
expected Elizabeth to feel foetal movements. But she was taking
large doses of opium which would have prevented morning
sickness and nausea, and reduced movements.

Robert was upset by the drama, not because the child had
been lost, but that Elizabeth's life had been endangered. He
blamed himself; he had been self-indulgent and irresponsible in
making her pregnant. Agitated, he hovered outside the bedroom door while the miscarriage was occurring. When it was
over he rushed into the room and 'threw himself down on the
bed in a passion of tears, sobbing like a child . . . '. He stayed by
her bedside, rubbing her, talking, reading to her, 'overset, –
overcome'. Elizabeth became more concerned for Robert than
for herself; he had virtually given up eating ' "tout de bon"
and I expected him to turn into a shade'.

They arrived in Florence on 20 April 1847 and moved into
temporary rooms. 'I was too weak when I came, to see anything,
and had to lie on the sofa and grow strong, while the Venus of
Medici stood two or three streets off – think how tantalising!' she

reported. But it was Robert's concern over her which really kept her confined to her room, she explained. He 'had suffered great anxiety about me, and it was only just to him to run no risk'.

By May she was going out to 'see all the glories', and planned to spend the summer in Vallombrosa 'with the monks', despite knowing that women were not allowed. Robert was unable to dissuade her, and after some trouble obtained a special letter of dispensation from the Archbishop of Florence. This failed to impress the Abbot of Vallombrosa and they had to leave the monastery and return home after three days, Elizabeth angry and elated by turn.

Elizabeth was now much stronger. Her good looks heartened Robert, and he wrote to her sisters of 'her rounded cheeks with not a little colour in them, and her general comparative . . . dare I write it . . . "plumpness" '. Others, who had not previously seen her, were less impressed. Mary Boyle,[5] who was one of their few visitors at that time, observed that she had 'never . . . seen a more spiritual face, or one in which the soul looked more clearly from the windows; clusters of long curls . . . framed her small delicate face, and even shrouded its outline, and her form was so fragile as to appear but an etherial covering'.

The lease on their rooms was coming to an end. Robert, frantically searching for fresh accommodation, discovered Casa Guidi, where he rented six rooms on the first floor for three months. The rooms were large and dark, although with high ceilings, and airy, and Elizabeth at once felt at home there. Outside the drawing room, facing the wall of the San Felice church and offering no view and very little light but complete privacy, was a narrow balcony or terrace, and here in the cool of evening Elizabeth enjoyed walking to and fro with Robert. They had to give up the apartment in October when the lease expired because, Robert informed Elizabeth, they could not afford the increased rent. She was irate with what she saw as Robert's misplaced parsimony, but he was adamant; he, after all, was responsible for their finances, and in the end she had to accept his decision. He was, as Elizabeth never ceased to tell her sisters, 'perfect', and she sometimes wondered, 'Where are such men in the world?'

They spent the winter in a tiny house on the piazza opposite the Pitti Palace – the Duke of Tuscany's residence – where she began to write *Casa Guidi Windows*. This was a political poem, and in it she gave voice to her idealistic belief in Italy's liberation from the Austrian yoke, and her admiration for Italian resistance. This was interrupted in February when she found she was pregnant for a second time.

In early March she miscarried again, after carrying for nearly four months. She was disappointed, but not seriously depressed.

> I have been ill [she told Miss Mitford a month later] but not as ill as at Pisa – and am now quite recovered, except as to having lost the hope which had made me glad again. There is no use in hoping. . . . For happier I am than I ever counted on being in *this* world – and if I had to choose between additional comforts, I should choose the smile of my own father to that of my own child . . . if I could choose either . . . oh yes I should and would.

They returned to Casa Guidi in May 1848 – now rented unfurnished to them at a rent they could easily afford – and almost at once Elizabeth again became pregnant. It is unlikely that she recognised this before August, for in mid July Florence became stifling and she and Robert set out for Fano. Finding that town much too hot for comfort they moved on to Ancona and Ravenna. Wanting a child it is unlikely that she would have risked a bumpy gruelling trip, liable to cause miscarriage, had she known she was pregnant. It is inconceivable that Robert would have permitted it: his wife was much too precious to risk. When he learnt of the pregnancy he insisted that she rest, that she reduce her letter writing – he had been convinced that the excitement of writing letters had contributed to the second miscarriage – and that she make a serious attempt to stop her opium.

On 10 October, kneeling on a chair, she overbalanced and pitched forward on to her forehead. 'Here's the end of keeping in the house for months together, to avoid shakings and strainings! One falls out of an easy chair into the arms of destiny.' The shock stunned her and caused a headache, but otherwise had no bad consequences. However, it caused Robert to redouble his attentions. A fortnight later Elizabeth felt movements, to her relief and excitement, which made her determined to end the opium habit. But it was a slow business, and the drug was not entirely stopped until the eighth month of pregnancy. If the withdrawal followed its usual course Elizabeth would have become moody and irritable during this time. In the last three months she fretted over the child's well-being and the possibility of it having been deformed or diseased by the opium. All the medical opinions on her own health were favourable and she had 'no misgivings, no fatal presentiments' about herself – only about the child.

At 2.15 a.m. on 9 March 1849, after twenty-one hours of labour, her son was born. The birth was uncomplicated, and Elizabeth was always in control of herself, 'never cried out once or shed a tear, acute as the pains were'. Her delight when told she had a healthy boy was immense, and 'after the rapture of hearing my child's first cry, I thought of nothing but of what was best for him'.

Not only did she suffer no postnatal depression, but so great was her relief at having produced a normal child that 'she rose up in a state of ecstasy so that she could scarcely be kept quiet'. Her premonitions had proved unfounded; the boy was perfectly formed and healthy. But she had doubts over her capacity to mother the child. She did not want to breast-feed or nurse him herself, and in this she was supported by her doctor. Temperamentally she was unsuited to breast-feeding, her uncertainty and anxiety would have been transmitted to the child and created endless difficulties. But over and above this was a superstitious fear that she 'carried a curse', and was liable to harm those she loved. The child was perfect, but for his continuing health and safety, 'the farther from me the better, surely! – it was enough that I had not injured him so far'. And so at first she preferred to look at him from a distance, rather than cradle him in her arms.

Robert, once reunited with Elizabeth and assured of her safety, was enthralled with his son, carried him triumphantly round the room, and praised him extravagantly. But his happiness was short-lived. Three weeks later, when Elizabeth was back on her feet, he had three letters in quick succession from his sister, first telling him that his mother was not well, then that she was very ill and finally that she had died. In fact she was already dead (from apoplexy) when Sarianna wrote the first letter. His sister had hoped to soften the blow for him by this stratagem.

Robert was shattered. 'I never saw a man bowed down in an extremity of sorrow – the depression is great. . . . when I leave him alone a little and return to the room I find him in tears,' Elizabeth wrote. He sat in a despairing heap, weeping profusely whenever he thought of his mother or a letter arrived from New

Cross. He lost his appetite, became thin and pale, was unable to sleep at night, and clung helplessly to Elizabeth.

Elizabeth must have recalled the lines Robert had composed at Fano, while they sat together in the church:

> . . . I would rest
> My head beneath thine, while thy healing hands
> Close-covered both my eyes beside thy breast,
> Pressing the brain which too much thought expands,
> Back to its proper size again, and smoothing
> Distortion down till every nerve had soothing,
> And all lay quiet, happy and suppressed.[6]

She encouraged him to interest himself in the baby, but this did not 'mend his spirits much'. He could barely bring himself to talk of the child in response to Elizabeth's eulogies on his looks and health: 'Such a lovely, fat, strong child, with double chins and rosy cheeks'. It was as though, for Robert, some dreadful primitive rite had been played out and his mother sacrificed in exchange for his son. He had feared that he might lose Elizabeth, but never his mother. The bereavement was totally unexpected and the rejoicing that had followed the birth had, by contrast, heightened his grief. When he had been most happy his mother had been dying, or was already dead. The joyous letter he had written, containing a snippet of the child's hair, was never seen by her.

It was not helpful to be told by Elizabeth that his mother had gone to her saviour, who in turn was *his* saviour. His mother was irreplaceable and he would never 'feel as he used to do'. He envied his sister who had been with their mother to the end. Elizabeth urged him to return to New Cross and be with his father and sister, but the idea was unacceptable to him. He could not bear 'to see his mother's roses over the wall, and the place where she used to lay her scissors and gloves'. Much as he loved him, his father was no substitute for his mother.

The bereavement showed a new aspect of Robert to Elizabeth; a dependency on her which was not dissimilar to her own on him. She was grateful to be needed; it strengthened her self-confidence and heightened her love for Robert. She understood, perhaps for the first time, the depth of his feelings for her, and the unstinted nature of his love.

Elizabeth's reactions to Sarah Browning's death, after the first shock, may have been mixed. The two women never met or, so far as is known, communicated directly. Elizabeth had admitted during the courtship how much she dreaded meeting any of Robert's family, fearing what they might think of her. She may well have felt uneasy about this. She assured Sarianna more than once that, 'Though I never saw her face, I loved that pure and tender spirit'. Selfconsciously, she added, 'Very bitter has it been to me to have interposed unconsciously as I have done and deprived him of her last words and kisses.' None the less she was probably relieved that it was no longer possible to meet. To exclude the possibility of Sarianna entertaining such an idea, Elizabeth told her, 'I feel that for the sake of my love for Robert she was ready out of the fulness of her heart to love *me* also.'

Elizabeth decided that a break from Florence was necessary. At first she had the greatest difficulty in persuading Robert, since he 'had no mind for change or movement', and only when she angrily insisted that she and 'the baby could no longer bear the heat of Florence and that for the health and safety of them both, she must and would go away', did he agree.

Showing determination and a sense of priorities, she left the baby with Wilson and the wet nurse at Casa Guidi, and took Robert off to explore the neighbourhood for a suitable holiday home. They eventually decided on Bagni di Lucca and rented for four months 'the highest house of the highest of three villages . . . which lie at the heart of a hundred mountains, sung to continually by a rushing mountain stream'. Then they hurried back to Florence, Elizabeth suddenly convinced that they would find the baby dead or dying and the house in ruins. But all was well.

She paused only long enough to organise her son's christening at the French Evangelical Protestant Church, choosing the names Robert Wiedeman Barrett. Robert was pleased by the second choice, his mother's maiden name (but with only one 'n' at the end), which would 'have pleased her so much'. Elizabeth later had 'a sort of regret for having called my child Robert. . . . For my part I don't much care to use beloved names over again.'

In their 'Eagles' Nest', amid the chestnut woods and beside the mountain stream, Robert's spirits slowly revived. Elizabeth recognised his needs, mothered him when he was sad, often accompanied him on his walks, and encouraged him to climb the hills on his own and 'lose himself in the forests'.

Elizabeth was in great health, 'wonderfully improved . . . and it seems like a dream when I find myself able to climb the hills with Robert. . . . I can do as much, or more, now than at any point of my life since I arrived at woman's estate.' Just as great was the change in her mind; she was assured and decisive, and above all believed in herself. She had shed the fear that she was in some way bad for Wiedeman and should keep her distance. She picked him up naturally and enjoyed cuddling and playing with him. When he cut his first tooth she was as excited as the wet nurse.

She and Robert walked together through the woods, meeting no one apart from a woodcutter or itinerant peasant, not needing to talk, mutually conscious of the harmony surrounding them. Elizabeth had never been so happy; it was not the frenetic happiness of past times, but a fuller joy, arising from the sense of communion with Robert. It was not that she loved Robert differently, or felt that his love had changed in any way. The difference lay in her certainty that she was loved without qualification. Robert's collapse and his obvious dependence on her had enabled her to see not only her own dependence in a new light, but how much of his strength was derived from her.

One day in September she suddenly said to Robert, 'Do you know I once wrote some poems about *you*?', and handed him the 'Portuguese sonnets' she had composed during the courtship. She knew from odd remarks he had made that he disapproved of 'putting one's loves into verse' but, if he was embarrassed, he hid his feelings. To Elizabeth he seemed 'touched and pleased'. Psychologically she had chosen the right moment to reveal herself.[7] Reading the forty-three sonnets celebrating their love was, among other things, therapeutic for Robert. The weight of grief began at last to lift and he turned back from the memories of his mother to Elizabeth and his son. He took a new interest in his son's activities and even criticised Elizabeth for taking risks with the child's safety. More important, he began to argue with her over the way she was bringing him up. Robert wanted English to be his first language, Elizabeth Italian. Since the wet nurse spoke only Italian the early outcome was hardly surprising. But Wiedeman, or Penini as he became known through his mispronunciation of his name, Pen for short, was still conversing in Italian two years later. Miss Mitford, when she saw the Brownings in London in 1851, was indignant that both parents spoke Italian to him.

Elizabeth's attitude to Pen became increasingly idiosyncratic. Like many mothers with their first child she looked on Penini as perfect, beautiful, intelligent and artistic, but this natural pride was to become elaborated and magnified into a veritable cult which affected his education, manner of dress, discipline and behaviour. She came to see him as an extension of herself, as the perfect being she had striven to be since childhood. All her ideas about Penini's upbringing were centred around this fantasy. He was to be the ideal child, neither boy nor girl, allowed to develop freely and without bias, his natural beauty and goodness of spirit controlling his development and never to be lost.

It has been said that Elizabeth tried to form Penini into a girl, but there is no good evidence for this. She wanted him to be 'natural' and to develop accordingly. The knowledge that Pen must grow up distressed her, for growth meant change and the risk of imperfection, and she tried her utmost to hold him back and preserve, or at least prolong, his infancy. Robert wanted him to be a normal boy and treated as one. Inevitably there were clashes between the parents over his upbringing.

Particularly pleasing for Elizabeth, and an indication of Robert's recovery, was his reawakened interest in poetry. They moved back to Casa Guidi in October, and during that winter he completed his first major work since his marriage: *Christmas-Eve and Easter-Day*, concerned with some of the religious issues of the day. The pair of poems were not popular – they sold only two hundred copies or so – but they heralded Robert's return to creative writing after three years of lying fallow. Elizabeth was much relieved – although fainthearted in her praise of the poems – for she had been concerned about 'Robert's idleness and mine'.

She was preparing to revise her poems for a new edition when she discovered she was pregnant for the fourth time. She was extraordinarily fertile, as intercourse must have been scanty during much of the time in Lucca, given Robert's depressed state. She was delighted. She wanted a girl, not only to complement Penini, but because she could ensure that a daughter would have and become everything that she had lacked. The woman who *craves* a daughter, and Elizabeth 'lusted' for one, invariably pictures an idealised version of herself, someone who is everything she senses she has failed to become.

At the end of November 1849, after six weeks' pregnancy, a miscarriage threatened. Elizabeth believed, in fact, that she had miscarried, 'but nobody would hear me speak', and her doctor persuaded her that the foetus was alive. By the end of December it was apparent that she had been correct, 'a disappointment and vexation certainly . . . only I have got over it now,' she wrote to Miss Mitford in April.

However, still hopeful, she resumed intercourse as soon as

possible and was pregnant by late March. But on 28 July, around sixteen weeks, she miscarried, and a severe haemorrhage ensued. She was packed in ice for two days and nights together, 'and feeling very doubtful in my own mind . . . I who am not easily alarmed . . . how it was likely to end'. Robert was up all night in a frenzy of anxiety, ministering to her every want, holding her hand and reassuring her, fanning her 'to keep off the fainting', and encouraging her to drink. Opium was certain to have been prescribed early in the miscarriage to calm and relax her; the dose comparatively small at first as her tolerance would have been low. She had been without the drug for over a year. She was frightened and clung to Robert. 'I don't want to leave the world, while Robert and Wiedeman are in it,' she repeated.

Robert was terrified by what he had seen, and the very real threat to Elizabeth's life. 'Four of these mishaps, beside the advent of our babe, amount to a serious drain on such a constitution as hers,' he wrote to Kenyon. Such a dangerous situation could not be allowed to recur; their active sexual life must finish. Elizabeth was forty-four, and still had another five years possibly, or even more, of childbearing life. There was no alternative in Robert's mind but to abstain. It seems likely that sexual intercourse stopped from this time. It is, of course, conjecture, but the fact that Penini usually slept in their bedroom during most of their marriage provides some support; so also does Elizabeth's denial to Miss Mitford of the possibility of another pregnancy, in 1852: 'I have not any prospect, nor have had since the bad illness in Florence nearly two years ago. . . .'

Elizabeth was long in recovering and remained thin and exhausted for several months. She was at first too weak to stand unsupported, and it was six weeks before she could even rise from her chair without help. Looking in the mirror she saw 'a perfectly white and black face, the eyes being obliterated by large blobs of darkness'. Robert carried her to the carriage and then on to the train, 'like an infant', and she was whisked away, with the rest of the family, to a hilltop villa outside Siena, with magnificent views and undisturbed quiet. There she gradually regained her spirits and strength, and even the knowledge that another pregnancy was impossible and the daughter she so much wanted could never be, failed to prolong her depression. This was all the more remarkable because after the miscarriage she learnt that a woman friend she much admired, Margaret Fuller, the Marchesa d'Ossoli, had been drowned, together with her husband and child, in a shipwreck off the American coast. This news recalled the memory of Bro's death, and she wrote to Miss Mitford that 'the arrowhead of anguish was broken too deeply into my life ever to be quite drawn out'. But there were no repercussions on her health as in the past.

There were at least two reasons for this. She was again consuming opium regularly, and this would have had a tranquillising effect. More important, she was excited by the prospect of visiting London in the New Year. The Brownings had not been able to return to England in their first year for lack of money, and each visit they had tentatively planned over the next two years had had to be postponed because of pregnancies.

Elizabeth was optimistic about the prospect of reconciliation with her father. None of her letters to him had been returned, which made her think that he had read them, despite not writing back. She was agog to see her sisters again, particularly as Henrietta had at last plucked up courage and married Surtees Cook in April 1850, having been secretly engaged since 1845.[8] (Unlike Robert, Surtees Cook had followed protocol and asked Edward Moulton Barrett for permission to marry. He had been told that in the event Henrietta would be excluded from the Barrett household and disinherited – and that had happened.) At first Elizabeth had feared that Henrietta's action would make her own reconciliation with her father more difficult, but later she changed her mind; he might, on the contrary, prove more responsive to the overtures of two rather than one outcast daughter.

Penini, now eighteen months, was a joy to his mother. Any remaining lassitude was shaken out of Elizabeth when Penini suddenly fell ill, with a twenty-four-hour fever, 'lying in a half stupor. . . . a silence . . . suddenly fell upon the house. . . . But God spared us'; he quickly recovered and resumed his boisterous ways. Penini continued to be the perfect child in Elizabeth's eyes, and she persisted in keeping him a baby for as long as possible, but eventually she had to decide to wean him from the wet nurse. It was an upsetting experience for mother and child, and she objected more strongly than usual to Robert's attempts to make him 'like a boy'. 'The truth is,' she confided to Arabel, 'the child is not like a boy. . . . he isn't exactly like a girl either. He's a sort of neutral creature, so far.'

They returned to Florence and settled down for the winter, Elizabeth to complete the second half of *Casa Guidi Windows*. She had written the first section after the 1848 uprising when the

Italian cause for freedom had looked set to succeed, and she had been immensely enthusiastic. Since then the Italians had collapsed and everywhere seemed to be submitting to the old tyrants. 'My faith in every species of Italian is . . . nearly tired out, 'she declared. 'I don't believe they are men at all, much less heroes and patriots.' Part II of the poem reflects her disillusion:

> From Casa Guidi windows I looked out,
> Again looked, and beheld a different sight.

Her mind, in truth, was on her hero in Wimpole Street, her father, for their plans for London were almost completed. They had sufficient money; Kenyon had made them a yearly allowance of £100, and Robert had arranged to sublet Casa Guidi during their absence.

Hopes and Disappointments,
1851–1857

They all set out for London, via Venice, on 3 May 1851, intend-
ing the journey to be a grand tour. Elizabeth was excited from
the moment she left Florence. Robert described her as being at
the 'very height of her health', and she was certainly extraordinarily energetic and enthusiastic. Much of this, one may
guess, arose from her hope that she would be reconciled with
her father. Everything looked good. 'Never had I touched the
skirts of so celestial a place,' she cried at the sight of Venice. She
'longed to live and die there . . . never to go away.' She and
Robert had 'coffee every evening at half past eight on St Mark's
piazza to music and the stars'. They travelled everywhere in
gondolas, visited the opera house, saw a play (Elizabeth insisting on bringing Penini, as part of his education in aesthetics, to
Robert's irritation and no doubt that of the audience, since he
had to be removed before the end), and spent too much money
for Robert's peace of mind.

Unlike his wife, Robert was far from well and was not
enjoying himself. He could not sleep – always a sign of anxiety
with him – and was unusually irritable. He dreaded returning
home and being reminded of his mother. The thought of staying
at New Cross, surrounded by objects which he associated with
her, weighed heavily on him. But he kept his worries to himself.
He blamed his malaise on the food and damp climate, reasons
Elizabeth accepted, and chose not to look deeper. The explanation seemed the more convincing as Wilson was also unwell,
and continually sick. 'While I grow fat,' Elizabeth noted, 'Wilson
grew thin and Robert could not sleep at night!'

From Venice they went to Milan where, although she was
meant to rest before proceeding into Switzerland, Elizabeth
climbed the 350 steps of Milan cathedral to the 'topmost pin-
nacle', a considerable feat. Travelling through the St Gotthard
Pass, Elizabeth insisted on sitting on the outside of the coach for
a while, exclaiming with wonderment at the views despite the

intense cold and Robert's concern for her chest. She had never, she declared, seen 'the sublime before'.

Elizabeth was still exalted when they arrived in Paris, despite the downpour of rain for the first two days and the indifferent hotel. But gradually her high spirits subsided, and she began to feel trepidation at the thought of England. Robert was still despondent, and for a time they seriously considered not going there. 'Airs and hearts are against me in England,' she wrote to Kenyon. 'I feel here near enough to England. . . . were it not for Arabel I would stay in Paris by myself, and beseech Robert to take Wiedeman with him to New Cross . . . and that proves how I am feeling.' Robert would never have agreed to such a plan, and would willingly have stayed in Paris with her, particularly as his father and sister were prepared to come to Paris to see them. It was not possible for Arabel to do the same, her father would never have agreed, and Elizabeth's desire to see her sister was so great that they decided they must go. However, they changed their plans, which had been to stay at New Cross, and Elizabeth wrote to Arabel to ask her to find them rooms near her. After much discussion Robert decided that 'he would visit his own home by himself and get it over with'. He dreaded putting his wife and child 'into the place of his mother'.

They left Paris on 22 July and crossed the Channel; the deleterious effect on Elizabeth's health was immediate. 'My first step ashore was into a puddle and a fog,' she wrote, 'and I began to cough before we reached London. The quality of the air does not agree with me. . . . For nearly five years I have had no such cough nor difficulty of breathing. . . . I get so much paler every day. . . . Robert begins to be nervous about me.'

She was, of course, desperately anxious to hear from her father, but no word came. She was reunited with Arabel – and Henrietta, who came up from Somerset for a week – and saw her each day. Several times she went with her to Wimpole Street, sometimes with Penini, and took risks, half hoping and terrified that she might meet her father face to face. On one occasion she was in Arabel's room when her father returned earlier than expected, and she heard again his well-remembered footsteps on the stair, and his voice. She had to wait, trembling, until the family was at dinner before she crept past the dining room and out of the house. She arrived home late, distressed and exhausted, to Robert's irritation.

Unable to bear the silence she eventually wrote to him, asking yet again for forgiveness. When there was no reply Robert wrote a 'manly' letter, which Elizabeth was convinced would move him. She was shocked, as was Robert, when 'a very violent and unsparing' reply came, accompanied by all the letters she had written to him over five years, unopened. Some of the envelopes had been sealed with black wax, which could have signified she was dead, but this had had no effect. For a time Elizabeth was distraught. The brutality of her father's rejection left her miserable and without hope.

Her difficulties were now increased by Wilson having a fortnight's holiday with her parents in the Midlands. Penini, not unnaturally upset when his mother substitute took herself off, became fractious and difficult and very demanding of Elizabeth who had never before had to cope alone. At first he would not let her out of his sight without setting up a loud wail. Arabel proved her worth and Penini gradually allowed himself to be comforted and even taken alone by her to Wimpole Street.

Robert worried and fussed over Elizabeth, but he now had other concerns on his mind. He had been to New Cross and overcome his scruples and been reunited with his father and sister. Elizabeth had accompanied him at least once and been received 'most affectionately' by Sarianna and old Mr Browning. They had all dined together and afterwards walked in the fields. Penini was an enormous success and both his aunt and grandfather fell in love with him. More to the point, Penini rapidly took to his 'Nonno', as he named his grandfather, and delighted in his company.

Meanwhile Robert was learning, to his astonishment, that his father was engaged in an affair. Nearing seventy, Robert Browning senior had become infatuated with a neighbour, a handsome widow, twice married, and some thirty years younger. He had already proposed to her and was writing her impassioned and imprudent letters. It was somehow in keeping with his naïve innocence that, so soon after his wife's death, he should turn to another woman and make a public exhibition of himself.

The prospect of his father remarrying was extremely painful to Robert. It amounted in Robert's mind to a betrayal of his mother's memory. Robert had always maintained that a man or woman could love deeply once only in a lifetime; and as for marrying a widow, the notion was thoroughly repugnant to him.

Elizabeth was firmly on her husband's side. Only a year earlier she had written to her neighbour criticising a mutual acquaintance who had just remarried: 'A second marriage after

149

such love! And she a Swedenborgian, believing in the eternal validity of marriage! . . . it is monstrous.' But in the last year of her life she modified this view sufficiently to accept that there was a possibility that Robert might marry again after her death.

After two months in England Elizabeth was thin and pale and prone to bouts of breathlessness. Robert was enjoying the social life, meeting his old friends, and making new ones. In Elizabeth's view 'he would have been capable of never leaving England again had such an arrangement been practical to us'. She was exhausted, and overcome by the weather and her father's unforgivingness. She was thankful to leave England on 25 September, and felt better as soon as she reached Dieppe. Bitterly she wrote, 'Where love of country ought to be in the heart, there is the mask of the burning iron in mine, and the depth of the scar shows the depth of the root in it. . . . I wasn't made to live in England, or I should not cough there perpetually.'

For Elizabeth, the visit to London had been a disaster. True, she had been reunited with her sisters, and the breach with her brothers had mostly been healed, but she was as far from her father as ever, and her hope of reconciliation almost gone. She was miserable.

She and Robert half hoped they might live permanently in Paris, where they could readily receive or visit their relatives, and 'have art and literature', and above all (absent in Florence) 'that continual beat of mind'. They settled into a spacious second floor flat overlooking the Champs Elysées.

They remained in Paris until July 1852, and during these nine months important developments took place in their lives. Elizabeth grew more assertive, as though needing to establish her authority in the marriage, perhaps attempting subconsciously to show that she could do without her father. But at the same time she was searching for a father figure other than Robert, someone she might place on a pedestal and admire.

Louis Napoleon had been elected President of the Republic in 1848. Elizabeth had been in Florence at that time, when she had had some doubts about him, fearing that he might not be a strong enough character to lead France. His three-year term was now coming to an end, and not having been able to change the constitution to allow him to stay in power, he staged the *coup d'état* of 2 December.

She marvelled, watching from the windows of their apartment, to '. . . have the great heartbeat of the world' before her. It was 'thrilling' to see the troops pouring into Paris 'in a real sunshine of Austerlitz, and the immense shout of soldiers and people through which Louis Napoleon rode on horseback under our windows . . .'. They heard the heavy cannonading in the distance, and she and Robert sat up until the early hours; '. . . one shrank,' she confessed, 'from going quietly to sleep while human beings were dying in heaps . . .' A few days later her tenderhearted solicitude had been replaced by a degree of callousness: 'The people never rose,' she assured Henrietta. '– it was nothing but a little popular scum, cleared off at once by the troops — . . .'

Louis Napoleon could now do no wrong in her eyes. Robert, on the other hand, strongly disapproved of his actions and had a 'personal hatred' to the man. He had, of course, always loathed despots, but one wonders how much of his suppressed dislike of Elizabeth's father – whose idealised qualities Elizabeth had projected on to Louis Napoleon – contributed to some of his antipathy for the President.

They quarrelled increasingly over his behaviour. 'Robert and I are not as one as we are accustomed to be on the subject,' she confessed. 'Robert hates all Buonapartes, past, present, or to come, but then *he* says *that* in his self willed pettish way, as a manner of dismissing a subject he won't think about. . . .'

Robert was unable to bring himself to compromise, or back down. There were now moments when he became angry with Elizabeth, although he was rational enough when writing to his brother-in-law George. 'Is it not strange that Ba cannot take your view, not to say mine and most people's, of the President's proceedings? I cannot understand it – we differ in our approach of facts too – things that admit to proof. . . .'

Louis Napoleon III was one of the 'seven distinct issues' which came between the Brownings during their marriage.[1] 'In our profoundly different estimates of thing and person,' Robert claimed, 'I go over them one by one, and must deliberately, and inevitably say, on each of these points I was proved to be right and she wrong. And I am glad that I maintained the truth on each of these points, did not say, "What matters whether they be true or not? Let us only care to love each other".' The storm created by Napoleon III was to go backwards and forwards until Elizabeth's death. Among the other six issues were probably her consumption of opium, against which Robert persistently canvassed until the last years, and Penini's upbringing.

Apart from Penini's speech, which at this time was largely an unintelligible mixture of Italian, French and English, his long golden curls, white felt hat trimmed with feathers and ribbons and blue satin brim, and long white gaiters, 'ridiculous tiny trowsers', and elegant shoes, attracted stares in the street, and Robert was constantly being asked, to his chagrin, whether the child was a boy or a girl. Penini was to remain 'extravagantly undifferentiated' until his mother died, when he was twelve, despite Robert's protests and occasionally Penini's own. The more attention the child attracted the better Elizabeth was pleased: he was the living embodiment of her perfect marriage. He could rarely do wrong and when Robert corrected him she invariably rushed to intercede.

A less contentious issue was Elizabeth's desire to meet George Sand. 'I won't die, if I can help it,' she promised, 'without seeing George Sand.' Robert obtained a letter of introduction from Mazzini, the Italian republican, which, after much haggling between husband and wife was delivered to Sand and led to an invitation to call. Elizabeth, who was in a state of great excitement – even more so after she was kissed by Sand on the lips – discovered she liked her, but 'did not love her . . . and was not disappointed'. They called twice more, once when Sand was out, despite Robert's reservations about the company she kept: 'Crowds of ill bred men who adore her à genoux bas, betwixt a puff of smoke and an ejection of saliva.' Robert, Elizabeth considered, 'was really good and kind to let me go at all. . . . He didn't like it extremely, but, being the prince of husbands, he was lenient to my desires and yielded the point.'

In January, Elizabeth was dismayed to learn that Miss Mitford's recently published *Recollections of a Literary Life* included a section on herself, and the devastating effect on her of Bro's drowning. The *Athenaeum* reviewer of the book quoted the piece on Elizabeth, and when the magazine reached Paris she reacted histrionically, threw a fit and declared that she was too upset to read it. Robert comforted her, read her suitable extracts, and commiserated with her over Miss Mitford's treachery in betraying her confidences. An element of comic relief was introduced to the drama when a French professor, lecturing on English writers, distorted the account and 'produced a tragedy about a fiancé, which would have done honour, Robert says, to Dumas himself . . . and final residences in "magnificent palaces of the Medici" called Casa Guidi'.[2] This was sufficiently humorous to curb Elizabeth's distemper, and after a flurry of letters, Miss Mitford apologised and was forgiven. It was a measure of

Elizabeth's greater resilience, and Robert's more robust influence, that the incident did not prostrate her, as it would have done in the past.

Robert's father and sister visited them for three weeks in November. His father was having second thoughts about his engagement and appealed to Robert for help. He described how an immoral Mrs von Muller had made a dead set at him, and Robert became so indignant that he immediately wrote to her, demanding she stop chasing his father. This was followed by a letter from his father, breaking off the engagement and accusing Mrs von Muller of 'misconduct from the time she was a girl', including bigamy.

Mrs von Muller brought an action for breach of promise and defamation of character, which was heard at the end of June, just before the Brownings arrived on their second visit to London. The case attracted considerable public attention and was widely reported in the newspapers. Mr Browning's love letters were read out in court, provoking much mirth. Many began, 'My dearest, dearest, dearest, dearest, dearest much loved Minnie', and professed the deepest love. Far from being the grasping woman described by Robert Browning senior, Mrs von Muller was shown to be a woman of exemplary character, and her suitor a ridiculous 'old dotard in love'. Damages of £800 were awarded against him, a considerable sum when weighed against his annual salary of £350.

Elizabeth was ashamed to think of her father reading the newspaper accounts of the case and grimly smiling to himself. Robert was touched on the raw and extremely upset. For such a private man to have his family affairs exposed to the public gaze was painfully humiliating. But he never wavered in his loyalty to his father. The old man was unable to pay the damages and, to save himself from financial ruin, had to leave the country hurriedly. He resigned from the Bank (on two-thirds salary pension) and Robert took him and Sarianna to Paris, found them accommodation, and comforted the 'poor victim'.

Robert was exhausted after his exertions and the strain of the case. 'The vexation of it all is immense,' Elizabeth reported. The 'strange and calamitous visitation' had grieved him 'as few things could'. But the 'visitation' may have had an effect in releasing his creative energies. Apart from *Christmas-Eve and Easter-Day*, dull stuff, he had written almost nothing since leaving England, a humbling thought to the man who had dedicated his life to being a poet. There were doubtless a number of reasons for this block, the most obvious being the tedious, time-consuming business of settling into Florence and organising Elizabeth's comforts. But a prolonged writing block has a psychological cause at its base, and in Robert's case this is most likely to have involved his mother.

Robert's courtship had had a profound effect on the Browning family and particularly his mother. She was in pain much of the time towards the end of it, and severely incapacitated, and worry over her son must have been a major cause. Robert had not been in love before he met Elizabeth, and no one had ever come between him and his mother. Now, his time and energies were devoted to Elizabeth, visiting her, arranging visits, writing letters, thinking of her and the future, and talking to his mother about her. He had shared his hopes and fears and frustrations with his mother from the start; Elizabeth's attempts to prevent him doing so had been met with such vehemence that she had quickly desisted. His mother had always accepted his right to choose whatever life he wanted. She had never stood in his way or opposed him once he had made up his mind.

She had acquiesced in his wish to marry Elizabeth, despite not having met her, and never once, so far as one knows, raised any protest over his plans. She was the ideal confidante for Robert, and it was understandable that, while he poured out his feelings to her, he overlooked, in the strain and excitement of events, the pain he inevitably caused her; not least because she was about to lose him from home.

In Italy he thought of his mother every day and wrote home regularly. Never in his life, he said on the first anniversary of his marriage, 'from his joyous childhood upwards, had he enjoyed such happiness . . .'. Yet he missed his mother and must have regretted that she could not be with him and Elizabeth and imagined the pleasure she would have from seeing him again.

His mother's death had destroyed those possibilities. His grief had been terrible but in the end, with Elizabeth's help, he had begun to make peace with himself. *Christmas-Eve and Easter-Day*, which he wrote nine months afterwards, were personal poems in that they dealt with religious issues over which he and his mother had disagreed; they represented, perhaps, an attempt on Robert's part to make amends to his mother for his teenage rebellion and return to his 'joyous childhood'.

The anxiety he displayed when he first returned to London, and his reluctance to visit New Cross, suggested he had not yet fully resolved his old conflicts and guilt. He was finally freed from these barriers by his father's affair with Mrs von Muller. It was as though a gale had arisen and blown through the Browning family and in the process cleared away the remains of his guilt. He could now be released from the hold of his mother, and freed of her inhibitory influence. The effect was quickly evident in his new-found source of poetry.

That winter was bitterly cold and Elizabeth only occasionally went to parties. She was unwell and depressed from her experiences in London; 'I grew thin,' she reported to Henrietta. She stayed indoors and encouraged Robert to attend functions on his own: 'He might as well be in Florence if he shuts himself up here.' Robert enjoyed himself, without the old uneasy feeling that he should be at Elizabeth's side all the time. More important, he began to write. He made what at first sight seemed a rash New Year's resolution to write a poem a day. That he was able to complete at least seven poems at the beginning of 1852 was a clear sign that his creativity had returned. One of them, 'Childe Roland to the Dark Tower came', was written one suspects in a dreamlike state.[3] It has a disturbing effect on the reader, and its meaning is unclear; Browning himself confessed that he did not really understand what the poem signified. It is, perhaps, a description of Robert's journey to self-knowledge, the dark tower being his subconscious, and an affirmation of his future triumph.

> There they stood, ranged along the hill-sides, met
> To view the last of me, a living frame
> For one more picture! in a sheet of flame
> I saw them and I knew them all. And yet
> Dauntless the slug-horn to my lips I set
> And blew. 'Childe Roland to the Dark Tower came.'

Elizabeth was glad to see him working. She had become increasingly critical of his lack of industry, and had repeatedly urged him to take himself in hand and force himself to write – Elizabeth herself always found writing extremely easy – but Robert was emphatic that he could not do this; for him writing was a chore, and he *had* to have the desire first. Elizabeth always had faith in Robert's poetic power, but she was keen to see her belief translated into sales and widespread renown. She desired this not only for Robert's sake but, one suspects, to show her father that she had not been mistaken in her choice of husband.

Her distress over her father was never far from the surface, although largely disguised by exaggerated reactions to events, political and personal. In the spring she had an attack of what could have been pleurisy, with cough and pain in the side, brought on by the cold weather and perhaps psychological factors. She told a friend how she had 'turned into the likeness of a ghost and frightened Robert from his design of going to London'.

Robert's cousin, James Silverthorne, died on 25 May 1852. Robert had earlier heard that he was seriously ill; indeed, on reading the news he had burst into tears in front of Elizabeth. The two men had been close friends since childhood and his cousin had been best man at his wedding. Elizabeth knew how strongly Robert wanted to be present at his funeral. Yet despite her chest having almost recovered, she panicked at the thought of his leaving, collapsed breathless and fainting, and persuaded Robert that she was too ill to be left. Robert's instinct to care for her was so strong that he cancelled his trip, in spite of appeals from his sister to reconsider the decision. It was unreasonable behaviour, given how fond Robert had been of Silverthorne. One may excuse Elizabeth on the grounds that she was still very depressed and insecure on account of her father, and therefore needed Robert's presence, but Robert was aggrieved. He would not be so readily persuaded another time.

The Brownings returned to London in July 1852. Wilson again went off to visit her parents, this time for three weeks, and Elizabeth was left with Penini, helped out by Arabel. Henrietta, pregnant for the second time, came to stay for a week. Once again Elizabeth paid frequent visits to 50 Wimpole Street and risked encountering her father. One evening she delayed her departure until so late that she actually saw him walking up the street as she was starting to go down it, and only avoided meeting him by turning briskly into a side road. Penini, who was usually with her, naturally became infected by his mother's nervousness, and was convinced that some kind of evil demon inhabited the house in the evenings.

Her longing for reconciliation mounted until she could no longer contain herself and she wrote her father a pleading letter. This time he read it, since she received a reply which was so cold and merciless that for the time being she banished every hope she had of reconciliation.

When Wilson returned the Brownings embarked on a hectic social life. They lunched with Ruskin and his wife Effie at

Denmark Hill, and admired his collection of Turners. Jane Carlyle brought her revolutionary friend Mazzini to meet them, and Elizabeth was immediately impressed. 'Oh, what a fuss the Brownings made over Mazzini the other day!' commented Mrs Carlyle. 'My private opinion of Browning is, in spite of Mr C's favours for him, that he is "nothing" or very little more "but a fluff of feathers!" *She* is *true* and *good*, and the most *womanly* creature.' She was to alter her opinion of Elizabeth within a few years: 'She does not grow on me.'

Robert went alone to the christening of Hallam Tennyson, as Elizabeth was unwell, or perhaps too depressed and exhausted to go. Henrietta's second child, a girl, was born at the end of September, the news of which made her envious, and increased the sense of misery and futility which continued to grip her. She had grown thin and ill. 'All I have,' she wrote, 'is detestable weather and horrible cough.' The fogs made it difficult to breathe. On 12 October they left for Paris and Florence.

They were rash enough to cross the Mont Cenis. The cold became intense and 'together with the necessity of travelling three nights without once undressing, I was nearly extinct before we got to Turin'. When they reached Genoa Elizabeth broke down and 'had to remain at the hotel for ten days, just fit to lie on the sofa. . . . Every breath brought the life back to me – but I *wanted* life . . . for the continued night fever and cough had worn me to the bone literally. You never saw such a spectral thinness! Poor Robert was horribly vexed. . . .'

Once back in Florence she relaxed, her despair over her father waned, and she forced herself to eat and take cod-liver oil by the spoonful to please Robert. She recovered her weight and health with striking rapidity away from London. It was 'a load thrown off'. She was delighted to be back 'in the old nest, still warm, of Casa Guidi, to sit in our own chairs and sleep in our own beds'. She had endured enough of literary society. Robert, on the other hand, took a while to adjust to Florence; he 'said most strongly that the place is dead and dull and flat'.

The winter of 1852–3 was warm, and Elizabeth was contented. She and Robert worked steadily and without interruption. Elizabeth had begun to write *Aurora Leigh*, the novel–poem she had been planning since completing 'Lady Geraldine's Court-ship' in 1844. Robert worked on the poems that were to make up *Men and Women*, 'lyrics with more music and painting than before, so as to get people to hear and see'. They wrote in separate rooms and did not discuss their day's work with one another, a sensible practice for two such artists. Each needed room and time to themselves; Elizabeth maintained strongly that 'an artist must have or make time for himself for good work'.

Socially they went from one extreme to another. Robert never went out in the evenings, 'just as we had never known Paris'. People occasionally called or came to tea – 'a few intelligent and interesting persons such as [Frederick] Tennyson [Alfred's eldest brother] and [Robert] Lytton . . .'.

Frederick Tennyson was an eccentric man who was preoccupied with arcane religious matters and dabbled in spiritualism. Robert Lytton was enthusiastic about table-rapping, and 'visionary enough to suit' Elizabeth, 'which is saying much'. Elizabeth was beginning to be attracted to spiritualism, and sought out the company of like-minded people.

Spiritualism in one form or another, levitation, table-rapping and turning, spirit writing and painting, apparitions, had swept America in the 1840s and was now beginning to make inroads into Europe. Paris society, during the winter of 1851–2 had been buzzing with stories of spirit comings and goings.

Elizabeth had long been interested in the supernatural. She had been impressed by claims for mesmerism – which had held the field before spiritualism – and especially the manner in which Miss Martineau, suffering it was said from incurable cancer, had been cured by the application of 'animal magnetism'; put into a 'magnetic trance' twice a day for some months, until finally restored to health. The case, Elizabeth firmly declared, 'will settle the question of the reality of magnetism with a whole generation of infidels'. The sceptics' argument that the effects of mesmerism came about through suggestion and illusion could not apply to Miss Martineau, who was no 'weak willed woman [with] a nervous affliction'. Strangely, Elizabeth was too nervous to allow herself to be mesmerised for a cure. 'I understand that in cases like mine the remedy has done harm instead of good, by overexciting the system.' And when, in 1845, a friend asked her for a lock of hair to be sent to a Parisian practitioner, she 'shook . . . with horror . . . I . . . the most excitable person in the world and nearly the most superstitious. I should have been scarcely sane at the end of a fortnight'. Still, she was emphatic that, 'I have long been a believer in spite of Papa.'

She had no such horror of spiritualism. She took to it like a duck to water. Perhaps her readings of Swedenborg, that extraordinary genius who turned mystic and saw the heavens and the hells, and was able to converse with angels and spirits, prepared her for spirit communication. And, unlike mesmerism, where the participant went into a trance and lost control of himself, the spiritualist retained his conscious hold.

Robert was of the same mind as Elizabeth's father, that the subject was pure 'humbug' and the practitioners 'charlatans'. Disagreements between husband and wife, even at this stage, were sometimes warm. Robert refused, in the absence of clear proof, to believe stories of furniture rising and floating across the room without being touched, whereas Elizabeth was disposed to accept uncritically their veracity.

Robert, if the poem 'Mesmerism' can be taken as an expression of his views, seemed to look on the whole supernatural business as profane, regarding it as wrong for one soul – all souls belonging to God – to dominate another.

> First I will pray. Do Thou
> That ownest the soul,
> Yet wilt grant controul
> To another, nor disallow
> For a time, restrain me now!
>
> I admonish me while I may,
> Not to squander guilt,
> Since require Thou wilt
> At my hand its price one day!
> What the price is, who can say?[4]

But, 'profane or not' Elizabeth was resolved to explore the mystery. She declared, in good Swedenborgian style, that she was less interested in what the spirits 'are capable of communicating, than of the fact of there being communications. . . . They seem abundantly foolish, one must admit. There is probably, however, a mixture of good spirits and bad, foolish and wise, of the lower orders, perhaps in both kinds.'

Spiritualism attracts people who are unhappy and guilt-ridden. Those who want urgently to make contact with relatives or close friends who have 'passed over to the other side' are usually seeking reassurance that they are still loved, the wrongs they perpetrated are forgiven, and that in the end they will all be happily reunited, without blemish. The spiritualists' question 'Are you all right Harry?' means 'Are you at peace with me?' among other things. The comfort of feeling 'watched over' by a loving spirit is immense, and it is logical for the spiritualist to ask for advice and guidance. But there are evil spirits as well as good ones, as Elizabeth knew well from her readings and conversations. We have no idea what questions she asked during her séances, and one wonders how she would have reacted to spirit advice to shed Robert in order to regain her father's love. An emphatic refusal, for certain, but it would have disturbed Robert had he heard.

Elizabeth, from her earliest years, was prone to depression, and ready to assume that she was somehow responsible for the misfortunes which befell those she loved, perhaps her mother's death, certainly Bro's. She frequently felt bad and wanted reassurance that she was loved and forgiven. To learn, on her last visit to London, that her father no longer felt affection for her had had a catastrophic effect on her mood. It was useless for Robert to tell her that her father's love was only hidden. She wanted reassurance that she was not thoroughly bad and harmful. Robert could tell her that she was not, that *he* loved her through and through, but he was not her father and could never speak for him, never fully takes his place.

Spiritualism alone offered her hope. She had to contact her mother and Bro, her uncle Sam, her grandmother, to learn that she was loved, and seek peace and forgiveness through them. On all sides she heard accounts of the living communicating with their beloved dead and being comforted, and she wanted the same.

Perhaps if she had been able to discuss her intimate feelings and thoughts with Robert her need for spirit communication would not have become so powerful. But Robert was curiously incapable of exploring Elizabeth's deeper thoughts, despite his closeness to her and the insight he had into people's behaviour. That he tried and failed is suggested by Elizabeth's statement in her last year, 'My husband calls me "peculiar" in some things. . . . I can't articulate some names or speak of certain afflictions – no, not to *him*, – not after all these years! It is a sort of *dumbness* of the soul. Blessed are those who can speak, I say. But don't you see from this how I must want "spiritualism" above most persons.'[5]

More than anything else, more than Penini's upbringing, or Napoleon III, spiritualism created a rift between the Brownings. Robert bitterly resented being cut off from an important part of her life and not being able to replace her father in her emotions, and he feared she would come under the influence of unscrupulous practitioners. Later, as spiritualism increased its hold on her and she became more suggestible, Robert came to dread its effects on her health, mental and physical.

Robert's fears were far from groundless. Elizabeth's excitability and hysteria were all too often enhanced by séances, when she moved from the world of reality into her dark inner one, often aided by opium. She was over-susceptible to the influence of other spiritualists. Some, like Mrs Eckley, were frankly dishonest. Others were involved with her in a kind of *folie à deux*, like her maid, Wilson. Wilson, after watching a séance, discovered she could 'spirit write', and demonstrated her ability to Elizabeth. Seated beside her at the table Wilson's hand became stiff and cold and the pencil formed letters whose meaning she was unaware of while writing. On one momentous occasion she wrote 'Mary Barrett. Mama', which aroused considerable expectation, but nothing significant followed, despite numerous sessions together.

The summer was spent at Lucca, at Bagni Caldi, and both Brownings continued to write, between long walks and donkey-back expeditions and visits from friends. Elizabeth was remarkably well when they left for Florence at the beginning of October: 'Such a summer we have enjoyed here, free from burning heats and mosquitos . . .'.

In November 1853 they decided to spend the winter in Rome. The journey, which took eight days, was easy and enjoyable, and according to Elizabeth they were all in happy mood on arrival. Yet clearly something had upset Robert – extra opium, talk of spiritualism, the presence of Louis Napoleon's soldiers in Rome, what it was is guesswork – for he was in a state of 'bilious irritability' on arrival, and next day, without advance warning to Elizabeth, shaved off his beard and whiskers. Knowing how much Elizabeth admired his beard and saw it as adding to his good looks, Robert's action in removing it can only be viewed as an aggressive and at the same time assertive act. To shave off a beard that has been present for many years is always momentous, and suggests strong desire for change and a new persona.

Elizabeth was aghast. 'I *cried* when I saw him, I was so horror-struck. I might have gone into hysterics and still been reasonable; for no human being was ever so disfigured by so simple an act. Of course I said when I recovered breath and voice, that everything was at an end between him and me if he didn't let it grow again directly.' Robert's open rebellion subsided. The beard was allowed to grow, but it was now grey in place of its former luxuriant black, to his chagrin and Elizabeth's amusement.

More shocks were to follow. Almost at once their friends the Storys – the husband an expatriate American lawyer turned sculptor, who was to become one of Robert's closest friends, his wife and two children, who had been their near neighbours in Lucca and preceded them to Rome – appealed to them for help when their son Joe, a little older than Penini, became ill with gastric fever. They hurried to the house, but Joe died within a few hours.

For once Elizabeth reacted sensibly and calmly to death – the first she had ever witnessed. But her initial support for the mother was soon replaced by panicky concern for Penini's safety as the Story daughter Edith and her nurse both developed the disease. Her fears were hardly unfounded and it took considerable reassurance from the doctors, and a reprimand from Robert, to persuade Elizabeth that Penini was not in serious danger and they need not immediately leave Rome. Edith and her nurse recovered. But Rome was spoilt for Elizabeth, 'all this has blackened Rome to me'. The remainder of her stay did nothing to change her opinion. 'I don't like Rome, I never shall,' she wrote more than once.

The weather in Rome that winter was exceptionally mild and Elizabeth went out most days, and visited St Peter's, attending mass there on Christmas Day, the Sistine Chapel, the Forum and the Coliseum. She and Robert met large numbers of English and Americans living in or visiting Rome and they were much in demand socially. Robert went out increasingly on his own in the evenings; Elizabeth accompanied him only occasionally. She went with him once to a musical soirée, where she spent her time sitting by the fire and talking spiritualism to a fellow guest, while Robert, in the midst of a large circle of acquaintances and people determined to meet him, conversed loudly and continuously. Elizabeth often entertained friends interested in spiritualism, without Robert, when the latest manifestations of the spirit world would be gravely discussed and the table sent 'panting and shivering'. Robert was not at ease in such gatherings, and when present was liable to spoil the séance by his attitude of disbelief; furniture would not move and the spirits would fail to reveal themselves when he was present.

They became friendly with the Kemble sisters, Fanny and Adelaide. On one occasion they went on a picnic in the

Campagna, 'three carriages full of people!' It was a merry occasion and after the meal a walk was proposed. The party set out, but Elizabeth unexpectedly stayed behind. It seems strange that Robert was separated from her, and it may have been that she was sulking, but whatever the reason, he immediately returned and sat beside her for the afternoon. Fanny Kemble applauded Robert's actions. He was the only man she had ever known, she said, 'who behaved like a Christian to his wife'! It was of course inconceivable that he would have left Elizabeth behind. However much they might disagree their essential closeness never altered and Robert never neglected his wife's comforts.

But Robert was now capable of standing up to his wife over issues he regarded as important. Edith Story had not fully recovered from the illness of November and continued to have fevers. Hoping that a change of air would do her good, the Storys set out from Rome for Naples in early April. They had gone a short distance only when Edith collapsed and lay insensible, seemingly dying. William Story, who hero-worshipped Robert, and was curiously dependent on him, sent an urgent message to him, pleading for him to join them immediately and be with them when their daughter died. Robert responded, and instantly prepared to leave home, whereupon Elizabeth raised various objections, and Pen burst into piteous howls; Robert could do nothing to help Edith, she maintained; the Storys had their own physician; Robert had already done more than enough for the Storys that winter; he ran the risk of catching the disease and dying himself or passing it on to his own child. The row was noisy and angry, but Elizabeth was unable to make Robert change his mind.

As it happened Robert found Edith to be very much better than expected, stayed that night only with the Storys, and hurried back to Elizabeth next day. Elizabeth, who had spent an anguished, sleepless night, was not in a mood to forgive him quickly. Still seething, she described the incident to Arabel and castigated Story for his 'lack of manliness and fortitude'.

Their work, during the six months' stay in Rome, had not progressed as planned. Not a line had been added to *Aurora Leigh*, and her only poem was 'Plea for the Ragged Schools of London', written at the request of Arabel. Robert's sole production was the short poem 'The Twins', which he included in *Men and Women*. The two poems were published in pamphlet form and sold at a bazaar in 1854 to raise money for Arabel's charity, 'a refuge for young destitute girls'.

Elizabeth was glad to leave for Florence at the end of May. She was irritable with Robert, and anxious over Penini who had grown wan and was now 'a delicate, pale little creature'. Robert was also unhappy. He regretted his overstretched social life, 'having not been without social engagement for each evening for many a week now', which had kept him apart from Elizabeth, and interfered with his writing. 'The place is ill-starred, under a curse, seemingly,' he declared ominously.

Robert had intended to visit London again in the summer of 1854, but had to abandon the plan for lack of money; not only had they spent too much in Rome, but neither the allowance from Kenyon nor Elizabeth's 'ship money' had arrived. There was insufficient even to go to Lucca for the summer, and they had to brave out the heat of Florence in Casa Guidi. In fact, this was to their advantage. Elizabeth and Robert both worked hard on their books. Robert was capable of working with great intensity and speed when he was in the right mood and under sufficient pressure, as he now was. He wrote to his friend Story, 'I am trying to make up for wasted time in Rome and setting my poetical house in order.'

Elizabeth was heartened by the change in Robert, and relaxed into a happier frame of mind. She was no longer interrupted by visitors, as in Rome, and was able to concentrate on *Aurora Leigh*. Her interest in spiritualism took a more quiescent form. Wilson's automatic writing had dried up, and her enthusiasm too, for she was engaged in an unspiritual love affair with their Italian servant Ferdinando, whom she would marry next year.

Elizabeth read Robert's new poems, which she thought 'magnificent', and discussed and criticised them with him. It was a peaceful time for them, although Penini was still liable to cause ructions. Elizabeth taught him reading and writing, but as she did not believe in anything that smacked of compulsion or punishment, it was hardly surprising that he played up and that progress was slow. Robert taught him music and to play the piano, and here Penini did as he was told and learnt quickly. He knew that if he disobeyed his father he would be punished, despite Elizabeth's interventions, and he respected Robert's authority and wanted to please him. Elizabeth acknowledged the benefits of taking a firm line, but she proved incapable of change and continued to spoil Penini.

Politically the Brownings were in accord at this period.

Tuscany was quiet, but in March 1854 England and France, engaged in the Crimean War, had signed a treaty to save Turkey from Russia. This had pleased Elizabeth; it was 'good for each nation, and for the general civilisation of the world, especially England'.

The disasters and loss of life in the Crimea, and the general chaos and inefficiency that characterised the war made Robert 'frantic' over the way the English were making fools of themselves 'in the face of Europe'. He advocated abolishing the system of privilege in the British Army. 'Army officers should be properly selected and trained, not chosen because they were "Lord Nincompoop's" youngest sons.' Louis Napoleon III's sun continued to shine and he could do no wrong in Elizabeth's eyes. So incompetent did the British seem to the Brownings, and Lord Aberdeen's government in particular, compared to the French, that for once Robert agreed with Elizabeth over Napoleon. When the war ended in September 1855 both felt that the French way of life was superior to the English.

Elizabeth had met Florence Nightingale in London in 1852. Her reaction on hearing that she was being sent to the Crimea in charge of a group of nurses was one of indignation.[6] 'I do not consider the best use to which we can put a gifted and accomplished woman is to make her a hospital nurse,' she wrote to a surprised Mrs Jameson. 'Every man is on his knees before ladies carrying lint, calling them angelic shes, whereas if they stir an inch as thinkers or artists from the beaten line (involving more good to general humanity than is involved in lint) the very same men would curse the impotence, of the very same women. . . .' She was already expressing this feminist viewpoint in *Aurora Leigh*. Robert, one suspects, had no *strong* feelings concerning women's rights, for or against, unless it concerned tyranny, and the subject never caused any disagreement.

Elizabeth's peace of mind was interrupted in September by the news that her father had been knocked down by a cab, and his leg seriously injured (in fact the injury was not severe, although the shock to a seventy-year-old man probably was). She panicked at the thought that his life might be in danger and wrote frantic letters to her sisters: 'You know how I must have felt about the accident in Wimpole Street. I can scarcely talk to you about it.' The bitterness and despair that had been with her since reading her father's letter in 1852 were instantly replaced by concern, and her longing for reconciliation returned as strong as ever. She dreaded the possibility of her father dying before the rift was mended. Her peace of mind required knowing that he loved her. She wrote him 'a little note' and, intent that he should read it, took the precaution of having the envelope addressed by Penini and posted by a friend in London. But she received no reply. Robert tried as usual to cheer her, without success, and she lost weight.

Elizabeth's gloom was increased by the news in December that Miss Mitford was dying, after a long illness. The two had continued to correspond after the marriage, and they had had a warm reunion in London in 1851, but the old intimacy was no longer there. The account of Bro's drowning in her memoirs, although forgiven by Elizabeth, had left a grievance and, more important, Miss Mitford had never been able to overcome her antipathy for Robert and his poetry. But she had been a very dear close friend, and the news of her death in early January came as a blow. The effect was the more serious because Elizabeth herself was ill.

The winter of 1854–5 was exceptionally cold for Italy, with 'snow and frost, together with a bitter wind'. Elizabeth's depression after her father's accident was succeeded at the end of the year by 'the worst attack on the chest I have ever suffered from in Italy. . . . for a month past or more I have been ill . . . now the exhausting cough and night fever have gone . . . but [I am] much weakened and grown thin'. There was no blood when she coughed, no loss of voice as in other attacks, and hardly any pain in her side. But she was reluctant to eat, and sleep became difficult. One may suppose that the dosage of opium was increased.

Robert was a devoted attendant. He kept the fire stoked all night in the bedroom, provided a continuous supply of hot coffee, and drove himself into a state of near exhaustion. Elizabeth worried about him, in turn, and urged him repeatedly to sleep for a few hours. But Robert always seemed to thrive on Elizabeth's sickness. He did not of course want her to be ill. What he liked was the re-creation of her total dependence on him. There was now no room in her mind for her father when she was sick, and nothing separated him from Elizabeth. Robert, and to a much lesser extent Penini, occupied her thoughts. The illness made her feel very close to Robert. 'If it had not been that I feared much to hurt him in having him so disturbed and worried, it would have been a very subtle luxury to me, this being ill and feeling myself dear. . . . Do not set me down as too selfish,' Elizabeth told Sarianna. She did not prolong her invalidism. She obeyed Robert and took cod-liver oil and allowed her weight to increase. 'I don't give up,' she declared. 'I mean to live on and be well.'

Robert's poems were ready for the publishers and in June they set off for London. This time Elizabeth did not anticipate reconciliatory moves by her father. She was excited at the prospect of meeting the American medium Douglas Dunglas Home, who 'is turning the world upside down in London with this spiritual influx'.

They spent only seventeen days in Paris (long enough to arrange for the marriage of the Protestant Wilson to their Roman Catholic servant Ferdinando) before crossing the Channel. Robert and Elizabeth seemed very much in harmony. Robert raised no objections to their accepting an invitation to a séance with Home on 23 July from the Ryder family, with whom he was staying. The Ryders were well-to-do friends of Mrs Jameson; their twelve-year-old son Wat had recently died.

But Robert was apprehensive of Elizabeth's reactions to the séance.[7] His natural antipathy to spiritualism was confirmed by his first impression of Home, who, he said, affected 'the manners, endearments and other peculiarities of a very little child indeed – speaking of Mr and Mrs Ryder as his "Papa and Mama" and kissing the family abundantly – he professes timorousness, "a love of love" – and is unpleasant enough in it all . . .'. But, he added, 'I observed nothing offensive or pretentious in his demeanour beyond the unmanlinesses I mention, which are in the worst taste.'

The séance began at 9 p.m., with everyone seated around the table. The table turned several times and lifted from the ground, a hand, loosely clothed in white folds of muslin-like material, appeared from the edge of the table and moved about, an accordion was played by invisible hands, Elizabeth's dress, near the waist, was several times 'slightly but distinctly uplifted in a manner I cannot account for – as if by some object inside', and raps were heard, which were recognised by the Ryders as coming from Wat. Robert felt a hand touch his knee and 'a kind of soft and fleshy pat' on his own hands. The *pièce de résistance* of the séance was the setting of a wreath of clematis (earlier constructed by Home) on Elizabeth's head by a hand which 'pushed . . . or pulled it, off the table, picked it from the ground, brought it to my wife . . . and put it on her head'.

Robert was unable to explain these phenomena, but he was

Elizabeth Barrett Browning

certain they were brought about by trickery, and that Home was
a charlatan. Elizabeth, on the contrary, was 'confirmed in all my
opinions. To me, it was wonderful and conclusive; and I believe
that the medium present was no more *responsible* for the things
said and done, than I myself was.'

A bitter quarrel took place when they returned home, Robert
having worked himself into a fury by now. Neither husband nor
wife was prepared to compromise and next morning Robert
announced his intention of confronting Home and the Ryders,
and thrashing the whole business out with them. Elizabeth was
appalled and begged him not to, but he was adamant and there
and then asked for a meeting. Home declined, pleading illness,
but a few days later he and Mrs Ryder unexpectedly called on
the Brownings. They were shown into the drawing room.
Robert shook Mrs Ryder's hand and pointedly ignored Home.
He was, according to Home, 'pallid with rage'. Elizabeth stood,
'pale and agitated', as though re-enacting one of her father's
outbursts, until Home went to her and she took his hand. Seeing
that, Robert lost control of himself. He harangued Mrs Ryder for
her complicity in the deception, and then turned furiously on
Home, his movements 'like those of a maniac'. Home tried to
protest, but reasoned discussion was not possible and eventually the visitors made a hurried departure. Elizabeth touched
Home's hand despairingly as he left, apologising repeatedly.
'Dear Mr Home, I am not to blame. Oh dear! Oh dear!'

Elizabeth showed her resentment by ostentatiously hanging
the clematis wreath on her dressing table where it stayed until
Robert, in a moment of fury, flung its withered remains into the
street. Home's name was taboo in the house, and Elizabeth
warned Henrietta never to mention the medium in her letters
(which Robert normally read).

Robert's antagonism to spiritualism was so extreme that one is
led to look for an explanation other than that Elizabeth needed to
be protected from herself and unscrupulous practitioners. The
most likely explanation is that Robert came, in a roundabout
way, to associate spiritualism with Edward Moulton Barrett. His
outright rejection of his daughter had had a devastating effect,
and Elizabeth's interest in spiritualism had grown steadily from
that time. It was unfortunate that Robert never delved into
Elizabeth's mind and her deep need to be at one with her father.
He must have been distressed when Elizabeth turned to spiritualism for relief from her unhappiness rather than seeking

solace through him. By the mid 1850s, he was, one imagines, furious with his father-in-law for his seemingly cruel behaviour, but Robert was in a difficult position because he was, after all, responsible for the rift. He knew it would be unwise to rail against Edward Moulton Barrett too strongly. An outburst might temporarily relieve Robert's feelings, but was liable to do more harm than good if it provoked Elizabeth into proclaiming her father's essential goodness. His anger mounted, and was increasingly displaced on to spiritualism.

Spiritualism now evoked such a passionate reaction in him that Elizabeth sometimes feared what might happen – she had been terrified during Douglas Home's visit. She told her sister that Robert thought her 'very wrong' to continue to believe in the spirit world. Yet the more Robert criticised and tried to persuade her to abandon the practice, the stronger was her compulsion to communicate with the spirits. At times it must have seemed to Elizabeth as though Robert had taken on some of the qualities of her father – who also regarded spiritualism as poppycock. Robert came to realise that he was making no headway and was only antagonising Elizabeth, and he decided to retreat. His hostility remained, but he came to control his temper and accept that he could not dictate to Elizabeth. 'Robert promised me he would be "meek as maid" for my sake,' Elizabeth told Henrietta, and that even if he met Douglas Home in the streets 'he would pass without pretending to see'.

Circumstances determined that their third visit to London was quieter than the others. Robert was busy revising and correcting the proofs of *Men and Women*, helped by Elizabeth who had temporarily put *Aurora Leigh* to one side. She disliked London as much as before. The weather was cold and wet, and she felt ill and depressed, 'hating and detesting this London which hangs weights on my very soul and sinks me to the bottom of things'.

Money was still short and she could not afford to visit Henrietta in Taunton. Arabel called each day and took Penini back to Wimpole Street. On one occasion he encountered his grandfather. He was playing in the hall with George, his uncle, shouting and laughing, when Edward Moulton Barrett came out of the dining room and stood looking at him for several minutes. Then he called George and went back into the room and asked whose child it was. ' "Ba's child," said George. "And what is he doing here, pray?" Then without waiting for an answer he

169

changed the subject. 'To hear of it thrilled me to the roots of my heart,' Elizabeth wrote, still ready to grasp at any straw coming from her father's direction. George and Arabel must have known their father was in the house, and presumably hoped that a meeting with Penini might soften his feelings. If so, their plan misfired, for he immediately arranged for the family to spend the rest of the summer at Eastbourne while he remained in London.

Arabel's angry reaction to the news was tempered by Penini agreeing to stay at Eastbourne with her. He went off excitedly but the visit was not a success. He missed his mother, and after rousing the household with his nightmares he had eventually to be returned to London. He remained difficult and fractious after his return and the Browning establishment was, one suspects, in an uproar for a while. Wilson had confessed to being pregnant – the baby was due in October – and hasty arrangements had been made for her to leave and have her child at her sister's home, and a temporary replacement had had to be found. All of this must have increased Elizabeth's tensions and Penini's insecurity.

Elizabeth received at about this time an invitation to stay with an old friend and correspondent, Mrs Martin, who still lived near Hope End. She refused, on the grounds that a visit there would be too painful: '. . . if I went there, the thought of *one face* which never ceases to be present with me (and which I parted from for ever in poor blind unconsciousness with a pettish word) would rise up, put down all the rest, and prevent my having one moment of ordinary calm intercourse with you, so don't ask me. . . . I could as soon open a coffin. . . . I never could get into that neighbourhood except to die, which I sometimes think I should like.' Elizabeth revealed, in this reply, her misery and desperate desire to communicate with Bro, to make direct contact with him. Bro alone, she seemed to be saying, could give her lasting peace, and if everything else failed she would abandon the living to be with his spirit. It was as well that Robert never read any of the letters Elizabeth wrote.

Elizabeth left London for Paris in mid October, after a 'most uncomfortable and unprofitable visit'. Yet she had been of great help to Robert over the last-minute changes in the poems, and the final preparations of *Men and Women* for the printers. Her high opinion of Robert's poetry had been confirmed and she was confident his new work would be widely praised. So too were others. Milsand – the French critic who was such a good friend to Robert and believed so strongly in his work – had told Elizabeth, she reported, 'that he considered the poems "superhuman" – Mark that! only superhuman.'

Men and Women was published on 17 November 1855, and Robert waited on tenterhooks for the reviews, confident that the collection would be well received. As poor reviews appeared through December and the New Year, his disappointment and bitterness grew. Many of the reviewers found the poems obscure, although a few were admiring. To Robert the critics were 'mostly stupid and spiteful, self contradicting and contradictory of each other'. Their 'zoological utterances' made him furious, as was apparent from his letter to his publisher: ' "Whoo-oo-oo" mouths the big monkey – "Whee-ee-ee" squeaks the little monkey and such a dig with the end of my umbrella as I should give the brutes if I couldn't keep my temper, and consider how they miss their nut[s] and gingerbread.' Robert was also considerably put out because none of his influential literary friends had come to his aid and praised the book or written anywhere of its merits. Ruskin had been imprudent enough to say that the poems were 'a mass of conundrums', and criticised specific pieces. Robert was, not unnaturally, offended and sent him a sharp reply: Ruskin was asking of poetry 'the explicitness and detail needed in a business contract'. His objections, Robert suggested, arose mainly out of his own ignorance.

Robert's demoralisation was profound, almost as great as after the failure of *Sordello*. Four years' work had seemingly done nothing for his reputation. All desire to write further poetry went, although Elizabeth, to distract his thoughts and occupy his time, suggested that he should revise *Sordello* and make it less obscure (not perhaps the most tactful of ideas). Robert immediately began to work on the poem but it was a case of flogging a dead horse, and he could not bring himself to continue. He began to draw and accompanied his father to the Louvre (his father had a ticket to sketch there) each day.

After thirteen days application [Elizabeth told Mrs Jameson] he has produced some quite startling copies of heads. I am very glad. He can't rest from serious work in light literature, as I can; it wearies him, and there are hours on his hands, which is bad both for them and for him. The secret of life is full occupation, isn't it? The world is not tenable on other terms. . . . So while I lie on the sofa and rest in a novel, Robert has a resource in his drawing. . . .

Elizabeth was now hard at work on the completion of *Aurora Leigh*, although she was far from well. The cough that had returned in London continued, and she was spitting blood, probably from the lungs. She spent much of November and December huddled over the fire. The flat which had been rented for them by friends turned out to be draughty, small and uncomfortable, and they moved into a larger and more pleasing apartment off the Champs Elysées. The winter was a mild one, but she remained sickly and Robert had to push her to eat adequately, and take supplements of cod-liver oil. By the end of February she had improved and had 'no blood or much cough . . . but was still not very strong' and easily tired. The lack of appetite had not been helped by the need to have five teeth extracted.

That she was able to continue working was remarkable, especially as Penini was still difficult. Without his beloved Wilson – the new maid must have been at least adequate, since Elizabeth made no serious complaints about her – and with no playmate, he was bound to be demanding of his mother's time. He shared his parents' bedroom, at first because of lack of space, but this arrangement persisted after they moved to the larger flat. 'He was so pathetic about it,' Elizabeth explained, 'that we would not lose him.' She continued her attempts to teach him to read, although it was time-consuming, frequently futile, and added to her exhaustion. 'He tears me to rags sometimes,' she confessed to Henrietta, after what must have been a particularly trying day.

She was uncertain how to bring *Aurora Leigh* to a satisfactory conclusion, and was worried lest the book should not be ready on time, but she could easily cope with such problems. Indeed, had she not been able to absorb herself in the novel–poem, she might not have been able to survive the combined strains of organising her son and Robert.

Robert went frequently into society, usually without Elizabeth. Once the dinner party included Cavour – soon to be one of Elizabeth's heroes – and George Sand. Elizabeth was too busy writing to be envious, and relayed Robert's description to Mrs Jameson with some amusement. 'George Sand had an ivy wreath round her head and looked like herself.' She was more likely to have regretted staying away from the baptism of the Prince Imperial at Notre-Dame, for she missed sitting near her hero, Napoleon III.

Robert was in a curious state of mind at this time. He believed in himself as a poet, yet for twenty-five years he had been comparatively unsuccessful in selling his work and attracting a wider reading public. He was bitter over his failure and as compensation, plunged into a busy social life where he was always welcomed. He had no incentive to write poetry and occupied himself in the daytime with drawing. He was unforgiving of the critics who had so obviously failed to understand his work. But he kept his angry feelings well under control and assumed an air of detachment. Perhaps it was these suppressed emotions that directed him to one of the Paris morgues where, from behind a protective screen of glass, he gazed at the already decomposing bodies of three men who had killed themselves. Seven years later he wrote about them in the poem 'Apparent Failures', which was published in *Dramatis Personae* in 1864. Elizabeth would not have liked it. Indeed, one suspects that she would not have been best pleased to have heard of his expedition to the morgue.

It is notable that this morbid side of Robert's nature is largely absent from *Men and Women*. Only after Elizabeth's death in 1861 did it begin to show in his writing. Just as the death of his mother seemed to allow his love poems to emerge, so perhaps he had to wait for his wife's death before he could express his angry feelings openly.

The Brownings returned to London on 7 July 1856. Elizabeth was by now well and active, and *Aurora Leigh* was almost completed. Much of their first month was taken up with preparing the poem for the printers. It consisted of nine books or sections, of 11,000 lines in all, and Elizabeth looked on it as 'the most mature of my work, and the one into which my highest convictions upon life and art have entered'. Robert praised it without stint, and showed no hint of the bitterness he still had over the reception given to *Men and Women*.

Elizabeth was too occupied at first by *Aurora Leigh* to devote much thought to her father. But as soon as the manuscript went off to the printers she began, as before, to visit Wimpole Street and run the risk of encounters. He soon learnt of the Brownings' presence, and immediately ordered his family to leave for Ventnor in the Isle of Wight. It was so clear an expression of his determination to maintain her exclusion from the family that her grief showed even to Penini. 'Mama,' the child declared, after learning that his grandfather was angry with his mother, 'if you've been very, very naughty – if you've broken china, I advise you to go into the room and say, "Papa, I'll be dood." ' A year earlier she might just have heeded his advice. She knew now that it would be futile.

Since Mr Barrett remained in London, the Brownings immediately packed their bags and joined the family at Ventnor. Although there was always the danger of her father making an unexpected appearance, Elizabeth enjoyed the fortnight they spent there. For the first and only time, she and Robert and Penini were able to take part in the Barrett family life. 'George and my brothers were very kind to Robert,' Elizabeth noted, 'and he is quite touched by it.' But pleasant as it was, the experience only served to highlight the fact that she was an outsider, and that her alienation from her father was absolute.

She was temporarily diverted from these thoughts by the need to correct the proofs of *Aurora Leigh*, and by news of the terminal illness of her beloved cousin Kenyon. He was dying at his summer house at West Cowes, on the other side of the island, and she and Robert and Penini spent two weeks with him, in effect paying their last respects, although Elizabeth tried to be optimistic about the outcome. She dedicated *Aurora Leigh* to him, but he was probably too ill to read the dedication when he received his copy. He died on 3 December 1856.

Elizabeth and Robert were saddened by his death. He had been of immense importance to them both, as adviser, friend, critic and supporter, and he had been instrumental in bringing the two poets together. He had played the rôle of substitute father to them and, in the end, treated them as if they had been his own children. His will put an end to their financial difficulties. Elizabeth was left £4500, and Robert £6500. Elizabeth was particularly grateful to him for bequeathing the greater sum to Robert. Her father, she learnt from Arabel, was 'much vexed'.

Opium in large amounts had continued to be necessary for Elizabeth. One suspects that she increased the dosage after Wilson left to have her baby, for she was depressed and physically unwell at that time. She now complained that the chemist had made a mistake in making up her 'amreeta mixture', so that it was too weak. She developed what sound to be withdrawal symptoms: 'I have a feeling people have in dreams, of being forced to run, for some great motive or other, and of not being able to move their legs . . . '. With the stronger mixture the symptoms disappeared and she felt more comfortable. What happened was that the first chemist had sent her the standard mixture purchased by the majority of his customers who dosed themselves only occasionally, which proved far too weak for her needs. She probably required at *least* 60 milligrams of morphine a day at this time to avoid withdrawal effects.

Aurora Leigh having been finished and the proofs despatched to the printers, a gap was left in her life. For the past year she had worked ceaselessly to complete it, and the work had occupied virtually all her energies and time. Spiritualism had taken second place, and even her father's hurtful actions had made less impact on her than before. Now the misery and emptiness she associated with London returned in full. She was depressed and restless, her cough increased, her weight fell. She was adamant that she could not wait in London, or even Paris, until 15 November, the publication day of *Aurora Leigh*. Wilson had returned, and was caring for Penini, having left her own child with relatives, and was prepared to travel to Italy with the Brownings. Fog was gathering, the wind was in the east, and her breathing was daily becoming more laboured. On 23 October they all left for Florence.

As usual Elizabeth improved rapidly all round once England was left behind. She was delighted to be home in Casa Guidi, and enjoyed 'the repose, the quiet'. She had absolutely no wish to go back again to London or Paris, at least for the moment: 'I couldn't bear it – it would drive me mad. . .', she told Henrietta.

Reviews of *Aurora Leigh* were not particularly good. The poem seemed cumbersome to the reviewers and the narrative strained. A few critics took her to task for 'immodesty' and vulgarity. Aurora Leigh is the child of a Florentine mother, who dies when she is four, and an English father. She is brought up in Italy until thirteen, when her father dies and she is sent back to England to live with a maiden aunt. There she is given a conventional upbringing, reads her father's books, thinks and develops feminist ideas. Her cousin Romney, in line to inherit the Leigh family fortune, falls in love with her and proposes marriage; but he expects her to give up poetry and help in his sociopolitical work and she turns him down, saying

I too have my vocation, – work to do.

Her aunt, shocked by Aurora's refusal, dies and Aurora moves to London to become a writer. Romney, continuing his good works, encounters Marian Earle, a working-class girl who has run away from home and is alone. He arranges to marry her, not from love but to demonstrate his belief that class barriers should be abolished. Marian fails to turn up at the church and goes to France, where she is raped, has a child, and is later traced and found by Aurora. The story becomes extremely convoluted and far-fetched and ends with Romney – who has become blind through his work – and Aurora marrying for love, and Romney acknowledging the value of Aurora's 'art'.

The book's main interest today lies in the way Elizabeth sets out her views on society's treatment of women, and the expectation that they take second place to men. How can a marriage be happy under such circumstances? she asked. She believed that a happy marriage was the happiest condition, but was only possible when partners had equal opportunities.

The public flocked to buy the book and the first edition was sold out within a fortnight, helped no doubt by the news that 'the mammas of England' considered it to be unfit to be read by their daughters. Five editions in three years was no mean achievement. Friends wrote congratulatory letters praising the book and the authoress. Ruskin congratulated Elizabeth on constructing 'the greatest poem in the language, surpassed only by plays of Shakespeare, but not by his sonnets'. Elizabeth took in the praise and for the most part ignored the criticism, which was an unusual reaction. She needed the acclaim to bolster her morale, to counterbalance the weight of her father's disapproval and silence. She had 'many sad and heavy thoughts this winter', she told Henrietta, and they were centred around her father and his reactions to the poem. 'I think so much of these things in reference to him, but I daresay he is absolutely indifferent to me and my writings.' Never before had she been so despairing of the future. Nothing was worthwhile as long as she remained in exile.

Her interest in spiritualism revived and she sought the company of fellow believers and listened avidly to their stories. Robert continued to stand back from the subject, and even accounts of Home's spectacular successes in Florence and Rome, while the Brownings had been in Paris, did not cause him to express anger and upset Elizabeth. But at heart he remained convinced that, 'no trick is too gross'.

Robert busied himself in gathering the reviews of *Aurora Leigh* as they arrived in Florence, and boosting his wife's spirits. 'That golden-hearted Robert is in ecstasies about [*Aurora Leigh*] – far more than if it all related to a book of his own,' Elizabeth wrote. That he admired the poem, and was delighted for Elizabeth's sake with its sales, is certain. But it was inevitable that some of the bitterness he felt over the reviews of *Men and Women* would surface. It was not in Robert's nature to complain or compare the reception of his poems with that accorded to Elizabeth. Instead he directed his anger against any reviewer who dared to criticise *Aurora Leigh*. 'Don't you mind them,' he declared, 'and leave me to rub their noses in their own filth some fine day' – a sentiment he was later to apply to 'Mr. Sludge. "The Medium" ', alias Home.

Meanwhile, Robert wrote nothing. While Elizabeth read endless French and German novels, Robert drifted aimlessly. He continued with his drawing, went out many evenings, and in the spring began to ride, a pleasure he had always denied himself until now because of the expense. He also went regularly to the Protestant Church at Florence, occasionally accompanied by Elizabeth. Elizabeth, like her father, was always highly critical of bad sermons, and described the preacher as 'the slowest . . . I have ever listened to', but Robert was not dismayed and continued to go, presumably reviving childhood memories and associations.

12

The Last Years,
1857–1861

In March 1857 Elizabeth heard that the Creole nurse who had cared for her and her father, and been her grandmother's companion, her 'beloved Treppy', had died. She was ninety, so the loss was hardly a surprise, but it added to the gloom at Casa Guidi. It did nothing to lessen the shock that followed. On 17 April Elizabeth's father died.

The news prostrated her. She lay on her sofa, shocked, incapable at first of crying or even talking, 'miserable to see'. She read and reread the letters from Arabel and George, announcing their father was ill, and then dead, without fully comprehending. 'I knew that this which we have suffered was before us to suffer,' she later told Henrietta, 'yet when it came it seemed insufferable as if unforeseen.' After a few days she was able to cry, which pleased Robert, but the tears did little to alleviate Elizabeth's misery. The knowledge that her father was dead without a reconciliation having been effected was impossible for her fully to grasp. 'I take up books – but my heart goes walking up and down constantly through that house of Wimpole Street till it is tired, tired.' She saw no one, apart from Isa Blagdon who called often, and refused to leave the house – until Robert threatened to carry her outdoors if necessary.

She clutched at any passing straw and drew momentary relief from what her father had said to Mrs Martin, when the latter had asked him to forgive his three married children; 'He had forgiven them, and . . . he even prayed for the well being and well doing of the three families. . . . Those were the words,' Elizabeth repeated to Henrietta. 'Let us hold them fast. He prayed for us.' At heart she was unconvinced. Spirit communication was the one channel to her father which was still open to her and gave her cause for hope. If she could be in touch with him in the spirit world she might learn that she was forgiven. 'My interest,' she said of spiritualism, 'grows deeper and deeper.' She might have to wait for her own death before she and her father were fully reconciled, but to know that he had forgiven her would release her from an intolerable burden of guilt and despair. 'In that world,' she said hopefully, 'spirits learn and grow faster.'

Robert felt helpless. At first he was fearful of the effect on Elizabeth of her father's death, '. . . strange and sudden and mournful. . . . So it is all over now, all hope of better things, or a kind answer to entreaties. Such as I have seen Ba write in the bitterness of her heart . . . now, here is a new grief not likely to subside very soon.' He encouraged her to weep, to eat adequately, to walk outdoors, even perhaps to take a larger than usual dose of opium to ensure a full night's sleep. Yet he was unable to share in what she was experiencing, her thoughts, her guilt. He understood her so well in everything except her past. She had given him several opportunities during the courtship to explore her psychic depths, but he had failed to seize them. 'The personality of my wife was so strong and peculiar,' he explained, 'that I had no curiosity to go beyond it and concern myself with matters which she was evidently disinclined to communicate.' He began to take a more optimistic view. 'I have no fear for the result,' he assured Mrs Martin after a month, although Elizabeth was still 'very weak and prostrated'. To Henrietta he confided that Elizabeth was 'no more shaken than was inevitable, and far less than I should have expected'.

As the shock lessened, Elizabeth began to bombard Arabel with pleas – to Arabel they appeared more like demands – to visit Florence, to live near them, to accompany them on holiday. She addressed her sister as though a helpless and irresponsible child, and at times adopted her father's autocratic manner. She was upset when her brothers and Arabel decided unanimously to leave Wimpole Street, each individual going his or her own way. She seemed to believe that the family home would continue unchanged, perhaps envisaging it as a shrine to her father, preserved after his death as her mother's room had been. But she rejected any idea of her and Robert going back to England. 'To go there and be quiet would be impossible . . . people tear us to pieces . . . I couldn't bear it. . . . It would drive me mad I think.'

Robert took her to Lucca in July, hoping that the change of climate and pleasant memories would help to lift her spirits. But the holiday was not a success. Robert was himself still depressed, restless and searching for social stimulation. He was not interested in poetry, and the novels that Elizabeth read mostly bored him. He bathed in the mountain streams and went for long walks, but nothing held his attention for long.

Elizabeth remained weak and preoccupied with memories of her father, but she tried her best to arouse Robert's interest and lift his morale. It was a case of the blind leading the blind. At this time neither seemed able to help the other.

Their difficulties were increased by Wilson having to return to Florence. She was seven months pregnant and when she complained of stomach pains everyone feared she was about to go into labour. As it turned out the child was not born until November, but the possibility of Wilson delivering in their small house at Lucca put Elizabeth into a spin and she took no chances. But she did not escape trouble, for Wilson's replacement, a young Italian woman called Annunziata, became ill with 'gastric fever' almost at once, and had to be nursed, and then Penini sickened which threw Elizabeth into a panic. As likely as not, Penini's sickness was nothing more than a reaction to Wilson's departure, magnified by his mother's overconcern.

It was at about this time that the Brownings met the Eckleys, a wealthy middle-aged American couple. Sophie Eckley wrote poetry, and was not only interested in spiritualism but claimed to be a medium. An intense friendship sprang up rapidly between the two women, and Mrs Eckley fell 'into a sort of love' with Elizabeth. She was embarrassingly generous with expensive presents and eventually Elizabeth had to avoid expressing a liking for any object in her company for fear it was immediately given to her.

Elizabeth was usually slow to form a close friendship, liking to understand the nature and interests of the person before committing herself. Mrs Eckley does not sound to have been an exceptional character. That Elizabeth took to her so uncritically was entirely due to their common interest in spiritualism, and to Elizabeth's morbid preoccupation with spirit communication.

In Florence Mrs Eckley called at Casa Guidi almost every day, discussed the spirits and conducted séances with Elizabeth. Clearly, significant and revealing communications were received through Mrs Eckley, because Elizabeth came increasingly under her sway and for two years had no doubts about her authenticity. Robert regarded her as a fraud and a liar almost from the start, and continually tried to warn his wife off her. It was reminiscent of the Home episode, and the more Robert nagged the more determined Elizabeth was to continue. Mrs Eckley 'cheated Ba from the beginning' Robert told Isa Blagden[1] when it was all over, 'and I say, in the bitterness of truth, that Ba deserved it for shutting her eyes and stopping her ears as she determinedly did'. Whether there were communications or visitations from Bro or Elizabeth's father is not known, but it seems likely that meaningful messages, or hints of them, materialised. Mrs Eckley, in the course of a two-year friendship with a depressed Elizabeth, must have learnt much about her, apart from what she had read and heard, and used it to effect.

Robert did not dislike David Eckley – he rode with him and looked on him as tolerable company – but he found it a strain to be polite to Mrs Eckley and keep his temper under control. It must have appeared to him at times as though he and Elizabeth were being taken over by the couple. They had to be dissuaded from accompanying the Brownings to France in the summer of 1858; only the plea of needing to be with their relatives saved them. After their return to Florence in October, they found the Eckleys waiting to learn of their movements before making their own plans. Hearing that the Brownings had decided on Rome they insisted that both families must travel in comfort together in the Eckleys' sumptuous carriage. Elizabeth, who had been depressed and anorexic during the summer holiday at Le Havre, now came to life. She and Mrs Eckley talked a great deal, Elizabeth pleased to be with her spiritualist friend again, although careful not to say too much in front of Robert. Her appetite improved strikingly, and when the party stopped in the middle of the day for their usual two-hour rest, she 'had a kind of second breakfast, eggs, tea and coffee – and then in the evening we dined'.

Robert seethed inwardly, amazed that his wife 'by some miracle would not see' the falseness of Mrs Eckley. 'You know,' he told William Story, 'that those inventions about "spirits", etc., were not at all more prodigious than the daily sprouting toadstools of that dunghill of a soul – lies about this, that and the others'. Robert was convinced that David Eckley knew this, and 'resolutely shut his eyes and said black should be white. . . . I remember once inadvertently telling him something she had said about an invitation "she had reluctantly accepted to please *him*' – whereas, as he cried in amazement, "she had forced *him* to go purely to please her". I saw his face change, and was afraid he would go home and explode: not he! It was gulped down and ignored henceforth and forever.'

Elizabeth was shaken to her core when, in Rome in the spring of 1860, she discovered Mrs Eckley's 'extraordinary falseness of character', and at last recognised that she was a fraud. 'Oh if I could believe in the honesty of an inch of her or if she said she hated me; how much easier I should feel.'

How Elizabeth discovered the truth is unclear, as she was too distressed to give details in her letters. Some flagrant act of deception may have been detected during a séance. There was perhaps a scene reminiscent of Mr Sludge,

> Now, don't, sir! Don't expose me! Just this once!
> This was the first and only time, I'll swear, –
> Look at me, – see, I kneel. . . .[2]

Recently, because of the poem 'Where's Agnes?'[3] which features a disguised Mrs Eckley, it has been suggested that the problem was a moral one and that Mrs Eckley was discovered to be involved in an affair. Elizabeth would certainly have been disturbed by such news, although her faith in her friend's mediumistic powers need not have been shattered. But all this was two years ahead.

Elizabeth came to life and grew cheerful when with Mrs Eckley. Away from her, during the winter of 1857–8 she felt exhausted and lacked zest for anything apart from spiritualism; 'the weight of the whole year, seems to have stamped out of me the vital spirit, and I am physically low. . . ', she wrote to her sister. 'For months I have done nothing but read French and German romances. . . .'

The atmosphere at Casa Guidi was one of boredom and apathy, interrupted occasionally by an outburst of irritability on the part of Robert. Neither Browning was moved to write poetry. Robert watched Elizabeth sitting dispirited by the fireside, pale and thin, withdrawn from him. She resented his wasting his time drawing instead of working at poetry. It was not how she had seen their literary life together.

Almost the last straw for Elizabeth was when Robert obtained a human skeleton to aid his drawing lessons. Elizabeth disclosed her feelings to her sister.

> He has made a great purchase of a skeleton and has discoursed upon it until he made me sick and dizzy . . . enlarging on the beautiful gutta-percha finishing of the joints, and the facility with which the head comes off and on – and how, two months ago, this was a Florentine of 36, straying, and eating perhaps, by Casa Guidi. Well – I have not seen it yet, I leave it

to you. I keep it on the 'outside' – saying, that if I tolerate Robert's bones in the house, he should my spirits. . . .

At this period Mrs Eckley was paying frequent visits, and adding to Robert's frustrations. Suddenly and dramatically he was struck down with a severe headache of a kind he had not had since his courtship days. So agonising was the pain that he was convinced that he was about to have a stroke. Such a headache for Robert was always a sign of suppressed anger, and of anxiety that he was no longer in full control of his life and needed to make changes. Elizabeth probably recognised this, but she was too tired and depressed to suggest remedies. 'I am a rag of a woman through weakness,' she wrote, 'but I have not had a cough as I had in England.' Nathaniel Hawthorne and his wife came to tea,[4] and the latter observed the 'deep pain furrowed into her face' from 'so much grief, so much suffering'. Her husband who, two years earlier, had found her to be 'more youthful and comely than I supposed', now saw her as 'a pale little woman, scarcely embodied at all'; she and her son seemed 'of the elfin breed'. By contrast Hawthorne perceived Robert as 'younger and handsomer' than when they last met. His wife noticed the sense of power and energy that emanated from him, yet mixed with an air of uncertainty, as though unclear as to the direction his life was taking.

Their tentative plans to spend the summer of 1858 in London were changed on medical advice – and, in all probability, some reluctance on the part of Elizabeth to return there now that 50 Wimpole Street had been given up and the family separated. Instead they decided to go to Paris and then on to a French seaside resort for a sea-water cure. Money being comparatively plentiful for the first time during their marriage, they travelled slowly and in 'unbridled extravagance' by first-class express coach from Marseilles to Paris, arriving there on 4 July. Elizabeth revelled in the luxury of having a carriage to themselves and the freedom to stretch full length across the seats. Travel usually improved Elizabeth – apart from the changing scenery she liked the absence of news – and by the time she reached Paris she felt much better. 'I am like another being from what I was two months since, so much better and stronger in all ways. . . . But still I can't do much. I break suddenly like a stick at a certain point and it comes early.'

In Paris they were joined by Robert's father and sister, and after a fortnight they all set off to find accommodation on the

French coast. Robert had chosen Etretat, '. . . very pretty, and the coast picturesque with fantastic rocks',[5] but the price of their lodgings was exorbitant, their room had no view, and Elizabeth objected to the beach being overlooked and the absence of any privacy for her to bathe there. In fact her doctor had told her 'not to bathe when we arrive at the sea – neither in hot or cold baths; but to use the salt water at home . . .'. They moved on to Le Havre and took a house near the sea. Robert, who would as soon have stayed at Etretat, had mixed feelings; '. . . the ugliness of everything in immediate view is surprising – but you have it all to yourself, and the sea-faringness of the place is good and interesting,' he told Isa Blagdon.

Old Mr Browning and Sarianna had rooms in their house, and a week or so later Arabel and George, and then Henry and his new wife arrived. Elizabeth had looked forward to having 'cosy chats' with Arabel, who was 'so well and so cheerful' but the presence of Sarianna, forever chattering and rarely giving the sisters an opportunity to be alone together, was a source of irritation. She disliked 'creeping down' each day to a bench on the seashore, and she longed to be back in the peace and comfort of her room at Casa Guidi.

Robert was equally bored and 'out of spirits'. He found the Barretts unstimulating company, but most of all he objected to the manner in which his day was taken up with trivia. 'What is to say about such a dull life as this daily one of ours?' he asked Isa Blagdon. 'I go mechanically out and in and get a day through – where not ten minutes have been my own – so much for your "quantities of writing" – I began pretty zealously – but it's no use now: nor will the world very greatly care.' Robert's bitterness over the reception of his work was never far from the surface. For three years he had written virtually no poetry and it was difficult to imagine doing so until his frame of mind changed.

Both Robert and Elizabeth were thankful to return to Paris in late September. Elizabeth had benefited physically, was stronger and able to walk reasonable distances. They spent two weeks in Paris before the weather turned cold and then set out for Florence. During most of the fortnight Elizabeth had had Arabel to herself for virtually the first time, and much of their talk must have centred around their father and his attitude to his children at the end.

When she reached Florence Elizabeth was feeling depressed and again weary. After a month the Brownings moved to Rome for the winter of 1858–9. Robert flung himself frenetically into social life, accepting two or three engagements in one night. He was rarely at home in the evenings. 'He never dines out now – except when he does,' Elizabeth commented caustically.

I mean there is not unfrequently an exceptional occasion – now he dines out somewhere out of friendship – now to meet someone extraordinary, – and now to eat something extra-ordinary – such as a roast porcupine . . . and a delicate luxury of a whole dinner 'dressed in garlic'. For my part I shall muse on separation when Robert returns . . . or rather I shall beg him not to return.

The idea was laughable, or rather lachrymatory, but Elizabeth's sentiments suggest an unhappy concern over the increasing divide in their lives, and for Robert's artistic integrity. She went on, 'Robert is lost to me and himself. If once a fortnight we have an evening together we call it a holiday, both of us. . . .'

She continued to be disappointed by his lack of interest in poetry, and regarded the three hours a day he spent in the studio of his friend Story, learning modelling, as wasted oppor-tunity: 'I grudged a little the time from his own particular art,' she wrote. On the other hand she avoided openly criticising him for she recognised his need for occupation; '. . . an active occupation is salvation to him with his irritable nerves, saves him from ruminating bitter cud, and from the process which I call beating his dear head against the wall till it is bruised. He has an enormous superfluity of vital energy, and if it isn't employed, it strikes its fangs into him.'

Elizabeth spent much of the winter shut up in her 'poky' warm room. Robert believed she was 'decidedly better', but she had little zest for anything outside spiritualism and politics. She still did not like Rome; it was 'an unhealthy place', with too much 'reckless dissipation. . . . For a residence, give me my Florence'.

She became excited by the political events that unfolded at the end of 1858, and their importance for the cause of Italian freedom. She hero-worshipped Cavour, now prime minister of Piedmont, as well as Louis Napoleon, and neither could do wrong in her eyes. She castigated England for not being more openly supportive of Italian unity. When Austria declared war on Piedmont in April, and France came to that country's assistance, Elizabeth was ecstatic. 'Louis Napoleon has acted . . . sublimely,' she declared.

They returned to Florence in late May, fearing to be trapped in

Rome by the hostilities, and found French troops encamped there. Elizabeth was convinced she was about to witness the liberation of Tuscany and the unification of Italy. At this time she and Robert were in agreement politically, despite Robert's continued reservations about Napoleon. In June news came of the victories against the Austrians at Magenta and Solferino, and Elizabeth became hysterical with excitement. Her letters and conversation reflected 'her passion and feverish obsession'. To care so intensely for such matters was more than reason allowed; it was 'a malady and a doom'.[6] The strain on her was great. She could not sleep, had no time for food, lost weight, and talked interminably of Italy's suffering and Napoleon III's greatness. Her 'insistent voice and fixed eye', betrayed her fanatical concern. Italy's freedom was surely identified in her mind with her own escape and freedom and the consequences. Louis Napoleon was the strong man, the substitute for the father for whom she had continually craved.

Politics and spiritualism absorbed her interest. They were, for her, complementary activities. At a séance she sat silent and withdrawn, absorbed in her memories, waiting hopefully for a sign of recognition, or better, of acceptance from the spirit world. In the field of politics she became outgoing and outspoken, proclaiming her principles and praising her heroes. Within that combination her neurotic needs were momentarily satisfied, her grief over her father's unforgiving attitude and his death temporarily displaced.

Robert, watching and listening to her, must have been worried by what he saw. He too was interested in the unfolding political scene, but he took a more balanced view of events and the personalities involved. Perhaps to induce Elizabeth to take a less extreme stance, he suggested, after the French victories, that they should each write a poem on the Italian question, and publish the two jointly. When she showed him her ode to 'Napoleon III in Italy' – subsequently published in *Poems before Congress* – 'he observed that I was gentle to England in comparison with what he had been, but after Villafranca he destroyed his poem'.

On 8 July, Napoleon III and Franz Joseph, the Austrian Emperor, met at Villafranca and agreed on peace. It was an unexpected end to the war, and appeared to vitiate almost all the gains made. Venice would remain Austrian. Cavour resigned after making a terrible scene; he 'seemed almost to have lost his mind.'[7] Elizabeth collapsed and took to bed.

The notion that Napoleon III was a coward and had retreated from the risk of a general war (Prussia had massed 400,000 troops on the borders. England was hostile) was, for Elizabeth, inconceivable. She agonised for a time, and made Penini take off the Napoleon medal he wore, but then decided that the fault lay with England – 'I will never forgive England the most damnable part she has taken in Italian affairs, never' – and Napoleon was not really to blame.

The strain proved too much for her:

> . . . after all that excitement and exultation, that walking on the clouds for weeks and months, and then the sudden stroke and fall, and the impotent rage against all the nations of the earth – selfish, inhuman, wicked – who forced the hand of Napoleon and truncated his great intentions . . . I was struck, couldn't sleep, talked too much, and at last this bad attack came on.

It was the worst attack on the chest she had had in Italy. Violent palpitations and an exhausting cough developed. 'For two days and nights it was more like angina pectoris, as I have heard it described; but this went off . . . and kept me *only* very ill, with a violent cough all night long.' The symptoms could well have been due, at least partly, to a panic attack brought on by the excitement and anger induced by events.

Robert nursed her with his usual devotion. He was 'perfect to me. For more than a fortnight he gave up all his nights' rest to me.' She remained excitable, however, and after three weeks Robert and the doctors decided that she must be moved to new surroundings. She was like 'a dark shadow' when she left for Siena, carried everywhere by Robert and torn by coughing and bouts of breathlessness.

She was blistered, fed with asses' milk and, no doubt, liberal amounts of opium. Every excitement was avoided, and talk of politics forbidden. After ten days Robert reported that she was stronger, although 'she takes no solid food yet – except a canary bird's allowance of toast at breakfast. She cannot walk alone – but still she *is* better and sits here by my side . . . in a delicious silence: she can't write, can't hear Pen's lessons, can't see anyone.'

She returned to Florence in October, 'recovered in appearance', although she 'constantly felt on the edge of a precipice, as if too much exertion would plunge me down'. As ever, illness brought them close together and she felt safely dependent again on Robert. Both were relaxed and 'buoyant of general spirits'.

They travelled south to Rome on 28 November 1859. Robert was still very much the nurse and kept all the carriage windows open. 'I enjoy the journey much – so evident is the advantage to Ba – these long doses of fresh open air which she would have made no effort to swallow in Florence.' Rome, in December 1859 was almost empty of foreigners, a few Americans only were visible. There were rumours that the French garrison troops were about to leave Rome and there was 'an expectation of fighting'.

Robert and Elizabeth were enthusiastically acclaimed as poets and friends of Italy on arrival there – Elizabeth again grew excited and a visit to Castellani, the jeweller, to view the much-talked-of swords that had been designed to present to Napoleon III and King Victor Emmanuel from grateful Romans, pushed her over the edge and she relapsed. 'All my bad symptoms came back. Suffocation, singular heart action, cough tearing one to atoms. A gigantic blister let me crawl out of bed at the end of a week. . . . I feel myself brittle.'

Elizabeth was able to complete her new volume of poems, hardly more than a pamphlet, *Poems before Congress*, which was scheduled to be published in March. It consisted of eight poems, mostly composed just before and after the peace of Villafranca, glorifying the heroics and sacrifices of the Italian people and their struggle for unity, and lauding Napoleon III, while berating England and Austria. Among the poems was one she had already published in America, 'A Curse for a Nation', which cursed the American slave states for condoning slavery. Understandably, given the tone of the other poems, the critics thought she was really cursing England, and Elizabeth was upset when her old friend Henry Chorley, of the *Athenaeum*, reprimanded her for being unpatriotic. A heated correspondence ensued, with Robert joining in and taking the chance to shower vituperations on the critics. On the whole, however, the poems had the reception she expected – and invited. She had written to Mrs Jameson in February 'of my thin slice of a wicked book. . . . Everyone will hate me for it, and so *you must* try hard to love me for more to make up for that. Say it's mad, and bad, and sad; but *add* that somebody did it who meant it . . .'.

Alas, Mrs Jameson had little opportunity to read the book, for she died a few days after its publication. The news took Elizabeth by surprise, and at first she was 'greatly moved by it'.

The loss was 'a blot more on the world for me', but Robert thought 'the pain can be only of the less bitter sort'. This was wishful thinking on Robert's part for Elizabeth had long looked on Mrs Jameson as a very close friend in whom she could confide. She spoke of 'losing (as far as the loving can lose whom they love, as far as death brings a loss) that great heart, that noble human creature'.

The shock was all the greater since it coincided with the discovery of Mrs Eckley's falseness, and the consequent disintegration of the comforting spiritualist world that woman had created for Elizabeth. Elizabeth's basic beliefs in spiritualism remained, however. They were far too strong to be destroyed by mere human weakness and culpability.

Robert changed his ways during the 1859–60 winter in Rome. He continued to model with Story, but went out little, and spent much time writing poetry, to Elizabeth's gratification. Perhaps this was due to the scarcity of social entertainment, or perhaps his concern over Elizabeth's health had made him resolve to spend more time with her. It is strange that he began the drafts of 'Mr. Sludge, "The Medium" ' and 'Prince Hohenstiel-Schwangau, Saviour of Society'[8] at this time, subjects on which he and Elizabeth differed to a bitter extent. It was probably to 'Mr. Sludge' that she referred when she wrote in May 1860 that Robert was 'working at a long poem' of which she had not yet seen a line. Robert himself mentioned that he conceived 'Prince Hohenstiel-Schwangau', a critical monologue dealing with Napoleon III, in 1860, in Rome.

Elizabeth's letters contained no specific references to these poems, and it is unlikely that Robert showed or discussed them with her. She would not have taken kindly to attacks on her almost hallowed belief and her heroes. This was the one safe way by which Robert could release the anger he felt for spiritualism and Napoleon III, and what he saw to be their disastrous effects on Elizabeth. It was still impossible for him to have a reasoned discussion with his wife on either of these topics. While she remained so frail and prone to hysterical outbursts it was incumbent on him to preserve the peace at home. Tactfully he sat in his room and worked at his poems, and agreed with Elizabeth that the unification of Italy was in sight.

They went to Siena for the summer of 1860. Elizabeth was fatigued by the journey, but enraptured by news of Garibaldi's successes in Sicily: 'All modern heroes grow pale before him,' she told Sarianna in an enthusiastic letter. But Garibaldi did not compare with Cavour or Napoleon in her eyes, and she later qualified her praise. 'He is not a man of much brain,' she confided.

Elizabeth was now writing with extraordinary vigour and freshness – sitting under 'my fig tree' behind the house which she drew with pen and ink the last day she was ever at Siena. 'Bianca among the Nightingales' was written at this time,[9] a poem unlike anything she had composed before. It has intense passion and sensuality. It rings out like a clarion call, announcing that, frail as she is, she is as passionately alive as Robert. 'Where's Agnes?' was also written then. But the surge of creativity was abruptly halted by the news that Henrietta had incurable cancer of the womb, and was in great pain. Elizabeth became frantic with worry, and could think of nothing but what her sister's suffering must be. Even the news of 'our triumphant Italy' was immediately trumped by the idea of her 'great pain at this moment perhaps'. She wanted to hurry at once to England to comfort her, but was firmly dissuaded.

They returned to Casa Guidi on 11 October, but even spiritualism offered little relief when weighed against the agony of her sister. Cavour's invasion of the Papal states and the Piedmont army's advance on Naples momentarily diverted her attention and brought back a gleam to her eye, but this was short-lived. She put her feelings into letters to George and waited on tenterhooks for news from him.

Robert took to opening all letters from England, to prepare Elizabeth for the worst before reading them to her. Henrietta's condition steadily deteriorated and the end was obviously approaching. Robert looked at Elizabeth's thin, huddled frame and decided that they must leave for the warmer climate of Rome at once, before her sister died, and a new crisis was precipitated.

Their post was inadvertently held back and for days there was silence. Robert tried to make out that no news was good news, but his attempts at protecting his wife did more harm than good. In the end he had to telegraph George Barrett and Isa Blagdon to learn that Henrietta had died ten days earlier, on 23 November.

'You know Ba's ways,' Robert told Isa. 'She will get over this, as other losses, in time; but she has endured and is still enduring sorrow enough.' It was surely Robert's anxiety for Elizabeth that made him take this somewhat brutal line, rather than insensitivity. He had said much the same after her father's death and yet, three years on, she still continued to mourn him. Only the year before Henrietta's death Elizabeth had written that, 'None of the old days go past without a throb of pain in love. There are things too dear to talk of sometimes – I remember always.' Had Robert been able to unlock the door to these memories and share them Elizabeth might have regained a zest for living which had died with her father. Now, she lived more in the past than the present, and more for Robert's sake than her own.

'It is a great privilege to be able to talk and cry; but I *cannot*, you know,' she wrote. 'I have suffered very much, and feel tired and beaten. Now, it's all being lived down; thrown behind or pushed before, as such things must be if we *are* to live.' Here she was surely echoing Robert. Her real feelings were 'not forgetting, not feeling any tie slackened, loving, unchangeably, and believing how mere a *line* this is to overstep between the living and the dead. . . . I am weak and languid. I struggle hard to live on. I wish to live just as long as and no longer than to grow in the soul.'

Robert was relieved that Elizabeth could be 'persuaded to eat a little, listen to talking, attend to Pen'. She was 'good and reasonable!' He continued to be optimistic. 'She will get over this grief in some respects but it wears her still. . . . I continue to intercept letters, and read as much of the contents as she can bear . . . or rather, she obliges me to do this – refusing to see them when they come, if I am out of the way.'

Elizabeth's behaviour encouraged her dependency on Robert, and was reminiscent of her attitude to her father before her marriage, which had contributed to their suffocating closeness. But Robert did not intend her to become too dependent on him again. He kept his distance. Despite his wife's misery he went to parties, rode for several hours a day, and continued to model with Story.

Elizabeth spent much of the winter shut up in her room, reading, seeing a few visitors, and writing. She was pleased by letters from Harriet Beecher Stowe, who described how she had communicated with her dead son Henry through the spirits. This gave her fresh cause for hope. She continued to follow politics eagerly. She was as attentive of Penini as ever, but he was almost twelve years old now and beginning to look unmistakably like a boy, and to think and behave like one. He still slept in his mother's room, but this could not continue much longer.

A furious row broke out between Elizabeth and Robert over the seemingly trivial matter of raising a subscription to Mrs

Jameson's two sisters. Elizabeth was keen to give money, but Robert dug his heels in and refused. He regarded the sisters as parasites who had worried Mrs Jameson to death. 'Ba shall not contribute a farthing thereto,' he thundered. She knew how awful they were and 'this time I mean to have my way.' The Jameson sisters were, one suspects, an excuse for Robert to be decisive and for once give vent to the frustrations and fears that had accumulated as he watched Elizabeth, 'so thin and weak', improve 'so slowly'.

Elizabeth recognised what the quarrel signified and backed down. She had, by this time, a good understanding of Robert's psychology and the ways he reacted to different strains. She told Sarianna of his enormous superfluity of vital energy, which turned against him if underemployed. 'He gets out of spirits as he was at Havre. Nobody understands exactly why – except me who am in the inside of him and hear him breathe. For the peculiarity of our relation is, that even when he is displeased with me, he thinks aloud with me and can't stop himself.'

There was, however, that darker side which Robert kept to himself and hid from Elizabeth – or which Elizabeth took care to hide from herself – concerned with suffering and death. In June 1860, walking through the open-air market of the Piazza San Lorenzo in Florence, Robert had bought a vellum-bound collection of letters, manuscripts and briefs concerning a seventeenth-century *cause célèbre*, *The Old Yellow Book*. It set out 'the entire Criminal Cause against Guido Franceschini, Nobleman of Arezzo, and his Bravoes, who were put to death in Rome, 22 February 1698, the first by beheading, the other four by the gallows. Roman Murder-case. In which it is disputed whether and when a Husband may kill his Adulterous wife without incurring the ordinary penalty'.[10] Utterly absorbed by the gruesome details of the case he read the volume 'from written title page to written index', until by the time he had reached Casa Guidi he 'had mastered the contents, knew the whole truth'. Four years later he was to commence writing *The Ring and the Book*.

Robert, in his enthusiasm, must surely have told Elizabeth of his find. 'She never took the least interest in the story, so much as to wish to inspect the papers,' he told Julia Wedgwood, which suggests that along with 'Mr. Sludge, "The Medium"', and 'Prince Hohenstiel-Schwangau', he had to keep his ideas from her. Miss Wedgwood could no more sympathise with his choice of subject than Elizabeth. 'Do you remember,' she asked, 'once saying to me that your wife was quite wanting in – the scientific interest in evil? – I feel as if that interest were in you unduly prominent.'

But Robert was still the lover, as well as husband and nurse, in her eyes. 'He is not thin and worn, as I am. . . . and the women adore him everywhere far too much for decency. In my opinion he is infinitely handsomer and more attractive than when I saw him first, sixteen years ago.' She was not jealous of other women, or so it seemed, for Robert never gave her any serious cause – although he would spend three or four evenings a week without Elizabeth, being entertained by Isa Blagdon at her home at Bellosguardo – and she understood the workings of his mind too well to entertain such fears. She was more jealous of a friend such as William Story, who encouraged him to model and thereby to neglect his poetry. But she came to recognise that such work made Robert happy and reluctantly condoned it.

Robert had suggested they should spend the summer of 1860 with his father and sister in France. It was three years since they had all met, and the old man was now approaching eighty. Elizabeth agreed reluctantly. 'I should prefer vegetating here in Italy among the hills – I am really fitter for it in body and soul – only there's a clear duty in the case.'

She was still profoundly depressed. So many of her friends had died and crossed that 'thin line'. Robert more and more led his own life and had his own thoughts. Penini was growing beyond her control. 'He sleeps in my room still, and says "Goodnight, darling", before he goes to sleep – but all must end as other sweet things do.' She, who had been the centre point of the family, was no longer necessary. She ate less and less and became so thin that the six-day journey from Rome to Florence was painful and exhausting, and every jolt of the carriage bruised her. Robert realised that she was in no condition to travel to France, and proposed they spend the summer in Italy, but she urged hysterically that he and Penini should go together to Paris and leave her alone at Casa Guidi: 'I feel more fit for going to Heaven sometimes.' Irritated, Robert abruptly dismissed such an idea.

They reached Florence on 5 June. Next day she heard of the death of Cavour. 'I can scarcely command voice or hand to name Cavour. That great soul who meditated and made Italy has gone to the divine Country,' she wrote to Sarianna. 'If tears and blood could have saved him to us, he should have had mine. I feel yet as if I could scarcely comprehend the greatness of the vacancy.'

193

Elizabeth Barrett Browning

She wept profusely, which in itself was therapeutic, but the morbid associations that scurried into her mind on the occasion of death prostrated her and she withdrew into herself. She began to pick herself up after a week and Robert noted that she was regaining strength. The weather turned increasingly sultry and Robert considered leaving for Siena at once. But Elizabeth refused to go out; in desperation he urged her to walk with him on the verandah. 'We used, you know, to walk on this verandah so often – come and walk up and down once. Just once.' She came to the window and took two steps on it, but it fatigued her too much, and she went back and lay down on the sofa. Part of her fatigue was no doubt the result of her extreme thinness, even perhaps from vitamin deficiency, but there was undoubtedly an element of wilfulness, wanting to draw attention to herself.

A week later Robert returned home to find Elizabeth sitting with the windows open, taking tea with Isa Blagdon – who had warned her against the draught. She caught cold and a cough developed which stopped her sleeping, despite increased opium. During the next night she suddenly became much worse and 'it really seemed as if she would be strangled on the spot, and that for six hours together'. Robert rushed for a doctor, who administered mustard plasters to her breasts and back, and put her feet into hot water and mustard, and induced her to cough up the offending phlegm. She felt much better, and the doctor 'supposed the difficulty was over and that sleep now would mend all', which meant, in all probability, that he prescribed yet more opium. He found 'one lung was solidified – the right', and suspected a lung abscess, but Elizabeth, not unreasonably, laughed at him. 'The *left*, Dr Chambers would have it – it's the old experience I've had in plenty – they don't understand.'

She improved, but Robert had been shaken by the experience and was once more intensely solicitous. He carried her to the sofa in the drawing room each morning, where she read or dozed and occasionally tried to talk politics with Isa before Robert forbade it. She ate no solid food, and Robert had to feed her spoonfuls of broth. At times her mind wandered, which Robert attributed to the larger quantities than usual of morphine. But he was able to hold a reasonable conversation with her and they decided it was times to move from Casa Guidi to a larger home, and talked of their plans for the summer next year. She reassured him that 'it is merely the old attack, not so severe a one as that of two years ago – there is no doubt I shall soon recover'. On the last night she 'sat up by herself, cleaned her teeth, washed her face and combed her hair without the least assistance –'.

She slept heavily and brokenly, watched over by Robert. At four o'clock she awoke in such a way that Robert was sufficiently alarmed to send immediately for the doctor. She smiled when he proposed to bathe her feet: 'Well, you *are* determined to make an exaggerated case of it!' Then she closed her eyes as though she had fallen asleep. Robert bent over her, whereupon she opened her eyes again, threw her arms around him, and kissed him repeatedly, exclaiming, 'My Robert – my heavens, my beloved.' He laid her down and she continued to kiss the air with her lips. 'How do you feel?' he asked – 'Beautiful.' Her eyes closed again, but he felt impelled to lift her up. 'Then came what my heart will keep till I see her again and longer – the most perfect expression of her love to me within my whole knowledge of her. Always smilingly, happily, and with a face like a girl's – and in a few minutes she died in my arms; her head on my cheek.'

It was 29 June 1861.

Epilogue

Grief takes many forms. Robert dealt with his by containing the memories of Elizabeth, the pleasures and pains of their intense relationship, in the depths of his mind. He could not forget but he could distance feeling.

So he lived for another twenty-eight years, protected from remarriage as securely as if Elizabeth had been alive.

> Life is stocked with germs of torpid life; but may I never wake
> Those of mine whose resurrection could not be without earthquake![1]

Appendix

The Moulton Barrett Children

Born

1806   Elizabeth (Ba): married 1846. Died 1861
1807   Edward (Bro): died 1840
1809   Henrietta (Addles): married 1850. Died 1860
1810   Mary: died 1814
1812   Samuel (Sam): died 1840
1813   Arabel: died 1868
1814   Charles (Stormie): married 1865. Died 1905
1816   George (Georgie): died 1895
1818   Henry (Harry): married 1860. Died 1896
1820   Alfred (Daisy): married 1855. Died 1904
1822   Septimus (Sette): died 1870
1824   Octavius (Occy): married 1859. Died 1910

Notes and References

I am indebted to Edward Moulton-Barrett for allowing me to see and use letters in his possession written between 1798 and 1855 by his great-great-grandfather and family members and acquaintances. Apart from these, the book is based on the widely available letters and works listed in the bibliography. For the most part I have not given the precise sources of quotations; there are a great many and often their source is apparent; to have provided references for every quote would have made the book unnecessarily ponderous.

In the early chapters I have relied heavily on the letters lent by Edward Moulton-Barrett. Like everyone concerned with Elizabeth Barrett Browning, I am both grateful and thankful to the dedicated industry of Philip Kelley and his co-editors in collecting Elizabeth's letters.

Of the books on the Brownings the most useful, for my purpose, have been Jeannette Marks's *The Family of the Barretts*, *The Book, The Ring, and the Poet* by William Irvine and Park Honan, *Robert Browning: a life within life* by Donald Thomas, Daniel Karlin's *The Courtship of Robert Browning and Elizabeth Barrett*, and *The Brownings and France* by Roy E. Gridley. Margaret Forster's *Elizabeth Barrett Browning*, which is the most up-to-date account of the poetess, was not published, unfortunately, until this work was almost completed.

My understanding of Elizabeth Barrett Browning's poetry has been greatly helped by Alethea Hayter's *Mrs. Browning. A Poet's Work and its setting*, and Angela Leighton's *Elizabeth Barrett Browning*. John Maynard's study of Robert Browning's early life was an invaluable introduction to his nature.

CHAPTER 1 Edward Moulton Barrett, 1785–1828

The Barrett ancestry is lucidly described by Jeannette Marks in *The Family of the Barretts*.

1. Thomas Jones was remarkable for the attention he gave to his pupils and his kind and guardian-like interest in their welfare and conduct. Additional to his views on slavery he wrote a pamphlet against duelling, maintaining that no man had a right to pierce another 'to the heart' and that duelling was 'much more connected . . . with barbarism than civility'. Quoted from Jeannette Marks op. cit. (pp. 285–6).

2. Yellow fever and malaria were endemic in the West Indies at that time.

3. Jeannette Marks (op. cit.) cites as evidence a poem written by Elizabeth at that date (p. 349).

> A joy was pulsing at my heart
> As I looked o'er the sea, –
> For dearest eyes were gazing there,
> And *they* were close to *me*!
>
> Nathlesse gone Time did visit me,
> And memory bared his face –
> To tell me of the absent love,
> And of the absent place!

CHAPTER 2 Elizabeth, 1806–1821

Descriptions of Elizabeth's youthful character come from her early diary, from letters from her mother and from Elizabeth to Miss Mitford and Robert Browning.

1. Elizabeth's feminist views began to form at an early age, largely centred around marriage. She had a 'loathing dread of marriage as a loveless state, and absolute contentment with single life as the alternative to the great majorities of marriage' – written to Miss Mitford, 19 December 1846.

CHAPTER 3 The First Illness, 1821–1823

1. Mary died aged four and was buried in a vault in Ledbury Parish Church. Elizabeth was about nine at the time. She never mentioned Mary in her extant correspondence. Both her parents were later interred beside her.

CHAPTER 4 Hope End, 1824–1832

Hugh Boyd's background is based on Barbara P. McCarthy's introduction to Elizabeth's letters to Hugh Boyd.

1. Elizabeth Moulton lived at 63 Baker Street, Marylebone, London, at this time.

CHAPTER 5 Sidmouth, 1832–1835

1. The account of George Barrett Hunter (despite his second name he was unrelated to Elizabeth) relies on Betty Miller's article 'Miss Barrett and Mr. Hunter', published in the Spring 1951 number of the *Cornhill Magazine*.

2. The lines are from *Aurora Leigh*, Book 9, lines 656–9.

3. These lines are taken from 'A Seaside Walk'.

4. Bro was sent out to Jamaica by his father to assist his uncle and to gather first-hand information on conditions on the estate, following the abolition of slavery. Although he satisfied his uncle he did not provide much help to his father after his return. Fear of being sent back for a longer stint may have influenced this.

CHAPTER 7 Torquay, 1838–1841

1. Jane Hedley was the youngest of the four remaining Graham-Clarke sisters.

2. Flush accompanied his mistress to Florence and gained a freer life, became a martyr to fleas and gradually lost his hair. He died peacefully in 1854, aged fourteen.

CHAPTER 8 London, 1841–1845

1. Elizabeth, encouraged by Robert Browning, turned down the proposal.

2. In his *A New Spirit of the Age*, Horne gave expression to his frustration: '. . . we should not be in the least surprised, could we lift up our ear out of our grave a century hence, to hear some learned Thebans expressing shrewd doubts as to whether such an individual as Miss E. B. Barrett had ever really existed'. From William Irvine and Park Honan, *The Book, The Ring, and the Poet*, p. 145.

3. From Tennyson's 'Mariana'.

4. Mrs Julia Martin lived near Hope End. She was a few years younger than Edward Moulton Barrett. Elizabeth always liked her but never

felt intellectually attuned. It was after moving away from Hereford-shire that their warm and intimate correspondence developed. Mrs Martin encouraged Elizabeth to stand up to her father and gave her and Robert Browning full support when they married. 'They are true friends whom I love,' Elizabeth told Henrietta after meeting the Martins in Paris in 1852. Later Mrs Martin tried to persuade Edward Moulton Barrett to forgive his three children who had married against his wishes (see p. 178).

5. This is Alethea Hayter's opinion. But see note 8, Chapter 12.

CHAPTER 9 The Courtship, 1845–1846

1. From John Maynard, *Browning's Youth*.

2. Alfred Domett. From John Maynard, op. cit.

3. Mrs Jameson, who also lived in Wimpole Street, called on Elizabeth in 1844. They quickly became close friends and, perhaps because she knew and liked Robert, Elizabeth was able to confide in her, much more so than in Miss Mitford. She remained a close friend of both Brownings until her sudden death in 1860.

4. Although they had not met for over eight years, Hugh Boyd remained an important friend to Elizabeth. Her sisters had visited him regularly and carried messages to and fro, and Elizabeth continued to write and send him her work.

5. Elizabeth was saddened. She wrote three sonnets to his memory, 'His Blindness', 'Legacies', and 'His Death, 1848'. The last lines of the latter are:

> Steadfast friend,
> Who never didst my heart or life misknow,
> Nor either's faults too keenly apprehend, –
> How can I wonder when I see thee go
> To join the Dead found faithful to the end?

CHAPTER 10 Flight to Pisa and Florence, 1846–1851

1. There is no clear understanding of Arabel's sleeping arrangements. She may have slept on the settee on which Elizabeth sat or lay during the day. She was never in the room when their father entered, late at night, to commune with Elizabeth. Perhaps she had a curtained-off alcove. Whatever the arrangement it must have been highly inconvenient for Arabel.

2. *Aurora Leigh*, Book 5, lines 14–16.

3. 'A Woman's Last Word', from *Men and Women*.

4. 'The Confessional', from *Dramatic Romances and Lyrics*.

5. Mary Boyle was a niece of Lord Cork, see William Irvine and Park Honan, op. cit., p. 244.

6. 'The Guardian Angel', from *Men and Women*.

7. Robert Browning, in a letter to Julia Wedgwood some years after Elizabeth's death, referred ambiguously to the 'strange heavy crown, that wreath of sonnets'.

8. Captain William Surtees Cook was a comparatively penniless cousin, allowed by Edward Moulton Barrett to visit the house freely, as a member of the family. Elizabeth and her brothers treated him badly at first, but later they respected him, especially after he faced his future father-in-law. This is well described by Elizabeth, see *The Letters of Robert Browning and Elizabeth Barrett Browning*, postmarked 26 January 1846.

CHAPTER 11 Hopes and Disappointments, 1851–1857

1. Robert Browning wrote to Isa Blagdon on 19 September 1867, six years after his wife's death: '. . . . . . abcdefg. There. Those letters indicate *seven distinct* issues to which I came with Ba, in our profoundly different estimate of thing and person. . . . as for *seeing* the truth, it seems to me such angelic natures don't – and such devilish ones do.'

    Edward McAleer suggests the seven issues might be spiritualism, Napoleon III, Mrs Eckley, Mrs Trollope (Robert could not stand her social pretensions), the method of raising Pen, the subscriptions for Mrs Jameson's sisters, and their own marriage which Elizabeth at first opposed. I would replace the last with Elizabeth's dependence on opium. Robert struggled hard to persuade her to abandon the drug, although he failed signally.

    Neither partner was inclined to compromise over issues on which they felt strongly. Robert confessed to Julia Wedgwood that, 'I think myself dreadfully in the right, all the while, in everything', while Elizabeth chose to see and hear what she wanted.

2. Well described by Gridley in *The Brownings and France*, p. 131.

3. Robert claimed to have written the poem in one day. Robert Browning, *The Poems*, Vol. 1. Notes p. 1117.

4. 'Mesmerism', from *Men and Women*.

5. Written to Harriet Beecher Stowe in 1860, and quoted by Jeannette Marks, op. cit. (p. 626). Mrs Stowe was interested in spiritualism. Her son had died and she claimed she was in contact with his spirit.

6. Elizabeth's letter to Mrs Jameson was written in February 1855. Four months earlier in a letter to Henrietta, she had been less critical of Miss Nightingale: 'She called on me when we were in Welbeck Street and sent me some flowers afterwards. A pretty and high accomplished woman – even *learned* she is – and she is acting greatly on this occasion, together with other women.'

7. The séance, and Robert's subsequent encounter with Home, are based on Betty Miller's account in *Robert Browning: A Portrait*.

CHAPTER 12 The Last Years, 1857–1861

1. Isa Blagden was a close friend of both Brownings. She lived at the Villa Bricchieri in Bellosguardo, just outside Florence and within walking distance of Casa Guidi, where she entertained her many friends. Robert saw her as a 'bright, delicate, electric woman'. She was small and dark, unmarried in her late thirties, had been born in India, and was reputed to have had an Indian mother; no one seems to have known her background for certain. She wrote indifferent novels and occasional poetry and lived on a small income.

   She was warm-hearted, down to earth and witty, enjoyed gossip and discussing books, music and politics. She was particularly important to Robert, who visited her three or four times a week in the last years of Elizabeth's life (encouraged by his wife). He often unburdened himself to her and spoke of his troubles; alongside Story Isa was probably his closest confidante. Robert loved her deeply although he made it plain that marriage was not an option. After Elizabeth's death Isa helped him to collect himself and Pen together and accompanied them as far as Paris. Their correspondence continued until her death in 1873.

2. 'Mr. Sludge, "The Medium".'

3. 'Where's Agnes?' was written in 1860, during Elizabeth's upsurge of creative writing.

4. *Nathaniel Hawthorne: a biography* by Arlin Turner, Oxford, Oxford University Press, 1980.

5. Quoted from Gridley, op. cit., p. 199.

6. Henry James, 'William Wetmore Story and His Friends', Vol. II, p. 53.

7. Denis Mack Smith, *Cavour*, London, Methuen, 1985, p. 174.

8. Robert Browning, *The Poems*, Vol. 1, Notes pp. 1163 and 1176.

9. Conceivably these last poems could have been written under the influence of large doses of opium.

10. Quoted from Donald Thomas, *Robert Browning: a life within life*, p. 219.

Epilogue

1. The lines are from 'La Saisiaz'.

SELECT BIBLIOGRAPHY

Poetry

The Poetical Works of Elizabeth Barrett Browning, Oxford, Oxford University Press, 1920

Robert Browning, *The Poems* (2 vols), edited by John Pettigrew and T. J. Collins, Penguin Books, Harmondsworth, 1981

Biographies and critical studies

Berridge, Elizabeth (ed.). *The Barretts at Hope End: The Early Diary of Elizabeth Barrett Browning*, London, John Murray, 1974

Browning, Vivienne. *My Browning Family Album*, Ascot, Springwood Books, 1979

Corkran, Henrietta. *Celebrities and I*, London, Hutchinson, 1902

Forster, Margaret. *Elizabeth Barrett Browning*, London, Chatto & Windus, 1988

Gridley, Roy E. *The Brownings and France: A Chronicle with Commentary*, London, The Athlone Press, 1982

Hayter, Alethea. *Mrs. Browning, A Poet's Work and its Setting*, London, Faber & Faber, 1962

Hewlett, Dorothy. *Elizabeth Barrett Browning: A Life*, London, Cassell, 1953

Irvine, William and Honan Park. *The Book, The Ring, and the Poet*, London, The Bodley Head, 1975

James, Henry. 'William Wetmore Story and His Friends', from *Letters, Diaries and Recollections*, 2 vols., Edinburgh, Blackwood, 1903

Kaplan, Cora (introduced by). *Aurora Leigh and other poems*, London, The Women's Press, 1978

Karlin, Daniel. *The Courtship of Robert Browning and Elizabeth Barrett*, Oxford, Clarendon Press, 1985

Kelley, Philip and Hudson, Ronald (eds.). *Diary by Elizabeth Barrett Browning: The Unpublished Diary of Elizabeth Barrett Browning 1831–32*, University of Ohio Press, 1967

Leighton, Angela. *Elizabeth Barrett Browning*, Brighton, Harvester Press, 1986

Marks, Jeannette. *The Family of the Barretts: A Colonial Romance*, New York, Macmillan, 1938

Maynard, John. *Browning's Youth*, Harvard University Press, 1975

Miller, Betty. *Robert Browning: A Portrait*, London, John Murray, 1952

Orr, Mrs Sutherland. *Life and Letters of Robert Browning (1891)*, ed. Frederic G. Kenyon, London, Smith Elder, 1908

Taplin, Gardner B. *The Life of Elizabeth Barrett Browning*, London, John Murray, 1957

Thomas, Donald. *Robert Browning: a life within life*, London, Weidenfeld & Nicolson, 1982

Ward, Maisie. *The Tragi-comedy of Pen Browning 1849–1912*, London and New York, Sheed & Ward and The Browning Institute, 1972

Letters

Curle, Richard (ed.). *Robert Browning and Julia Wedgwood. A Broken Friendship, as revealed in their letters*, New York, Frederick A. Stoakes Co, 1937

Erskine, Mrs Stuart (ed.). *Anna Jameson, Letters and Friendships*, London, T. Fisher Unwin, 1915

Freeman, Ronald E. and Landis, Paul (eds.). *Letters of the Brownings to George Barrett*, Urbana, University of Illinois Press, 1958

Heydon, Peter N. and Kelley, Philip (eds.). *Elizabeth Barrett Browning's letters to Mrs David Ogilvy, 1849–1861*, London, John Murray, 1974

Huxley, Leonard (ed.). *Elizabeth Barrett Browning: Letters to her Sister 1840–1859*, London, John Murray, 1929

Kenyon, Frederic G. (ed.). *The Letters of Elizabeth Barrett Browning*, 2 vols., London, Smith Elder, 1897
The Letters of Robert Browning and Elizabeth Barrett Browning, 1845–1846, 2 vols., London, Smith Elder, 1896

McAleer, Edward C. (ed.). *Dearest Isa: Robert Browning's letters to Isabella Blagdon*, Austin, Texas, University of Texas Press, 1951

Elizabeth Barrett Browning

Learned Lady: Letters from Robert Browning to Mrs Thomas Fitzgerald, 1876–1889, Princeton, Cambridge, Massachusetts, Harvard University Press, 1966

McCarthy, Barbara P. (ed.). *Elizabeth Barrett to Mr Boyd – Unpublished letters of Elizabeth Barrett to Hugh Stuart Boyd*, London, John Murray, 1955

Raymond, Meredith B. and Sullivan, Mary Rose (eds.). *The Letters of Elizabeth Barrett Browning to Mary Russell Mitford, 1836–1854*, 3 vols, Wacko, Texas, The Browning Institute and Wellesley College, 1983

Shackford, Martha Hale (ed.). *Letters from Elizabeth Barrett to Benjamin Robert Haydon*, Oxford, Oxford University Press, 1939

Townshend Meyer, S. R. (ed.). *Letters of Elizabeth Barrett Browning addressed to Richard Hengist Horne*, 2 vols, London, Richard Bentley & Son, 1877

Index

Aberdeen, Lord, 165
agoraphobia, 20–1
Annunziala (maid), 180
anorexia nervosa, 27–30, 67, 68, 83, 85
Arnold, Thomas, 6
Artaud, William, 24
Asolo, Italy, 95
Athenaeum magazine, 76, 79, 80, 89, 152, 188
Austen, Jane, 19
Avignon, France, 130

Barrett, Alfred (brother), 25, 48, 50
Barrett, Arabel (sister), 68, 70, 79, 145, 156; early illness of, 26; at Sidmouth, 50, 53; social life in London, 58, 59; restrictions at home, 63; and death of Edward, 73; and E's courtship and marriage, 111, 125, 133; with E and Penini in Wimpole St, 148, 149, 156, 169; at Eastbourne, 170; and death of father, 178; leaves Wimpole St, 179; at Le Havre, 184
Barrett, Charles (Stormie) (brother), 57, 84
Barrett, Edward (great grandfather), 1, 2, 4, 5, 8
Barrett, Edward (Bro) (brother), 14, 23, 37, 102; early education of, 15; and McSweeney, 16, 18, 19; at Charterhouse, 24, 25; with E in Gloucester, 30; visits Boyd with E, 34; tutors younger brothers, 48; in Sidmouth, 49, 50; in Jamaica, 1833–5, 54, 56, 57; in London, 59, 60, 63; in Torquay, 66, 67; love affair of, 68, 69; drowned in boating accident, 72, 74, 75, 82; E's need for substitute for, 98, 101, 111
Barrett, Edward Moulton (father), 1,

25, 26, 28, 30, 33, 59, 61, 64, 67, 70, 73, 79; early life in Jamaica, 4, 5; at Harrow School, 5, 6; and Cambridge, 6; marriage of, 7, 8; and Hope End, 8, 10, 11; financial difficulties of, 12, 13, 43, 44, 45; death of wife, 36, 37, 38, 39, 41; cholera of, 46; and sale of Hope End, 48; at Sidmouth, 49, 52; and emancipation of slaves, 55–6; moves to Wimpole St, 57; alienation from E, 113, 114; and E's elopement, 126, 127; disinherits Henrietta, 145; refuses reconciliation with E, 149, 156, 165–6, 168, 169, 174; death of, 178–9; attitude to E, 16, 17, 21–2, 23, 71
Barrett, Elizabeth (grandmother), 30; marriage of, 2, 3; separation from husband, 4, 15; closeness to E, 42; death of, 42
Barrett, George (brother), 66, 100; law studies of, 57, 58; and E, 75, 86, 87, 114, 126; and E's elopement, 129; rapprochement with, 133; and Robert Browning, 111, 151; at Wimpole St, 169; in Ventnor, 174; and Le Havre, 184; and death of father, 178; and Henrietta, 190
Barrett, George Goodin (great uncle), 5, 6
Barrett, Henrietta (sister), 14, 30, 50, 66, 100, 178, 179; at Hope End, 21, 22, 25; early illness of, 26; and Boyd family, 34, 39; and death of mother, 36; nurses E, 42; in London, 59, 61, 62; and Bro, 68, 72, 73; at Wimpole St, 101, 103, 111, 117; and E's elopement, 125, 129, 136; marriage of, 145; with E in London, 148, 156, 157;

Index

Barrett, Henrietta, continued
correspondence with E, 151, 155;
death of, 190, 191
Barrett, Henry (brother), 45, 48, 184
Barrett, Judith (great grandmother),
2
Barrett, Mary Moulton (née Graham-
Clarke) (mother), 9, 25, 30;
marriage of, 7; and Hope End,
10–11; and financial problems, 13;
devotion to E, 17, 102; illness,
death and burial of, 35, 36, 38
Barrett, Mary (sister), 26, 36
Barrett, Octavius (Occy) (brother),
50
Barrett, Richard (E. M. Barrett's
cousin), 55, 73
Barrett, Samuel (brother), 50; in
Jamaica, 56, 61, 64; death of, 70, 71
Barrett, Samuel Moulton (uncle), 4,
5, 7, 8, 70; at Cambridge, 6; MP,
11; litigations of, 12, 13; and Bro,
56; death of, 63, 66; will of, 69
Barrett, Sarah (aunt), 3, 5, 6
Barrett, Sarah (great aunt), 2
Barrett, Septimus (Sette) (brother),
30, 49, 50, 71, 73
Bath, 49, 51
Bathampton, 47, 51
Bayley, Miss, 77, 120
Beacon Terrace, Torquay, 66, 69
Bells and Pomegranates (pamphlet), 95
Blagdon, Isa, 178, 180, 184, 190; and
Robert, 193; and E's last illness,
194
Bourges, 130
Boyd, Annie, 36, 39; and E, 41, 45,
47, 51; marriage of, 62
Boyd, Hugh, 32, 62, 72, 74, 98;
correspondence with E, 33; first
meeting with, 34, 35, 37; E visits,
39, 40; Mr Barrett's jealousy of, 41,
42, 43; moves to Ruby Cottage, 44,
45, 46; moves to Bathampton, 47,
48, 49; visits E at Sidmouth, 51, 52,
56; moves to Hampstead, 58, 59;
renewed friendship with E, 76, 77,
78, 79; disagreement with E, 84;
visit from E, 121; and E's marriage,
125
Boyd, Mrs Hugh, 36; and E, 39, 45,
47, 51
Boyle, Mary, 137
Brighton, 10, 78
Browning, Elizabeth Barrett, family
background of, 1–13; birth of, 14;
childhood and first poems of, 15–
16; studies Greek and Latin, 18–
19, 24; adolescence of, 25; first
illness of, 26–31; and Hugh Boyd,

33–6, 37–8, 39–42, 44–5, 46–8, 49,
51–2, 62; and sale of Hope End,
44–8; at Sidmouth, 49–55, 57; and
George Hunter, 52–5, 78–9; moves
to London, 58; and John Kenyon,
56–61; develops tuberculosis, 64–
5, 66, 67, 71; in Torquay, 66–75;
literary career of, 76–8; admirers
of, 80–2; and Robert Browning, 89,
90; and his beard, 161–2;
correspondence with, 96–101; first
meeting with, 102–4; courtship,
105–25; marriage of, 125–6;
elopement of, 126–7; journey to
Pisa, 128–30; honeymoon, 130–6;
miscarriages of, 135–6, 138, 143,
144; illnesses of, 166–7, 172, 187;
anxieties and agoraphobia of, 20–
1, 27, 35; anorexia nervosa of,
27–31, 67, 68, 83; opium habit of,
85–8, 135, 144, 145, 174–5; in
Florence, 136–8, 147; pregnancy
and birth of son, 138–9; and death
of mother-in-law, 140–1; and
Penini, 142–3, 151–2; trip to
London, 147–50; in Paris, 150–3,
155, 156, 170, 176, 183–4; return to
London, 153, 156–7; return to
Florence, 157–8, 164–7; in Rome,
162–4; third visit to London, 167,
169–70; completes *Aurora Leigh*,
172–3, 174, 175; fourth visit to
London, 173–5; returns to
Florence, 175–7; and Mrs Eckley,
180–2, 189; and Henrietta's death,
190–1; last days of, 193–5; attitude
to slavery, 1, 46, 74, 188; and
politics, 151, 165, 185–7, 189–90;
and religion, 22, 37, 74; and
spiritualism, 158–61, 167–9, 181–2;
temper of, 14, 15; appearance of,
14; room at Wimpole St described,
101–2; and Bro, 15, 19, 23–4, 66–7,
68, 72; death of, 72–3, 74, 75; and
Mother, 17–18, 25; death of, 36–7;
and Father, 16, 21–3, 24, 63, 67–8,
79–80, 111–12; hopes of
reconciliation with, 149, 156, 165–
6; death of, 178–9
Writings: Aurora Leigh, 54, 134,
157, 163, 164, 165, 169; reception
of, 175–6; *The Battle of Marathon*,
63; 'Bianca among the
Nightingales', 190; *Casa Guidi
Windows*, 145–6; 'A Curse for a
Nation', 188; 'De Profundis', 74;
'Essay on Mind', 33; 'Lady
Geraldine's Courtship', 90, 157;
'The Lay of the Brown Rosary', 68;
'The Mask', 73, 74–5; 'Plea for the

210

Index

Cook, Surtees, 145
Coxhoe Hall, Durham, 7, 9, 14
Crimean War, 165
Crow (maid), 66, 83, 84, 88
Curzon, Mr (minister), 43

David Lyon (trading ship), 64
de Barry, Dr, 66, 69, 70, 71
Denmark Hill, 157
De Quincey, Thomas, 85, 86
Dilke, Charles, 76

Eastbourne, 170
Eckley, David, 180, 181
Eckley, Mrs Sophie, 161; and E, 180, 181, 182, 183; disgrace of, 189
Etretat, France, 184
Exeter, 53, 71

Fenham Hall, Newcastle-upon-Tyne, 7, 9
Florence, 121, 135, 141, 180, 181; first visit to, 1847, 136; winter 1850 in, 145; winter 1851 in, 157; summer 1854 in, 164; autumn 1856 in, 175; autumn 1858 in, 184; spring 1859 in, 185; autumn 1859 in, 187; E's last days and death in, 193, 194, 195
Flower, Eliza and Sarah, 96
Flush (pet spaniel), 75, 79, 83, 84, 101, 126, 132
Franz Joseph, Emperor of Austria, 186

Garibaldi, Giuseppe, 189, 190
Gloucester Place, London, 57, 58, 60
Graham-Clarke, Arabella (Aunt Bell or Bummy), 66; at Hope End, 45, 46; at Sidmouth, 49, 50
Graham-Clarke, John, 5, 7
Graham-Clarke, Mrs (grandmother), 25
Greenwich, 6
Grey, Charles, 38
Gull, Dr William, 29

Hampstead, 58
Hanworth, Fanny, 96
Harrow School, 5, 6, 25
Hatch End, 90
Havannah (pet dog), 19
Hawthorne, Nathaniel, 183
Haydon, Benjamin, 77, 78
Hedley, Mrs (aunt), 113
Helena, Grand Duchess of Russia, 50
Hereford Journal, 38
Home, Douglas Dunglas (medium), 180, 182; first séance with E, 167,

168; Robert's dislike of, 168, 169, 189; successes in Italy, 176, 177
Homer, 19, 77
Hood's magazine, 106
Hope End, Ledbury, Worcs, 11, 21, 24, 55; purchase and reconstruction of, 9, 10; financial difficulties concerning, 12, 13, 39, 40, 42, 43, 45; E's first illness at, 25, 28, 30; and Woodland Lodge, 35, 36, 37; sale of, 46, 48, 49
Horace, 19
Horne, Richard Hengist, 80, 81, 90
Hunter, George Barrett (minister), 52, 59, 72; friendship with E, 53, 54, 55, 56; visits Wimpole St, 77, 78, 79, 81
Hunter, Mary, 53

Jago, Dr, 84
Jamaica, 13, 18, 63, 70; Barrett family estates in, 1, 3, 4, 5; slave trade abolished, 2; E. M. Barrett leaves, 5, 6; embezzlement litigation and financial problems in, 7, 8, 9, 42, 43; Bro in, 54, 55, 56
Jameson, Mrs, 132, 134, 165; friendship with E, 77, 121; in Paris, 128, 129; journey to Pisa, 130, 131; death of, 188, 189
Jones, Thomas, 5

Kemble, Fanny and Adelaide, 162
Kenyon, John, 76, 77, 113, 114, 129; friendship with E, 59, 60, 61; in London, 81, 84, 88; introduces Robert to E, 89, 90; social life with Barretts, 100, 101, 104, 106; and Robert's courtship of E, 117, 118, 121, 123; correspondence with Brownings, 144, 146, 148; death of, 174
Knowles, Sir Charles and Lady, 34

Landor, Walter Savage, 60
Ledbury, Worcs, 36, 38
Le Havre, 128, 184
London University, 94
Louvre, Paris, 129, 171
Lucca, Italy, 141, 161, 162, 179, 180
Lyon, France, 130
Lytton, Robert, 158

Macready, William, 95
Madeira, 2
Magenta, Battle of, 186
Malvern, 35, 38, 41
Martin, Mrs, and E, 85, 136, 170, 178
Martineau, Harriet, 158
Mazzini, Giuseppe, 152, 157

McSweeney, Mr (tutor), 16, 18, 24, 25
Milan, 147
Milsand (critic), 171
Mitford, Mary, 54, 87, 97, 102; meets E, 60, 61; friendship with E, 62, 68, 70; gift of Flush, 75; at Wimpole St, 76, 77; influence on E, 78, 79, 80; attempts to help, 81, 82, 83, 84; meets Robert, 89; and E's courtship, 106; correspondence with E, 138; and E's pregnancies, 142, 143, 144; *Recollections of a Literary Life*, 152; death of, 166
Moses (pet pony), 19
Moulton, Charles (grandfather), 2, 3, 4, 8
Moulton, Robert (great uncle), 8, 9
Muchet, Henrietta, 41
Murphy, Francis (tutor), 5

Naples, 95, 190
Napoleon III, 165, 188, 189, 190; E's admiration of, 103, 173; political career of, 150, 151, 185, 186; E's disillusionment with, 187
Newcastle, 5
New Cross, London, Browning family home in, 108, 120, 147, 148, 154; E refuses to visit, 124; death of Sarah Browning at, 139, 140; E visits, 149
New Monthly Magazine, 62
New York, 3, 4
Nightingale, Florence, 165

Old Yellow Book, The, 192
opium abuse, 85–7, 135, 144, 174–5
Orléans, 129
Orme, Mrs, 24

Paine, Tom, 16
Pall Mall Gazette, 79
Paris, 16, 125; Robert and E elope to, 128; 1851 visit to, 148; 1852 visit, 150; 1855 visit, 170; 1858 visit, 183, 184
Piedmont, 185, 190
Pisa, 121, 125; Robert and E in, 130, 131, 133, 134, 135
Pitti Palace, 137
Pope, Alexander, 16
Price, Sir Uvedale (landscape gardener), 31
Prince Imperial, 173
Prince Regent, 10

Reading, 60
Recollections of a Literary Life (Mitford), 152

Reform Bill (1832), 11, 39
Roanne, 130
Robinson, Mrs, 44
Rome, 181; 1853 visit to, 161, 162; 1858 visit, 184; 1859 visit, 188, 189
Ruby Cottage, Worcs, Boyd family at, 33, 34; Boyds leave, 35; and return to, 44, 47
Ruskin, Effie, 156
Ruskin, John, 156, 171, 176
Russia, 165
Ryder, Mr and Mrs, 167, 168

St Kitts, W. Indies, 92, 93
St Petersburg, 95
Sand, George, E's admiration for, 81, 103; meets E, 152, 172
Scarlett, James (Lord Abinger), 7, 8, 9
Scully, Dr, 71, 75, 82, 84
Shakespeare, William, 77
Sidmouth, Devon, 55, 56, 57, 78; Barretts move to, 48, 49, 50; Hugh Boyd visits, 51, 52; E meets G. Hunter in, 52, 53
Siena, 189, 190
Silverthorne, James, 118, 125, 156
slavery and abolition of slave trade (1807), 1, 2, 12, 55
Solferino, Battle of, 186
Southey, Robert, 65
Southampton, 128
spiritualism, 158–9, 160, 161, 176
Story, Edith, 162, 163
Story, Joe, 162
Story, William (sculptor), 181; in Rome, 162, 163; friendship with Robert, 185, 189, 191; E's jealousy of, 193
Stowe, Harriet Beecher, 191
Stratten, James, 58
Swedenborg, Emanuel, 158

Tennyson, Alfred Lord, 77, 89, 90, 102
Tennyson, Frederick, 158
Tennyson, Hallam, 157
Torquay, Devon, Barretts' visit, 50, 53; take up residence in, 65, 66, 71; Bro drowned in, 72, 73, 74
Treppy (nurse), 10, 26, 56, 178
Turkey, 165

Vallombrosa, Italy, 137
Vaucluse, France, 130
Venice, 95, 147, 186
Ventnor, I.O.W., 173, 174
Victor Emmanuel, 188
Villafranca, Peace of, 186, 188
Voltaire, 16

Index

Picture Acknowledgements

By courtesy of Mary V. Altham, page 3 above left and below
right. By courtesy of the Master and Fellows, Balliol College,
Oxford, page 5 below left, page 7 below left. Hulton Picture
Company, page 4 above left, below right, page 7 above left.
Mansell Collection, page 4 below right. Mills College (Depart-
ment of Rare Books and Special Collections), California, page 6
below. By courtesy of Edward R. Moulton-Barrett, page 2 above.
By courtesy of Captain Gordon E. Moulton-Barrett, page 3 above
right and below left. John Murray Ltd, page 5 below right.
National Portrait Gallery, London, page 6 above. New York
Public Library, The Berg Collection, Aston, Lenox and Tilden
Foundations, page 2 below. Victoria and Albert Museum,
London, page 5 above right. Wellesley College Library (Special
Collections), Massachusetts, page 4 above right and below left,
page 8.